MARILYN HORNE

The Song Continues

by

Marilyn Horne
with **Jane Scovell**

Discography by
Gina Guandalini, Michael Benchetrit
and Susan Landis

CD edited by Bill Park and mastered
by José Feghali from material provided
by Marilyn Horne, Michael Benchetrit
and others

GREAT VOICES
8

BASKERVILLE
PUBLISHERS

Baskerville Publishers, Inc.
2711 Park Hill Drive
Fort Worth, Texas 76109

www.baskervillepublishers.com

Library of Congress Cataloging-in-Publication Data

Horne, Marilyn.
  Marilyn Horne : the song continues / by Marilyn Horne, with Jane
Scovell.
    p. cm.
"This is a complete revision, with additions, of the biography
published in 1983 by Atheneum"—ECIP info.
  ISBN 1-880909-71-5 (alk. paper)
  1. Horne, Marilyn. 2. Mezzo sopranos—United States—Biography.
I.
Scovell, Jane, 1934- II. Title.

  ML420.H66A3 2004
  782.1'092—dc22

                                        2003023625

Manufactured in the United States of America

First printing, 2004

CONTENTS

CD CONTENTS

1. *La Traviata* (Verdi): *Parigi o cara* w. Jan Peerce. Hollywood Bowl Symphony Orchestra (HBSO) 1963 (Henry Lewis)
2. *La Bohème* (Puccini): *Donde lieta* HBSO 1963 (Henry Lewis)
3. *La Cenerentola* (Rossini): *Nacqui all'affanno* HBSO 1963 (Henry Lewis)
4. *Die Walküre* (Wagner): *Schläfst du, Gast?...Der Männer Sippe* w. William Cochran. Pittsburgh Symphony at Carnegie Hall (PS) 1972 (Donald Johanos)
5. *Die Walküre* (Wagner): *Du bist der Lenz* PS at Carnegie Hall 1972 (Donald Johanos)
6. *Wozzeck* (Berg): *Und ist kein Betrug* New York Philharmonic 1966 (Lucas Foss)
7. *Carmina Burana* (Orff): *In truitina mentis dubia* HBSO 1955 (Leopold Stokowski)
8. *Manon* (Massenet): *Adieu, notre petit table* HBSO 1966 (Henry Lewis)
9. *Cendrillon* (Massenet): *Tu me l'as dit* w. Frederica von Stade. New Jersey Symphony (NJS) at Carnegie Hall (NJS) 1973 (Henry Lewis)
10. *Cendrillon* (Massenet): *A la branche du chêne enchanté* w. Reri Grist and Frederica von Stade. NJS at Carnegie Hall 1973 (Henry Lewis)
11. *Semiramide* (Rossini): *Si, vendicato* at Carnegie Hall 1983 (Henry Lewis)
12. *Aida* (Verdi): *Ohimé! Morir mi sento* Salzburg Festival 1979 (Herbert von Karajan)
13. *Aida* (Verdi): *Spirto del nume* w. Nicolai Ghiaurov. Salzburg Festival 1979 (Herbert von Karajan)
14. *Aida* (Verdi): *Numi, pietà del mio straziato core* Salzburg Festival 1979 (Herbert von Karajan)
15. *Aida* (Verdi): *Radamès, Radamès...Ah, pietà!* w. Nicolai Ghiaurov. Salzburg Festival 1979 (Herbert von Karajan)
16. *Les nuits d'été* (Berlioz): *Absence* Edinburgh, 1964 (Charles Münch)
17. *Der Rosenkavalier* (Strauss): *Marie Theres'...Hab' mir's gelobt* w. Reri Grist and Frederica von Stade. NJS at Carnegie Hall 1973 (Henry Lewis)
18. *Danny Boy* La Scala 1975 (Martin Katz, piano)

FOREWORD

by
Terence McNally

At the height of her career, Marilyn Horne was called "the greatest singer in the world." I don't remember anyone having a serious problem with that designation, even a Callas fanatic or a Caballé groupie or a Sills aficionado like myself. If great singing means faultless technique, beauty of tone, ease of production, commitment to words as well as music, intelligence of interpretation and communication to an audience, then Horne clearly deserved that lofty appellation. She sang in a great age of mezzos, too, her competition was formidable, but she reigned supreme.

And now in the twilight of her performing years, she has seen no serious challenger to that title. Perhaps it is time to retire it as Ms. Horne herself graciously, gradually withdraws from the stage and recording studio. What she leaves behind—in fond memories and on countless recordings—is proof enough that the word "greatest" is the only one that describes the range of her staggering accomplishment.

She could sing anything. Not only could she sing anything but she could sing it well. Her bel canto portrayals were as suited to their composers as were recitals of German lied. After all, Horne's three B's were not the familiar ones; they were Bach, Berg and Bellini. If that were not evidence enough of her versatility, there were memorable evenings of Rossini, Verdi, and Bizet. From her legendary debut at the Met as Adalgisa to Joan Sutherland's Norma, she was adored by her audiences in a way that was unique.

We loved a lot of singers but Marilyn Horne was lovable as a human being as well. She always seemed one of us, no matter how god-like her singing. She was a diva you wanted to take care of. Men and women loved her. Straight men, too. Everyone did. She was sort of like Sara Lee.

But that isn't the whole story. Marilyn Horne has returned a hundredfold all the honors, high fees, best-selling albums, sold-out performances, standing ovations and adulation that have followed her these many years. Instead of counting her money and updating her scrapbooks, she has made the future of the American singer her number one concern by nurturing young talent through master classes and the Marilyn Horne Foundation, both of which present emerging talents in programs that are a model of their kind. I was personally the beneficiary of her generosity to the next generation when, at the San Francisco Opera, one of her protégés, John Packard, created the title role in *Dead Man Walking*, an opera by Jake Heggie for which I wrote the libretto. Truly, I can think of no other singer who has given so much back to the music.

Marilyn Horne the writer is much like Marilyn Horne the musician: honest, direct and vibrant with heart. Her singing always said "This is who I am." Her autobiography simply reveals the details of the woman we already heard in the voice.

Though it will not replace an actual Horne performance, nothing will, don't be surprised if you'll want a good stack of her CD's handy while you read these pages. I found myself listening to her Mahler, Bach, and Handel recordings in fresh contemplation of their quiet beauty. And then I needed a dash of florid Rossini singing to recall the great nights at the Met. After reading the last chapter and closing the book with a smile and a sigh, there was only one choice: her exquisite way with the music of Stephen Foster, especially "I Dream of Jeanie."

I won't say "enjoy." We already have for years. Read and remember. We were lucky to have been around for so much of this.

The old order changeth, yielding place
to new;
And God fulfils himself in many ways...

—Tennyson

PREFACE

In 1967, at the same time it was announced that Marilyn Horne would make her Opera Company of Boston debut in *Carmen*, I joined the OCOB's Board of Trustees. I knew the young mezzo from her brilliant recordings which I played over and over in the opera appreciation course I taught at Newton College of the Sacred Heart. (The students tended to confuse her with "Lena" Horne—then again they thought that Verdi's *La Traviata* was based on "Our Lady of the Camellias" by Dumas.)

Traditionally, a member of the board of trustees gave opening night parties yet as the *Carmen* approached, no invitation appeared. I asked the Company's Artistic Director, Sarah Caldwell, who was fêting Ms. Horne?

"No one," replied Miss Caldwell.

"You're kidding," I said. "Somebody's got to give a party for her."

"Okay, you give it."

The opening was barely a week away—little time to create a big party—nevertheless I agreed to do it for a select group of directors and trustees. Sarah Caldwell said she personally would invite Miss Horne and her husband, Henry Lewis, the conductor. I quickly called my friend Jacques Noe, a Boston restaurateur, and enlisted him to prepare a post-opera buffet.

On opening night, Jacques delivered a cake dazzlingly decorated with scenes from *Carmen*. I set out for the opera

ix

as he began preparations, assisted by a few of my students who had been pressed into service—and cautioned not to refer to Miss Horne as "Lena."

At the theatre, I found Sarah Caldwell patrolling the lobby. I proudly announced that the party was all set.

"Well, honey," she replied in her signature sepulchral tones, "that's nice, but Miss Horne isn't coming."

"What do you mean?"

"She said she can't come," answered Sarah, shrugging her shoulders and moving off.

I blocked her exit.

"When did you ask her?"

"Oh, ah...let's see...I guess I mentioned it... ah... I just went backstage and told her."

"No wonder she won't come," I fumed. "It's insulting! You can't ask the guest of honor at the last minute. You were supposed to ask her days ago."

"Well, honey, I just forgot."

"Sarah, I've gone to a lot of trouble. My friend Jacques is working overtime, so are my students. She's got to come!"

"Okay, you tell her."

And that's exactly what I did.

After the final curtain, Miss Caldwell ushered me into Miss Horne's dressing room, then disappeared quicker than you could say Georges Bizet.

Backstage at the Opera House (née the Loew's State Theatre) was a setting worthy of Dante's *Inferno*. Peeling, crumbling walls and dank dressing rooms, frequented by indigenous rodents as well as visiting singers, created an inappropriate setting for a resplendently arrayed trustee. I was wearing a designer evening gown, a long sleeved brown velvet top with yards and yards of white tulle cascading down from an Empire waistline—a Filene's Basement item I'd purchased for $79.99 with an original price tag of $600.

In those days you dressed up for the opera.

Marilyn Horne sat in front of a large mirror surrounded by light bulbs, most of which were out. She was draped in a make-up smeared robe. Her dark, close-cropped hair, wringing wet from the weight of the wig she'd worn for four acts, was pulled back tightly by a wide white band. Her face glistened with Albolene cream. She was a far cry from the glamorous gypsy she'd been portraying.

"Excuse me, Miss Horne," I began quickly. "I'm going to level with you. The minute I found out there was no party scheduled, I told Sarah and she told me to give it. Believe me, it's a privilege and an honor, but there wasn't time to send a formal invitation and Sarah promised to ask you right away and..."

The diva stood up, turned around and interrupted my plaintive recitative. A look in her blue eyes and a distance in her attitude told me her answer before she opened her mouth.

"Thank you, it's very kind of you, but I really have made other plans. I have friends with me and we're going back to the hotel. I'm sorry."

"Bring your friends," I squeaked.

"I'm sorry," repeated the singer emphatically. "I just can't."

"Isn't there anything I can do to make you change your mind?" I implored, moving toward her.

Still courteous, still cold as ice, she shook her head and said, "No!"

Raising her right arm, she brought it down in a theatrical gesture of finality. Her outstretched hand struck a coffee cup on the dresser. The cup flipped into the air and its contents, mud-colored tea, splashed over the front of my splendid white skirt.

"Shit!" cried Marilyn Horne before I had time to react. "I'm so sorry, I'm so sorry," she keened.

She leaned over and brushed furtively at the stains. I looked down at the top of her head. This was no longer a prima donna giving the brush-off to a dressing-room pest; this was one woman who had ruined another woman's dress.

She lifted her head. "I'm so sorry, forgive me," she implored. "What can I do?"

"Come to the party," I said unhesitatingly.

She looked at me for a split second then burst out laughing.

"Okay, okay, I'll come, but it's a helluva way to invite someone!"

Thus my dress was ruined and a friendship began—a friendship that led to a book about her life, and now to this more complete version. Although much has changed in the intervening years, certain basics haven't. Age cannot wither Marilyn Horne's warmth, intelligence, humor, and generous spirit; she brings the same candor to this version of her story as she did to the first. Some alterations have been made—a few stories emended, others added—still, it rings true. Twenty years ago readers were astounded at Horne's frank disclosure about an embarrassing and dreadful Christmas Eve in Germany. She wanted to leave it out of this edition, and though I understood her reluctance to include it, I begged her to let it remain. That episode epitomizes the tribulations that go into the making of a great star—the anti-glamour side which constitutes most of the artist's life. It also illustrates how ably she took matters into her own hands and did what had to be done. I'm glad she left it in.

I'd love to go on writing in my words, but this is her story and no one could better celebrate herself or sing herself than Marilyn Horne.

—Jane Scovell

ENCORE

Two decades have passed since *Marilyn Horne: My Life* was published. Twenty years ago, I was the mother of a teenage daughter, Angela, and the former wife of a brilliant musician, Henry Lewis. I also sang in opera houses all over the world. When Handel was performed for the first time at the Metropolitan Opera House, I had the honor of creating the title role in the opera, *Rinaldo*. Trust me, *Rinaldo* calls for a lot of bravura singing and with all due modesty, I was up to the task. At fifty, I still felt like an operatic "kid," raring to sing and ready for any challenge, including Handel.

I'm still raring to go—and, physically, better equipped to do so thanks to a hip replacement and double knee replacement surgeries. (Knee surgery, by the way, is almost a given for someone who made a specialty of male, or trouser, roles. I fell to my knees on the stage as regularly as Joe Namath did on the football field.) My knees may be willing but today, as I approach my seventieth birthday, a lot has changed.

On the personal side, I became a mother-in-law when my daughter married Andre Houle in 1996, and am now the doting grandmother of Daisy and Henry. My grandson was named for his grandfather who died in 1996. Henry Lewis's death was a terrible blow. Although we had been divorced for many years, we remained close, not only for our daughter's sake, but because we had shared so much together. We married in 1960 at a time when interracial

xiii

couples were not as accepted as they are today. For me, Henry's color never was an issue. Someone once commented admiringly on the manner in which Henry and I stayed friendly. "Let's face it," I answered, "I had a failed marriage, and I have a failed divorce." This is not to say that Henry and I were faithful to each other—far from it! Both of us were romantically involved with others. Put simply, while we couldn't live together, we never stopped loving each other.

On the professional side, ten years ago I established the Marilyn Horne Foundation dedicated to the preservation of the art of song, both classical and popular. The MHF continues to aid a new generation of artists and I'm proud of its achievements. I also have kept busy adjudicating vocal competitions and conducting master classes and giving private lessons, as well. In 1994, I was named Vocal Program Director at the Music Academy of the West in Santa Barbara, California. While I still maintain an apartment in New York City, I bought a home in Santa Barbara near my family. Actually, I'm right back where I started my career. A half century ago I was a student of Lotte Lehmann, then the Vocal Program Director at the Academy.

I stopped singing opera in 1996 when Henry Lewis died, a coincidence that I only recently connected. And, in January of 2000, at the Horne Foundation's annual January concert in Carnegie Hall, I announced my intention to stop singing classical music. At the same time, I ventured into the popular field. To this day, I delight in appearing either on my own or with others, such as Barbara Cook, Robert White, Don Pippin, Marvin Hamlisch and Richard Hayman, in programs featuring the songs of America's great composers, from Irving Berlin to Paul Simon. I always said that I'd know when to stop singing opera, but it's one thing to talk about knowing when to stop, and quite another to have to.

Years ago, a friend asked when I planned to retire. "At fifty," I answered. "The rest will be gravy."

At fifty, I upped the ante. I wanted to make it through Rossini's 200th birthday. I actually retired from singing opera on his 204th birthday and I honestly believe that what I've learned about coping with retirement might be of help to others, no matter what their field of endeavor.

That's enough for the present. I've offered the preceding as a prologue to the following pages—the updated version of my life story. We have a lot of catching up to do, so let the house lights dim, the curtain rise, and the song continue.

Da capo!

September 2003

PROLOGUE

Call me Jackie. My brother Dick gave me that nickname when I was born. He wanted a kid brother so badly he had the name ready, and my gender didn't alter his plan. So it's been "Jackie" ever since for family and friends. My dad had a pet name for me, too, he called me "Peanut," and when I was a very little girl, this is what he told me:

"Don't ever forget, Peanut. Whenever you think you're getting too big for the guy sitting next to you, remember, the only thing that separates you from the rest of the world, the only thing that makes you special, is a little piece of gristle in your throat."

Isn't it inspirational to be told your claim to fame rests on a bit of cartilage? That's the way my dad talked—matter-of-fact, straight out, with no embellishments. He made no bones about the fact that my gift was an anatomical quirk, and was just as direct in telling me what he expected me to do with it. I was to go to the top, and in order to reach the pinnacle I had to work—hard! From the beginning, there was no other way, and the result was, I became an international opera star bound to the Protestant work ethic of her youth. I had a purpose around which my life revolved, and that was to sing. Believe me, I worked my butt off. Sure, in many ways, I fought against it. As a kid I sometimes wanted to play, go to the movies, parties, baseball games, anything rather than practice—and I did do those things—but my singing came first. Consequently, I learned

1

early how to sacrifice. It's rough for a kid to know she's got responsibilities beyond the simple enjoyment of life, but the lessons my dad taught me stood me in good stead for over half a century of singing, a feat which might not have been possible had I not adhered to his principles.

My father, Bentz Horne, a pivotal figure in my life, was a semi-professional singer with a fine voice and I inherited my musical gift from him. People who don't know me might think I'm a bit tough, a bit brassy, someone who really speaks her mind. Well, to a certain extent that is part of me, but I didn't always speak my mind and sometimes I haven't been as tough as I should have been. I wasn't only a singer, I was also a woman.

As a singer, I went from Hollywood soundstages to grand opera houses, from genteel poverty to genteel riches, from boarding houses to palaces, from choruses to center stage. Nobody ever handed me anything. I had to study, work, and sing my heart out. I was lucky, too, but you have to take advantage of good fortune, and that I did.

As a woman, perhaps my struggles were even more arduous. In 1960, before Selma and Freedom Rides, before desegregation, before black became beautiful, I married Henry Lewis, a Negro, and America's unwritten apartheid threatened to stop my career before it began. Other repercussions followed. For many years our daughter Angela led a sheltered life surrounded and coddled by our friends in the entertainment world. Eventually, as a child of mixed heritage she had to come to grips with other peoples' reality. One particular incident, when she was a teenager, remained with me. Angela was at home waiting to hear from a couple of school friends whom she was meeting at the Plaza Hotel, along with the mother of one of the girls. They never phoned. The next day, the other girl called in tears to say that the mother refused to include my daughter. I got right on the phone with that woman and though she denied everything, she didn't fool me. Angela didn't whimper about the situation, she simply got mad at the stupidity of prejudice. She was born to that battle, and to a certain extent, even with all the advances in equal rights, my grandchildren have been born to it, too.

Henry Lewis and I were united in loving and caring for our child, but at the height of my career, my marriage failed. Like so many women, I had to learn to face life alone. Again, I was lucky, I had a career, but even that couldn't protect me from the torment of divorce, and the pain of finding and creating a place for myself as a single woman. I came out of it, though, and that's part of the story I want to tell.

We open in Venice.

September 1983

VENICE

On December 9, 1981, I arrived in Venice for my debut at La Fenice, the most beautiful opera house in the world, on whose stage Rossini's *Semiramide* and *Tancredi*, Bellini's *I Capulleti e I Montecchi*, Verdi's *Ernani*, *Attila*, *Rigoletto*, *La Traviata* and *Simon Boccanegra*, Stravinsky's *Rake's Progress*, and Britten's *Turn of the Screw* had their premieres. I was engaged to sing the title role in *Tancredi* one hundred and sixty-eight years after its premiere and a quarter of a century after my first visit to the city of liquid streets. In 1956, Igor Stravinsky had chosen me to perform there in an International Festival of Music. I was a twenty-two year-old unknown singer, alone in a foreign country, an ambitious, sassy, somewhat idealistic, single young woman, sure of her talent and determined to succeed. Twenty-five years later, I still was blessed with my voice, still ambitious and sassy, and, once again, single. I no longer was unknown.

Ten months before, Robert Jacobson, the editor of Opera News, had written, "It's that simple, Marilyn Horne is probably the greatest singer in the world." (If only it were that simple!) In a few months, the Rossini Foundation would present me with its very first Golden Plaque, calling me *"la più grande Rossini cantante del mondo"*—"the greatest Rossini singer in the world." Some might dispute that phrase, but who am I to argue with Italy? The medal was made all the more special because I was an American. In the past, the

4

very idea of a non-Italian receiving the honor would have been inconceivable.

Tancredi already had been a spectacular vehicle for me in Houston, San Francisco, Aix-en Provence, New York City, and Rome; still, the Venice engagement was especially meaningful. Because the opera—Rossini's first big triumph—and my international career began in Venice, it felt as if both *Tancredi* and I were coming home.

Ironically, though, for all my success with it my association with *Tancredi* nearly didn't happen. Until a scant two decades past, Rossini was known primarily for comic operas such as *Il Barbiere di Siviglia*; few appreciated the greater number of serious operas this prolific, versatile genius also composed—elaborate formal works such as *Semiramide, L'Assedio di Corinto*, and, of course, *Tancredi*, all of which I performed many times. Indeed, my efforts to revive his serious works had much to do with my receiving the Rossini medal. Reviving *Tancredi* posed some problems, however. At least two versions of the opera existed, one with a happy ending and one that was much more somber and downbeat.

Set in Syracuse in the ninth century, the story finds Amenaide, daughter of the lord of Syracuse promised to Orbazzano; she, however, is in love with Tancredi, son of the deposed head of Syracuse. (One thing is certain in opera: If a daughter's hand is promised to one man, she has to be in love with another.) Amenaide sends a message to Tancredi, telling him to return and take both the city and her heart. The letter is intercepted by Orbazzano and misread as a message to the leader of the enemy Saracens. Amenaide is forthwith condemned to death as a traitor. Although Tancredi believes she's guilty, to defend her name, he challenges Orbazzano to a duel and kills him. Then Tancredi learns that the notorious message was written to

5

him and not the enemy. He goes off to fight the Saracens and, in the happy ending created by a librettist catering to popular taste, the young lovers are reunited at the victory celebration. That upbeat conclusion didn't sit right with me. Musically, dramatically, and every other way it seemed wrong. I knew that another version existed in which Tancredi dies in battle but I had no idea where to locate it.

When the Houston Opera presented plans to stage a revival, I told them flat out that I would not do it unless they found the other ending. (That's my 'determination' gene at work.) Happily, Philip Gossett, a renowned musicologist, searched and searched—and finally unearthed it. When it was shown to me, I knew my instincts had been correct. Tancredi's death scene—mournful, noble, and moving—was in keeping with the opera's prevailing mood. This was the version I did in Houston and the one I would do in Venice.

Those unfamiliar with opera may wonder when I say that I played the part of a young warrior. Tancredi is a "trouser role," meaning that a woman plays the man. Indeed, my career was given quite a boost by my proficiency in pants parts, many of which are a legacy from the legendary "*castrati.*" The *castrati* were promising boy singers mutilated at puberty to halt certain primary and secondary sexual developments in order to produce a freak voice featuring a female timbre and range supported by the more powerful male physique. Such voices were capable of incredible vocal pyrotechnics. Little wonder that the *castrati* dominated the musical world from the mid-seventeenth century to the early nineteenth.

Rossini did write for one *castrato*, Velutti, but the fact is Tancredi was not a *castrato* role. It was written for a female, thus carrying on another tradition, that of using the treble voice for the leading male role. These parts usually were young men, often aristocrats, on or slightly over the brink of manhood and already commanders of armies. The essence of this delicate stage in development was thought best represented by women rather than by full-grown men. The vocal range, as a rule, calls for the low female register, mezzo or contralto. Because I essayed so many of these roles I was given the nickname "General Horne."

On a sunny Wednesday afternoon, General Horne reported for duty in Venice. I was met by representatives from La Fenice at the Marco Polo airport and whisked into the waiting taxi—a motorboat. We sped across the lagoon into "La Serenissima." No time to sightsee, though, rehearsals began the next day.

Opera rehearsals always include a *sitzprobe*—better known to Americans as the *alla Italiana*. The principals in the opera sit (*sitz*) down with the director and go through (*probe*) the score. My colleagues included Ernesto Palacio as Argirio, Lella Cuberli as Amenaide and Nicola Zaccaria as Orbazzano, a really unusual roundup of artists. Ernesto was Peruvian, Lella was a Texan, Nicola was Greek, and besides Lella and me there was a third American, not to mention a Yugoslavian. So many foreigners, particularly Americans, performing in Italy would have been unthinkable only a few years before. Once upon a time, you almost had to be Italian to sing opera, not only in Europe but here at home. American singers actually changed their names to sound Italian: Lily Norton from Farmington, Maine, went to Milan in the late nineteenth century and returned to sing at the Metropolitan Opera as 'Lillian Nordica.' (If I'd been around in those days, I'd probably have become 'Mafalda Corno.')

Although rehearsals went well, putting on an opera usually involves as much drama offstage as on—and *Tancredi* proved no exception. The Adriatic provided the first hurdle.

7

Venice is constantly on the verge of being engulfed and during the rehearsal period, the "*aqua alta*" (high water) actually lapped into the opera house. I was supposed to make my first entrance on the prow of a ship and from the way the canals were overflowing, I feared I really might sail in! Cast and crew wore waterproof boots and sloshed around during high tides like fishermen rather than musicians and technicians. The Roggiero crisis came next.

When the opera was revived in Aix-en-Provence one year before, many cuts were made including an aria for Roggiero, another pants role. The Venice production was supposed to be definitive, but the complete opera is monumentally long. A tribunal of Rossini authorities, desperate to preserve and, at the same time, trim down the work, decided to eliminate Roggiero's big aria. Understandably upset, the young American mezzo singing the role came to me.

"Please, please, Miss Horne," she begged. "This is my big chance and it's all tied up in that aria. If they take it away, then I have nothing to show. Please, my career is in your hands!"

Right—her career was in my hands. And she was a mezzo, to boot. I decided to help her anyway.

The next day, I spoke to the tribunal, assuring them that in order to truly honor Rossini, Roggiero's aria must be included.

"After all, gentlemen," I purred, "the Aix-en-Provence *Tancredi* was a provincial production. Are you going to follow the lead of the provinces here in the very house where *Tancredi* premiered? Are you going to butcher the master's work?"

The tribunal relented and the aria was restored.

"Length" posed another problem. During the first week, I was presented with a splendid gold-trimmed royal-blue cloak. Alas, it was way too long for me and I kept tripping over my feet. I complained to the dresser, who replied,

"Ah, but Signora, the cloak is long to give you the noble line, to make you look, how you say.... grand."

"Garbage," I responded (or words to that effect), "it's long because my understudy takes over the part when I leave and she's a foot taller than I am!"

Thus saying, I walked out of the dressing room. The next time I assumed the mantle, the hemline had been raised. Let me explain... I didn't make a fuss about the cloak because I wanted to act the prima donna; no way. Singing on an opera stage is such hard work that it's absolutely necessary to feel completely in command. If you have to worry about the length of a garment or the reliability of a prop, it can take the edge off your concentration, adversely affecting the performance. For the same reason, it's important to keep in shape physically.

Singing is a strain on the entire body, not just the vocal cords and diaphragm. You have to move onstage; you can't simply stand there if you're going to create a part. My onstage woes came from my legs, not my lungs. Rather than my breath giving out, I worried more about my knees caving in. I had a whole set of exercises designed to keep my muscles from cramping up; when I neglected them, I suffered the consequences. Stendhal wisely noted that Giuditta Pasta as Tancredi presented "the aspect of the warrior." A real artist must give this aspect. Costuming is as important as movement in this endeavor. When I portrayed a young warrior, I liked to stride like a soldier and I needed the proper footwear to capture the movement. For Tancredi, I brought along a special pair of boots, the most comfortable ones I owned. They had three-inch heels and were built up inside— and not just for comfort. Not for nothing did my dad nickname me "Peanut." I'm short, and on stage I needed every inch I could get. My size was especially evident when I played trouser roles. Adalgisa, Carmen, Rosina, Isabella, Cenerentola—all those gals can be five-foot two, but Arsace, Orlando, Orfeo, Neocle, Rinaldo and Tancredi need elevation. I liked to be at least as high as my heroines and thanks to my special boots I usually reached an altitudinal compromise—with a few exceptions. I could have piled up boxes and stood tiptoe on them, and I'd still have been looking at Joan Sutherland's neck.

All in all, the rehearsal dramas in Venice played themselves out eventfully, yet more or less normally for opera. However, another crisis was brewing, one of a distinctly personal nature.

I've mentioned that Nicola Zaccaria, a Greek basso, also was in the cast. I knew Nico very well. He was a friend, a close friend—in fact, my love. Our relationship began after my breakup with Henry and had endured despite a triumvirate of difficulties: Nico's estranged wife, my own feelings about whether or not I wanted a permanent alliance and my daughter's mind-set—Angela was wary of the situation. Understandably, she didn't want anyone stepping into her father's place. Nico didn't speak much English, but was fluent in French, which Angela spoke. Still, she barely talked to him. If Hell hath no fury like a woman scorned, second place has to go to a teenage girl whose mother has taken up with another man. The Greek male gives new meaning to the word "macho," yet Nico was consistently kind and counseled me to be patient. Angela would be joining us to spend Christmas in Venice and though I was eager to see my baby, her presence would be a mixed blessing. I desperately hoped for "peace on earth" that Christmas—but, all things considered, I wasn't banking on it.

The problem with Nico's wife was equally perplexing. Not legally divorced, they'd been estranged for many years—even so, I didn't relish being with a married man; I didn't see myself in the role of the other woman. Fortunately, my work kept me from thinking too much about it. The dilemma wasn't going to go away, though, a fact that was driven home to me quite forcefully about two weeks into rehearsal.

In its own destructive way, the floods battering Venice were quite exciting. One afternoon, after a rehearsal, I decided to brave the waves and visit San Marco. Nico was off somewhere so I walked down the Calle Seconda de l'Ascension. A dress shop on the corner caught my attention. Who could walk by without looking in the window? I was standing there, checking the display, when I felt a tap on my arm. Now, I was used to being stopped by fans, and usually I smiled and moved on. I tried to move on then, but the person caught me by the sleeve. I turned around and knew immediately that this was no ordinary fan.

She was about my height and nearly my size. She had a strong Mediterranean face with wrinkles lining the corners of her eyes and mouth. I guessed her to be in her late fifties, still handsome but with a real sadness in her eyes.

"You are la Signora Horne?" she asked.

"Yes," I replied.

"I must talk to you," she said. "I am Elefteria Zaccaria."

What a jolt! I hope my mouth didn't fall open when she introduced herself. Signora Zaccaria never had contacted me in all the years I'd been with her husband, now she was here in person. Okay, I'm from Bradford, Pennsylvania, out of Long Beach, California but I know how to be civilized in the European manner—meaning, when you meet your boyfriend's wife, much as you would like to, you don't turn and run—you talk. I suggested that we go to the nearby Bauer Grunwald Hotel. She nodded in agreement and as we walked to the hotel she linked elbows with me in the cozy way European women have of strolling together. Anyone seeing us would have thought we were two old chums.

We took a table in the nearly empty lobby of the hotel. I could feel her staring at me as I removed my coat and draped it over the chair. I remember wishing I looked a little snappier. I was wearing a tight-fitting turban and no makeup—perfect for rehearsal but lacking in style for a personal drama. Worse, I'd put on weight. Isn't it ridiculous? I wanted to look my best.

We ordered tea and indulged in small talk about opera and Venice. She was staying at the Hotel Ala. The Ala is in the Campo Santa Maria del Giglio, directly across the square from the Gritti Palace apartments. Guess who was staying at the Gritti? She didn't come out and say so, but obviously, she checked our itinerary and carefully chose her vantage point. The choice was made all the more obvious when she told me that her room had no television, radio or telephone. I'm sure she pointed out the deprivations to contrast her sparse surroundings with my deluxe quarters, quarters in which her husband also was ensconced. Sure enough, the main topic surfaced.

"You, Signora Horne, have everything—a great career, fame, money, a child. Why did you take my husband?"

I understood how she felt, I'd been through a separation and divorce myself, and in many ways I sympathized with this woman—up to a point. I didn't like the way she had followed me nor did I like having to explain what I didn't feel had to be explained.

"I didn't take Nico away. You were separated long before I met him," I said forthrightly, adding that I was not the first, nor the only woman with whom Nico had had a relationship. (I knew of at least two sopranos and a mezzo, which I didn't mention to her).

Nothing I said had any effect. When I finished, Mrs. Zaccaria asked me to give him up.

"Even if I gave him up," I answered as gently as possible, "do you think he'd go back to you?"

She was silent for a moment. "Signora Horne, I have nothing in my life besides Nico. What can I do? What shall I do?"

Again, I was being asked for help but this time it wasn't a question of "restoring" an aria for a colleague, this was real life. The Zaccaria marriage had soured, not because of me; all I could do was try to convince her that I was not an adversary.

"Look," I explained, "I've told Nico not to get a divorce on my account. I do not want to marry."

That statement seemed to relieve her and when an opportune moment arrived, I suggested that we part. I paid the bill and we walked out into the square. Mrs. Zaccaria and I embraced, kissed and wished each other well.

That was some tea party that afternoon in Venice! Nico was aghast when I told him of our meeting.

"How could she? How could she?" he kept saying.

I tried to explain to him that under similar circumstances, I might have done the same thing. I didn't blame Elefteria Zaccaria, what concerned me was her proximity. Angela was arriving the next day and I didn't want my daughter mixed up in this affair.

My life was not grand opera—it was soap opera.

The following afternoon, I arranged for a launch to meet Angela at the airport. I returned to the Gritti Apartments in the early evening and found my teenager settled in. "The Who" blasted from the tape recorder and assorted clothing was strewn about the room. We hugged and kissed but I sensed a bit of a frost on my little pumpkin. Nico discreetly stayed away from the initial mother-daughter meeting. Still, though we each had a separate room in the three-bedroom suite, his presence was obvious. When Nico arrived and warmly welcomed Angela she greeted him indifferently and went into her room. Nico shrugged his shoulders and smiled; I sighed and began to prepare dinner. Despite my hopes, the prospects for a truly merry Christmas didn't look rosy. Being a mother was far more difficult than being a Tancredi.

Nico stayed out of the picture for the next few days; he was up and out of the apartment by the time Angela and I arose. The two of us would lunch together then go our separate ways. My route was ever the same: to the Fenice to rehearse all afternoon. As the strains of *Tancredi* filled the opera house, the sounds of the "The Who," "The Police," and "The Beatles" reverberated in the Gritti. Although Angela didn't go out much without me, she was cautioned not to talk to strangers if she did go out—especially, I wanted to add, to middle-aged Mediterranean ladies. I needn't have worried. Signora Zaccaria never crossed our paths. Nico took her out a few times and unsuccessfully tried to persuade her to leave. She stayed—at a judicious distance. Occasionally, I'd catch a glimpse of her walking in the piazza. What a situation. Opera is full of good guys and bad guys but life isn't so clearly divided. Mrs. Zaccaria was an unhappy woman—and because of my alliance with her husband, I couldn't classify myself as a thoroughly wonderful human being. All I could do was hope for the best.

As my domestic drama surged on, my operatic drama continued to take shape. Some roles are naturals—you shine no matter what you do. Arsace in *Semiramide* is such a role, while Tancredi is cut from different cloth—the kind of role that gives you a run for your money. Both marvelous and hellish to sing, Tancredi has three big arias and three big duets. You've got to be "up" for the entire evening— especially at the end when the dying Tancredi is carried onstage to sing the final aria, horizontally!

14

"How do you do it Jackie?" Lella Cuberli asked me after the first full run-through. "How do you keep it up? I'm ready to collapse after the prison scene."

How? Lella didn't have Bentz Horne for a father. I had to keep it up.

On opening night, an eerie Adriatic mist smothered the city and as we set out for the theatre, I couldn't help thinking how many times bad weather accompanied my important appearances. Always before, it had brought luck; I certainly hoped this evening would be no exception. Speaking of luck, La Fenice had a special tradition; before every performance, a cat was let in and sent down the center aisle. I don't know where the custom came from but I thought it charming, a kind of good-luck token for everybody. That night, as usual, the audience assembled, the house lights dimmed, the cat came in on little fog feet, and the overture began. Backstage, I climbed into the prow of Tancredi's ship and sailed into my Fenice debut.

Vocally, everything went well—splendidly, in fact—but I've rarely been in a production where something doesn't go wrong. This time, the glitch showed up in the very last scene. I was carried in on the bier which was set down center stage. Lella, as Amenaide, approached and I raised my head to acknowledge her. As I did, one of the pillows propped up behind me dislodged and began to slide down my face. My body was draped with a heavy cloth, pinning down my arms—I was helpless. As Lella bent over me, I whispered frantically, "Get the pillow out of my mouth!" Quickly, she stepped between the audience and me and knocked the pillow to the floor as we began to sing. We finished the final scene to thunderous applause. One hundred and sixty-eight years after its premiere, *Tancredi* remained a hit.

The critics, distrustful of the predominately foreign cast,

were unanimous in their praise. The Communist newspaper wrote, "If we're going to do Rossini, then we must hire Marilyn Horne and pay her whatever she wants. She's the only one who can do it." It must have killed them to write that.

The second performance went even more smoothly—no pillow in the mouth—and it appeared as though I could stop worrying and enjoy myself. If only I could do the same back at the Gritti; I so wanted our Christmas to be joyous.

On Christmas Eve, Venice was clear, chilly and shimmering with light. A huge Christmas tree glowing with red, green and yellow bulbs, stood in front of the Accademia. Angela and I passed it on our way to Standa, the Woolworth's of Italy, where we bought decorations. Next, we picked out a sweet little tree near the Rialto, and then loaded up with cold cuts, cheeses, bread, cakes, and wine at the local grocery. We returned to the apartment and trimmed the tree together, laughing and arguing over what should go where, just as we had done at home for so many years. We put out our presents and then dressed for the celebration.

A small group of friends, Lella, and her husband, Luigi; Nico; Angela; Ernesto and two or three others, arrived. The party began. Angela was a perfect hostess, chatting and giggling—but not in Nico's direction. We ate, sang Christmas carols and watched the Mass from St. Peter's on television. The time came to open presents. Angela gave me a delicate gold pin with a white coral rose in the center. I gave her goodies from Paris, including enough clothes, accessories and makeup kits to take her into middle age. (I have a tendency to go overboard in gift giving. Marty Katz, my friend and accompanist said I bought everything in bulk). Angela unwrapped another present, a wallet from Balenciaga. It was from Nico. She held it in her hands for a moment and then looked over at him.

"Thank you," she said, smiling and nodding toward him. She was so genuinely pleased, I couldn't believe it. And, I was in for another surprise. A minute later, Nico retrieved a package from under the tree. Inside was an assortment of chocolate liqueurs and a card reading, "To Nico, Merry Christmas, from Angela." Her first gift to him and I don't know who was more pleased, Nico or I. Angela had called a truce for the holiday and it was my best present. She didn't make a complete turnaround; she wasn't about to become best friends with him, but I wasn't asking for big miracles. The mini-miracle was enough to make that Christmas Eve a happy one.

Angela left Venice on December 30. We'd had a good time together and gotten along with a minimum of mother-daughter outbursts. Having her with me had truly made my holiday perfect.

Only four more performances remained before the hem of Tancredi's cloak would be let down for the next singer. Next, I was off to Milan for recording sessions of *Barbiere*, after which I would return to New York for a new production of the opera at the Metropolitan.

My last *Tancredi* performance on January 11, 1982, was non-subscription. Opera lovers came from all over—not a seat could be had. The house was so packed the cat probably had difficulty getting in. Once more, I stepped into the boat and, along with the audience fell under Rossini's musical spell. I actually had to repeat the opening aria, a rare and very special moment for me.

During my performing years, I sometimes experienced a spiritual, mystical feeling when singing, a feeling that's difficult to put into words because it was so tied to the music and the text. At those moments, it seemed like a sublime peace enveloped me. Usually it happened in recital. In opera, so much is going on you can't fully give yourself over to the music, whereas in concerts, one brief song can bring rapture. At the end of this *Tancredi*, as I lay on the bier, I looked up and out into the gold and blue jewel-box theatre and that singular ethereal feeling came over me. I was in the Fenice, surrounded by glorious music, singing a role first heard nearly two centuries ago. I was a part of history, part of an unbroken tradition of song and as the curtain fell on the final hushed chords, I thought to myself,

"If you're up there listening, Gioacchino Rossini, thank you, and I hope you liked it."

I'd come a long, long way to that special moment. Like Tancredi and so many other heroes that I portrayed, I had a quest in life, a quest that began in Bradford, Pennsylvania.

BRADFORD

Bradford lies four miles below the New York State line in the Appalachian Plateau region, not far from the Allegheny River. The plateau, a land of great divides, covers almost the entire northern and western portions of the state. The terrain of deep valleys, broad flattop plateaus and glacial rocks is most beautiful in the fall when colors burst over the rolling hills. Talk about Middle America... Bradford was a perfect example of Small Town, U.S.A, and it's where I was born.

The Hornes, and my mother's family, the Hokansons, had been around for a long, long time. The Van Hoorn brothers came from Holland in 1626 and my maternal great-grandparents, Wilhelm and Hulda Hokanson, along with their children, including five-year old Emil, sailed from Smoland, Sweden in the late 1800's. Plenty of my relatives were here in Colonial times—an ancestor even fought at Bunker Hill. That's the plus side—on the other side, my grandmother Sadie Hokanson was an adjunct member of the Ku Klux Klan, which none of us knew until she died. While going through her effects, they found a card proclaiming her a female member in good standing. Lucky for her she died before my marriage.

My great-grandfather, Sam Huff, fought at Bull Run and my other great-grandfather, David Horn, fought with the Union Army at Antietam, Fredericksburg, and Chancellorsville. When the war ended, he returned to York,

Pennsylvania, married Sarah A. Morningstar, and had four sons: Samuel, who assisted his father in a prosperous plumbing business; Luther, a businessman who patented and manufactured something called the Laraphone; Arthur, a talented musician who studied piano at the Stuart Gipes Academy of Music and Languages in York and my grandfather, James Bentz Horn. An insurance salesman and piano teacher by profession, James married Ada Mae Prunkard. Their son, Bentz, was born in Pittsburgh on November 7, 1906. Three years later, on January 20, 1909, Dad's only sister Adelaide was born. Most immigrant families lop off letters or syllables from their names—not my dad. For some reason, before he got married, he added a final "e" to Horn. (I should talk; in junior high school I did my own ornamentations by adding a final "n" to Marilyn. I dropped it when I went to Germany in 1956, and it's been Marilyn ever since.) My mother, Berneice Hokanson, was one of six children born to Emil and Sarah "Sadie" Huff Hokanson. The others were Ernest, Kenneth, Violet, Florence and Genevieve. Thanks to them, I had twelve first cousins on my mother's side.

My parents became parents while still in their teens; neither of them finished high school. They were married on June 2, 1926 and their first child, Richard Bentz, arrived on February 27, 1927. Gloria Dawn was born on May 23, 1931 and yours truly, Marilyn Berneice, made her debut at 3:20 p.m. EST on January 16, 1934—not 1929 as was erroneously recorded some fifteen years ago and which I've been trying to correct ever since.

Our household was, with few exceptions, American Normal. I was baptized in the United Brethren Church. Later, I joined the Methodist Church because we all sang in its choir. Later still, Mother, Gloria, and I became confirmed Episcopalians—"Catholic Lite," as Robin Williams termed it—and attended the Church of the Ascension. Dad and Dick

20

remained Methodists. I attended church regularly until I went to Europe and became what I call a Christian humanist. After being a magpie in the Protestant sects, I settled down into agnosticism. I rarely go to church but from time-to-time, I'll drop in to sit with my thoughts.

I was born at the height of the Great Depression. My dad went from job to job and barely made a living wage; my mother worked and raised the family. She always said the worst moment came when she had to leave baby Richard with Grandma Horne and travel thirty-five miles to her job in Warren. The separation was financially necessary but emotionally devastating. Years later, when career demands forced me to leave my daughter in the care of others, I truly understood my mother's distress.

Our house had a small store in the front and though I don't remember those days myself, I gather that Mom and Dad ran a grocery. We lived on Elm Street until we became more secure financially. Then we moved around the corner to number 9 Avenue B—a real step up. Number 9 was the best house on the block. Mom worked like a trouper around the house and then went off to work. In her absence, Nanny Horne acted as official baby sitter. She was there when we came home from school for lunch and after school let out. She fixed our meals, ironed, cleaned, mended clothes, applied bandages and did anything that was necessary. She'd only gone as far as the eighth grade, but what she lacked in education she made up for in humanity. Argumentative as all get-out, Ada Prunkard Horne gave her grandchildren nothing but love.

Music surrounded me from the very beginning and it was my father who set the stage. Music was his passion—a natural affinity, since his family was so thoroughly musical. His father and his uncles taught piano, and all my uncles sang in barbershop quartets. Dad's wonderful tenor voice

21

got him around and he performed everywhere—from the Methodist Church to the United Brethren Church, to the Jewish Temple. My dad should have been a professional singer, however the Depression was hardly the setting for such a chancy career. A job was a job, the steadier the better, and Bentz Horne had to provide for his family. Ironically the five dollars a week he made as a soloist in the church choir was what kept us going through those lean years.

Gloria and I were trained in music from infancy and while Dad encouraged us, he never pushed us. If he was frustrated or looking to live artistically through his children, I never noticed. He wasn't a bitter man nor was he a stage "mother" in the show-biz sense; he simply wanted us to do our best. He set a very high standard, which I spent a lifetime trying to reach and maintain. My training bears witness to his expert guidance.

"It's not good to start singing too young, unless you really know what you're doing," Dad cautioned.

It's true. If you begin to sing early and without proper instruction you can ruin the throat muscles. When a singer's voice goes, it's not because the vocal cords have given out, rather it's because the muscles of the larynx have lost their elasticity—and that can be a direct result of improper training. (You've probably heard a lot about Maria Callas "losing" her voice—well I believe she was a victim of a number of circumstances including her tremendous weight loss. Also, she might have lost the "great will" that it takes to sing as a result of the "good life" Mr. Onassis showed her.)

My dad was either an optimistic pessimist or a pessimistic optimist; if I had to settle for one definition, I'd go for the latter. I rarely disagreed with him except perhaps for his rule that "singers have to sing, no matter what!" (He made me sing if had a cold, or worse.) In principle, Dad was right

22

but in practice I found that necessary cancellations often were a wiser course. On a few occasions, which I'll discuss later, I made the mistake of going on when I shouldn't have.

My earliest memories of childhood are of song, not the phonograph or the radio, but living sound and it was my mother, not my dad, who first brought live melody into my life. She sang in church choirs with Dad and taught herself to play the piano by ear. She could play anything.....in the key of C. I wish I'd inherited that talent! Every day she played and sang, warbling melodies from Stephen Foster to pop tunes—not, however, operatic arias. Her sister-in-law, my Aunt Maybelle, was a fine pianist, and I remember listening enthralled to her playing. The Hornes definitely had a reputation for musicality. Singing brings people together and one of the great tragedies of modern times is the lack of real music in the home. Stacks of song books have been replaced by piles of CD's and instead of gathering around the piano, we huddle in front of the TV screen where shows like "American Idol" are a poor substitute for making your own music at home.

My debut, meaning I got through a whole number, occurred at around eighteen months. Apparently, I delighted my parents with a garbled rendition of "Walking in a Winter Wonderland." My precocity wasn't surprising. I'd been talking for some time and according to family lore, uttered my first word at six months.

"Apple," gurgled little Jackie.

It figures that my first word pertained to food—the beginning of my lifelong romance with nourishment.

By the age of two, I could sing my mother's repertoire. Auntie Maybelle claimed that I sang in church at that tender age. I was the Shirley Temple of the Appalachian Plateau, a dimpled, singing, darling and soon made my public appearance at a political rally for Franklin Delano Roosevelt.

Although Bradford was a Republican bastion, the Hornes were dyed-in-the-wool Democrats. We may have lived through a depression and a war, but in my childhood this country had a kind of stability that generations since haven't known. It may have been a false sense of security but it was security all the same. The one and only President of my childhood was God to my generation—superhuman. Although, FDR was crippled by polio, he was protected not only by his staff, but also by the media. In those days, the press observed an unwritten law and only photographed Roosevelt seated or standing unaided. Thus, children of the thirties and forties had no idea of his affliction, nor did many adults. The "secret" was kept. Today, they'd be selling his crutches on e-bay. FDR was the hope and the light to people like my parents and they worked furiously for him. Every election they were out there, and every election when the rest of Bradford went Republican, the Fifth Ward District stayed firmly in the Democratic camp.

I began my "professional" career at an FDR rally, and once I started, my dad went to work in earnest. Recognizing the importance of proper vocal schooling, he began coaching Gloria and me the minute we opened our mouths in song. Then, at the age of five, I began studying with Hazel Bittenbender. Ramrod-backed, prim, her hair cut short as a man's, Miss Bittenbender sang out of the side of her mouth. I was only five but I knew that was a no-no. Miss Bittenbender made me stand in the middle of the room and sing "Bah bay bee bo boo" over and over until I thought I'd go mad. The most I can say for her method is she didn't do me any harm. I was about seven when I moved on to the next instructor, Clayton Brennaman, choir director of the Catholic Church. Mr. Brennaman kept my head tones going and didn't interfere with my vocal progress. At around eight, I started studying with Edna Luce, a local singer who had a small career in Buffalo. Mrs. Luce probably was in her seventies—and this time, Dad picked a winner. Edna Luce taught me the basic technique of breath support, the very foundation of singing.

The principle of support is simple: you stand erect—like those cartoons of the prima donna with the big chest and straight spine—and as you inhale air, and as the muscle across your diaphragm expands, you push out and shove to keep it there while, at the same time, you tighten the buttocks and push down—exactly as though you were relieving yourself. (Italian singers used to employ suppositories and take "*una purga*" the night before a performance....just to be on the safe side.) As a result, the muscles of the diaphragm and the back become very strong, like a brick wall. In singing, breathing in is really breathing out—a yoga principle as well. A good singer knows that support is the key. When Luciano Pavarotti, Joan Sutherland and I did our televised concert at Lincoln Center in March 1981, we filmed an intermission discussion during which we divulged what we considered the secret of singing. Each of us said the same thing, "breath support." Ironically, in order to fit the interview into the allotted television time-block, someone chose to cut out that section. Here was advice straight from the horses' mouths—three of the biggest singers in the business—and out it went to fit the exigencies of prime time!

Mrs. Luce's instructions remained with me throughout my career.... as did many of the things my dad had to say including a piece of wisdom he gave me at the start of my formal training.

"Peanut," he advised, "if you want to get people's attention and hold it, sing softly."

I would heed his words some forty years later at my Metropolitan Opera debut, with significant results.

I honestly don't know what life would have been like without singing. Music got me around. Through church work I got to know kids outside of my district and made friends all over the city. And while it may sound contradictory, singing did and didn't interfere with my childhood. Although I didn't want to do it, I enjoyed doing it—especially when Gloria and I were appearing on bandstands. Singing in the Children's Choir at the Church of the Ascension, where Dad was a paid soloist and Mom was a chorister, was okay, but even then I leaned to the secular life.

I was seven when Gloria and I went "on the road." The two of us, sometimes along with Dad, appeared at a variety of places for a variety of events at bond rallies, service clubs and in school programs. Gloria and I had a ball at those rallies performing with the Citizens Band. Dad was the featured soloist and then he'd introduce us. It wasn't long before the Horne sisters took the spotlight away from their father. People called out for the "little girls." The bandleader was embarrassed for my dad but Dad was pleased as punch. He reveled in our popularity and stood by beaming while Gloria and I dressed in our finest, faces scrubbed, heads thrown back, belted out "Over There" and "You're a Grand Old Flag" with unbounded patriotic fervor. God, it was fun! My first formal recital took place at Kane High School. I was eleven and in total heaven but I loved the bond rallies more than the formal concerts.

I wonder if my sister's memories are as joyous as mine. We were very different, Gloria and I, and became more so as the years passed. Gloria had a voice, too, but early on opted for marriage and children. Sadly her marriage dissolved before mine. A voice isn't everything and while at times I wondered whether my career was worth the sacrifices, nothing could stop me from seeking that career and singing all that glorious music.

26

"Give Jackie an inch and she'll take a mile—and then some," my Mom always said.

I was a dynamo kid, constantly on the move, running ahead. My height had something to do with my velocity. Being short, I had to figure out angles taller people don't think about. There were advantages to my size, though—I was always first in line, and right up front in group photographs. I was sassy and many pictures show me with my tongue sticking out or grinning mischievously, chin in hand. Gloria was different; she liked to work things out before reacting. I was all action; she was contemplative. We fought like cats and dogs and drove Mother to distraction. But, when the time came to sing, hostilities ceased; whatever the differences in our personalities, we were a singing team. And I remained a team player throughout my career. You have to blend in order to produce the best effects and that's as true for singing "You're a Grand Old Flag" at a bond rally as it is for singing "*Mira, o Norma*" in an opera house. Even when I stood alone on the concert stage, my accompanist was there at the piano and the combination made the success. I pride myself on my ability to work well with others. For example, I went through three generations of *Semiramide* partners: Joan Sutherland, Montserrat Caballé and June Anderson. Up and coming exponents of my repertoire often heard, "Too bad you're singing in the time of Horne," which is flattering, yet there's always room at the top. And while I fought like an Amazon to keep my position, I never battled with a fellow artist onstage. (I'm not including a youthful fling in *Hänsel und Gretel* when I developed an antagonism toward the soprano and took full advantage of the scene in which I chased her with a broom.) Those magnificent bel canto duets go so well because they're a combined effort, the concentrated energies of two protagonists working together to carry themselves and the listeners into a musical euphoria.

Okay, back to Bradford.

I was about eleven when I became interested in the Metropolitan Opera's Saturday afternoon broadcasts. Gloria listened to them avidly; I was more casual in my appreciation, I wanted to have fun. In winter, I went to the movies—I'd take Van Johnson over Jan Peerce any day—and when spring arrived, I had to play baseball. Baseball was my sports love; I just watch it now but in my childhood I played, first as a catcher—I know they stuck me behind the plate because of my build—then as a first baseman. I played in games at the Fifth Ward School, the same institution my dad had attended. Lorina Peterson, a favorite teacher, taught me two important things: good penmanship and the love of learning. Miss Peterson loved music, too, and in her honor I put "Bethlehem Babe," a lovely carol she taught me, on a Christmas album I made with the Mormon Tabernacle Choir.

I was eager to use my singing skills at school—unfortunately they were either too refined or too unrefined. I didn't make the grade school glee club because, according to the teacher, Sigrid Johnson, I sang too loudly. I did appear in musical skits and plays, though, and treasure the memory of my role as Jolly Molly in the fifth-grade Christmas play. I sang "Up in Santa Land" and my Dad had me put a high C at the end. I cracked on it and the audience laughed. That didn't stop me; I went for it again and hit it right on!

Instead of acquiring a reputation as a singer, I became known as a "cut-up." From this vantage point, the word brat comes to mind but, if I was a brat, it was a special kind; I never wanted to hurt others. Gradually, I discovered that cut-ups weren't taken seriously. No matter how hard I worked, all I had to do was make a joke and people would flap their hands and say, "Oh that child, she's such a scamp." I guess because self-control and discipline ruled my musical

28

life, I naturally liked to let go in my everyday life. For me growing up meant learning how to superimpose restraint on my natural ebullience.

The sole discordant note in the Horne household was the lack of funds. Neither of my parents cared about money for themselves, they were only concerned about their children. How could we fully realize our potential if we didn't receive the proper musical education? The problem grew as we did. Bradford had just so much to offer and as I approached my teens, Mother and Dad decided to take action. We had to move—to live someplace where Dick, Gloria and I could get the best in general education and musical training...for the least amount of money. The options were clear: California and New York had the best state-supported educational systems and between those two, the choice was even clearer. Dad and Mom never would have survived the rigors of big city life.

Thus, in 1945, in true pioneer fashion, we stuffed a trailer with our belongings—including a refrigerator which was more precious than gold in those early post-war years—attached it to our 1939 Plymouth and set off for California, the land of sunshine and free colleges.

CALIFORNIA, HERE I AM

Pennsylvania provided a sensible down-to-earth eastern environment for my early years and, for good or for ill, certain tenets never left me. Something holds me back when I really want to let go—a sense of propriety I don't want to lose which I call the "little girl from Bradford" syndrome. It kept me from doing things that might have made me better known but which seemed beneath my dignity. Even when I was at the top of my profession, I remained perpetually on the brink of being a household word. The fact is you have to be a bit outrageous in order to be outstanding, particularly in the classical music field. Enrico Caruso provides a good example of what I mean. The great tenor arrived in the United States hard on the heels of the elegant Polish tenor, Jean de Reszke, and many comparisons were made between the suave, courtly Pole and the bumptious, portly Neapolitan. When Caruso was accused of pinching a woman's backside in the Central Park Zoo, the press had a field day. Sure, the glory of his voice made Caruso a legend, but the little episode in the monkey house definitely gave his career a boost up the contemporary fame ladder. The truth is opera singers don't reach that many people unless they cavort for the media. In general, the public remains naïve about the selling of personalities. Does anyone believe great fame is not the result of great publicity? Every time a name appears, other than in reviews, it's been put there directly or indirectly via publicity. I know of very few artists who do not employ a publicist, which has its good and its bad aspects. On the plus side, your name gets around, your legend is built up and so are your fees. On the minus side, you can start believing your own publicity. Some artists spend more time making their name than doing their work.

I can't resist telling the story of an American soprano who suffered from PRM (Public Relations Mania). She had all the stuff—youth, talent, looks and a good figure. She'd been heavily publicized by a flashy agency and then went to Columbia Artists Management where Humphrey Doulens agreed to accept her as a client—if she did exactly as he told her.

"A woman of your stature, and the artist you can be, must not do cheap tricks for the public," he cautioned. "It's beneath your dignity as an artist and mine as an artist's manager."

The soprano acquiesced and a contract was signed. Doulens went to work planning a grand campaign, including a Time magazine cover. One day, he walked into his office and on his desk found a copy of the Daily News open to the rotogravure section. On a two-page spread he saw a photograph of his client, clad in a bikini, lying on the ground, with a sailor standing on her chest. The caption read: "Never Underestimate the Diaphragm of a Diva." The Diva's contract was revoked.

I don't tell this story to diminish the accomplishments of artists who become popular idols—that would be sour grapes—but you do pay a price. I've been on enough TV shows myself, from Arthur Godfrey to Dave Letterman, to realize how beguiling popular acclaim and adulation can be—and, how fleeting. After appearing on the Tonight Show, I never was asked about myself; rather the question invariably was, "what's Johnny Carson really like?" And while

I'm sure no one asked Johnny what I was like, in fifty, a hundred, maybe two hundred years, I hope that someone will turn on a machine and hear what Marilyn Horne sounded like. For this I honored and served my muse—and kept sailors off my chest.

Back to sunny California.

My parents, solidly established in their hometown, must have had trepidations about resettling; even so, they never let Dick, Gloria or me see their misgivings. Studies on the effects of moving tell us that the accompanying sense of upheaval often creates permanent damage to the psyches of children. My psyche wasn't permanently damaged although it was hard at first. Eventually, we all flourished in the new setting, even Dad although it was hardest for him to make the adjustment.

Not until we moved to California did I appreciate our country's topography. Geography be damned—when you lived in Bradford, Pennsylvania, America was hills, rivers and plateaus. Lush and lively Long Beach was a revelation and within months, I became a child of the surf. I fell in love with the climate and the ambiance; the novelty of coming home from school and jumping into the ocean never wore off. I still remember long walks home after parties, or dates, along streets flowering with night-blooming jasmine and magnolia trees, and hearing the soft sounds of conversation, most of them centering around who wanted a kiss goodnight and who was going to grant it. Life was sweet and simple then, absolutely a kid's paradise. I've lived in lots of places since, but California has remained the place for me.

At first, it wasn't quite a Garden of Eden, largely because of the housing shortage. My parents chose Long Beach because mother's sister Violet and her husband, Loran Ferguson, lived there. We moved in with them—a jolting comedown for the former residents of Number 9, Avenue B—and stayed for several months. Then, when Dad went back east to close out his affairs, Mom, Gloria and I—Dick had joined the Air Force—rented a room in a Mrs. Woodring's house. We had kitchen privileges, but the living wasn't easy with three of us jammed into tight quarters. Mom and Gloria slept in the bed, I occupied an Army cot. Six months later, Dad returned; now we were four.

We left Mrs. Woodring and moved into Mrs. Loma Murphy's home on Fifth Avenue. Dad and Mother slept in one room and Gloria and I had to make do on a fold-down couch in the living room. It wasn't very restful. Mrs. Murphy was not a kind landlady. Gloria and I had to be up and out early, or she would have folded us up in the bed.

That Christmas, Dad bought a tree which took up most of the bedroom. We decorated it as best we could and then stood around it, singing carols. Mrs. Murphy looked in at us and scowled.

"Well, maybe she's never seen a family enjoy Christmas before," Dad volunteered. "This might change her disposition for the better."

It didn't.

When Dick returned, Dad rented a small apartment from Mrs. Murphy. Although we had more space, conditions weren't much improved. Dick slept on a couch in the living room, I slept in a bed in my parents' bedroom and Gloria shared the back bedroom with Reva Abernethy, a young friend of mother's from Bradford. Reva came with my Dad when he returned and we took her in. Dad and Mom weren't savvy enough to buy their own place right away or at least grease someone's palm to get a decent rental. The fact that we were suffering while real estate went wild in post-war California made it all the more frustrating. In 1950, we moved into our own home, one of the happiest days of our lives. Then, after my brother Jay was born, Nanny Horne came West to join us.

I was enrolled in the seventh grade at George Washington Junior High School and vividly remember wanting desperately to belong, especially to the top echelon of students. Any kid who's been uprooted might have the same feeling, however, I was luckier than most. I had a special way of getting in; my voice broke the social barrier.

Seventh-graders took art in the first semester and I struggled with drawing and painting for which I had no aptitude. Second semester began and music replaced art. On the first day, we were required to perform en masse for the teacher. The class stood up and started vocalizing. After a few minutes, the teacher, Mrs. McCartney, tapped her baton on the desk. We stopped.

"I hear a voice back there," she said. "Continue singing, class."

We began again and once more were brought to a halt by the baton.

"I hear a voice!" reiterated the teacher.

Mrs. McCartney moved toward us a like a worm-minded bird, head cocked to one side, eyes darting over the rows of students.

"Who is that voice?" she cried. With one move, the kids turned and pointed to me.

"What's your name, young lady?"

"Marilyn Horne."

"Come up here, Marilyn, and sing for me."

Even as I stepped forward, I knew my acceptance ticket had been issued. Truly, it wasn't calculated—I've always known that my voice was my entrée. Naturally Dad had a comment on that subject:

"Just remember, Peanut, they only like you for your voice."

It sounds like a putdown but Dad really was trying to impress me with two things. (1) the importance of working hard to keep the voice going, and (2) the probability that others would disappoint me. Like Yeats's Anne Gregory, I've wished to be "loved for myself alone," but I'd be a fool if I didn't acknowledge my debt to that little piece of gristle in my throat.

Once word of my triumph spread, I became part of the George Washington social scene—invitations for parties, picnics and shows poured in. I became active in school politics, a mini-FDR, and when I ran for office, I usually won. I literally sang my way into everything. They said I sounded like Kirsten Flagstad, and I believed them. Imagine!

Meanwhile, Dad, who looked for opportunities in music the way Sherlock Holmes looked for clues in mysteries, discovered the Los Angeles Bureau of Music. Immediately, he wrote a letter to them extolling his singing daughters. The Bureau, a musical clearinghouse or melodic matchmaker, numbered Roger Wagner among its members. He was the director of the Concert Youth Chorus (eventually the Roger Wagner Chorale). Gloria and I auditioned and were accepted into the Wagner group. No one could have had a better apprenticeship! At the age of twelve, I joined an assembly of exceptional singers, among them Marni Nixon, whose career of dubbing singing voices in Hollywood films (Deborah Kerr in *The King and I*, Audrey Hepburn in *My Fair Lady*) would somewhat obscure her own talent; Harve Presnell, a big strapping baritone who appeared with Debbie Reynolds in *The Unsinkable Molly Brown*; and Bruce Yarnell, another gifted baritone. Bruce appeared in opera as well as musicals. What's more, he often flew his own plane to and from engagements. Bruce was a happy go lucky guy and flying was his obsession. The last time I saw him, we were appearing on separate stages in

Sioux Falls, South Dakota. We got together for dinner and of course he carried on about flying.

"For heaven's sake Bruce," I said to him over dessert, "why don't you stop flying the plane of yours around? The next thing you know, I'll read that you slammed into the side of a mountain."

Tragically, not long after, that's exactly what happened.

The Roger Wagner Chorale was an exceptional group, equally at home in a church, the Hollywood Bowl, the Shrine Auditorium or on Hollywood sound stages. Roger Wagner himself was as extraordinary as his eponymous organization. Born in Le Puy, France, he came to this country at the age of seven. His father, a Ph.D. in music and concertmaster at St. Brendan's Catholic Church, wanted a musical career for his son. Roger, however, was interested in sports and might have become a professional athlete had he not broken his arm in a high school football game. That accident turned out to be a lucky break for music. The senior Wagner immediately plucked his son out of Fairfax High and sent him back to France for further schooling. Roger studied at the Paris Conservatoire, and received his musicology doctorate cum laude from the University of Montreal. Oh, and he also picked up a silver medal in the 1936 Olympics as part of the French decathlon team! Upon his return to Los Angeles, Roger not only taught music, he coached basketball, baseball and track at Mount Carmel High and somehow found time to form a choral group. Alfred Wallenstein, conductor of the L.A. Philharmonic, persuaded Roger to turn his chorus professional, and the rest is history. The Roger Wagner Chorale was an integral part of musical life in Hollywood, on and off the movie screen. I'm so proud I was part of it.

In 1947, while singing at a Jackson Day Dinner with the Chorale, I met Eleanor Roosevelt. Herbert Stothart, MGM's music director, had set FDR's Inaugural Address to music and we performed "The Only Thing We Have to Fear." (I still remember it! But, who could forget those "lyrics?") After the performance, Dad, Gloria, and I sat on the stairs leading to the kitchen, listening to Mrs. Roosevelt speak. When she finished, I got up and marched right over to her and stood there tongue-tied. For once in my life, I was flustered. In the presence of that magnificent woman, I couldn't think of anything to say. I finally blurted out,

"Could I have your place card, Mrs. Roosevelt?"

"Of course, my dear," she said, adding modestly, "it's an honor to give it to you."

What a gracious woman she was, and what a lesson in genuine humility she provided.

Moments like this stayed with me always. I remembered what it was like to be on the other side of the autograph book, which is why I tried to accommodate everyone who asked for my signature or photograph. Sometimes there were unexpected results. Once, after a Boston recital, a young blind woman with a seeing eye German shepherd joined a line of fans in the Green Room. She introduced herself as Pauline and we chatted about music as the dog stood by quietly.

"Beautiful animal," I said. "May I pat him?"

"It's a she," answered Pauline. "Her name is Gloria and sure, you can pat her."

I reached over and gently roughed the back of the dog's neck. She responded like a music critic—didn't even wag her tail.

At Pauline's request, I took a program and wrote a message to her thanking her for coming. She thanked me and moved off. (I couldn't help wondering why a blind person would want an autograph.) A minute later, she returned, escorted by another woman who asked,

"Miss Horne, would you mind signing again?"

For a second, I thought she was using Pauline to get to the head of a rather long line. I was about to remonstrate when she handed me Pauline's program. I looked down and saw that I had written: "Dear Gloria, Many thanks for being with me today. Sincerely, Marilyn Horne." It may be the only time a dog received an autograph. Truly, I have nothing but appreciation for fans—human or canine—genuinely moved by performances, who ask for autographs.

At times, though, autograph hounds can become a little too ardent and bombard the artist with requests. They ask for enough signatures to fill a telephone book. After you're presented with nine or ten extra pieces of paper by dozens of fans and asked to write to persons not at the concert, you do begin to fuss a bit. You know that the autographs are going to be sold. In this instance, the artist isn't being picky when he or she says, "That's all." Lois Kirschenbaum was the queen of autograph seekers in the old days and because of her avocation, she became an institution. Lois often knew their schedules better than the artists themselves! One time, after I appeared with Renata Scotto, I went into Scotto's dressing room to say goodnight. As I left, Lois came running down the hall waving her arms, crying "Renata! Renata!" Lois, who's very nearsighted, pressed a pen and paper into my hand and then peered into my face.

"You're not Scotto!" she declared, and snatching back the autograph material, stormed away.

Remember the Judy Garland/Mickey Rooney films about kids having a high old time getting in and out of scrapes and putting on shows? Well, from George Washington through Polytechnic High School, I actually lived that life. I was popular, a good student and yes, still a cut-up. From imitations to asides, my lips were never sealed. In the eighth grade, I corrected the choir director's Latin pronunciation during rehearsals. She told Royal Stanton, Polytechnic's music director, that Little Miss Horne had a very big mouth. Mr. Stanton decided to take me down a peg or two and gave me low grades in choir. I got mad and quit. You can guess the rest. The a cappella group needed me more than I needed it. Soon the music director came around for a discussion. We worked out an amicable agreement and I returned to the fold. Royal Stanton was a great teacher and really broadened my musical horizons—later, we became good friends.

Here's what I learned as a result of my shenanigans: when you have an extraordinary ability, you can throw your weight around. In general, public school teachers of my day didn't know what to do with gifted students. As a result, nine times out of ten, I managed to get my own way. Luckily, proper standards were established at home and my parents made sure they were met. Otherwise, I would have been unbearable.

Gloria and I sang in the girls' choir at St. Luke's Episcopal Church and William Ripley Dorr, the choir director, became another mentor. Singing the choral works of Haydn, Beethoven and Bach gave me a deep and abiding appreciation of the great masters. California indeed was providing the musical education and stimuli Dad and Mother had anticipated.

From day one, my goal remained constant. One teacher at Polytechnic remembered our first meeting, a classic teacher- pupil confrontation.

"What do you want to be when you grow up?" she asked.

"An opera singer at the Met," I immediately replied.

Later, the teacher confided that she was both amused and bemused by my statement; I was the first California student she'd ever come across who didn't want to be a

39

movie star.

I may not have wanted to be a star, but movies were very much a part of my life, and not merely going to them, either. I became involved with films for real because of my work with the St. Luke's Chorus and the Roger Wagner Chorale. You see, films needed background music, and St. Luke's and the Wagner choirs were two of the groups that supplied it. Ergo, I began a behind the scenes movie career singing in the chorus. And while I was doing this, I attended classes on the MGM lot. (My classmates included Roddy McDowall, Claude Jarman, Jr., and a pretty teen-ager named Elizabeth Taylor.)

The first movie I worked on was *Joan of Arc*, a spectacular failure starring Ingrid Bergman. This quasi-religious epic reading of Maxwell Anderson's play, called for a background wash of liturgical music, a natural for the Roger Wagner gang. Although I was a bona fide member of the Chorale, I was underage and had to get special permission from the Screen Actors Guild to participate. (The dispensation, I might add, came long after my professional singing began—I got my first paycheck at age seven.) With this film I entered the "DooWah" years.

In movies, whatever the required music—liturgical, classical, romantic or pop—the "lyrics" remained the same and consisted of "DooWah, DooWah, DooWah." Television programs also incorporated the DooWahs. "I Married Joan," a popular sitcom of the fifties, became one of the first shows to employ the Wagner Chorale and we DooWahed for season after season. In one episode, Joan Davis and her TV husband, Jim Backus, were vacationing in Hawaii. Naturally, the chorus was supposed to provide appropriate island DooWahs. But, what's Hawaii without an electric guitar? The call went out with no immediate results. Production was held up as we sat around waiting for the guitar to appear—until yours truly came to the rescue.

"I can imitate an electric guitar," I told the choir director.

To demonstrate, I held my nose with my thumb and finger and pressed and released them against my nostrils while humming island tunes. Roger Wagner was delighted. Following a quick run-through, the DooWahs were recorded with me playing solo nostrils. I couldn't blow my nose for a week after that but, as Tosca sings, "*Vissi d'arte.*" P.S. If you ever catch a rerun of the Hawaiian episode of "I Married Joan," listen closely to hear, if I do say so myself, a mean electric guitar.

At fifteen, I became a paid soloist for the California Heights Methodist Church Choir. I didn't find out till much later that the conductor, Dorothy DeCoudres, actually paid my fifteen-dollar-a-month salary out of her own pocket. Not only that, she bought gowns for me so I'd be properly dressed for performances. (Ms. DeCoudres is one of two important Dorothys in my life—more on the other Dorothy, later.)

During my junior year in high school, I got the lead in the school musical, Lehar's *The Merry Widow*. My first appearance in operetta and I was the star! I barely knew what a bride was, let alone a widow, which didn't stop me from reveling in the role of the *lustige* Hanna Glawari. My girlfriend Joanne Pagones also was in the cast. Joanne had a sparkling personality and a lovely singing voice. We sang together at Rotary Club meetings and the like. We'd pick up ten dollars a performance plus reviews in the Rotary paper, eg: "The little vocalists Marilyn Horne and Joanne Pagones could not only sing, but are pretty." Joanne and I were so close that we kept our nighties at each other's houses in case we decided to stay over on the spur of the moment. One time, during an overnight at the Hornes, my Dad walked into the living room where Joanne and I were rehearsing.

He listened a bit and then pointed a finger at me and said, "You, the Met." Then, he pointed to Joanne and said, "You, Broadway." Dad was on the money. You know my story and Joanne actually appeared as Irene Malloy in *Hello, Dolly!* with Carol Channing. Eventually, Joanne gave up her career to devote time to her husband and his career. The Horne family certainly approved of her decision—she married my brother Dick.

The Merry Widow was a huge success. According to the local paper, "Marilyn Horne, as the Merry Widow, was convincing. Her vocalism had a dependable security, and as it went up, it acquired considerable resonance and brilliance." (They liked my high notes.) Royal Stanton generated much of the joy in *The Merry Widow*. I still have the program in which he wrote: "Jackie, You have made me very proud—I anticipate the brightest future for you, since you have so much and know so well how to use it. Be assured of my continuing interest in you and all you do." Royal Stanton was a very positive influence on my career and I remain grateful for his support and his friendship. We kept in touch until his death. (Recently, I saw his two daughters and we reminisced about the old days when I went to their house to rehearse. They were just kids at the time but they remembered.)

All told, 1950 was a banner year. Besides T*he Merry Widow* and the Rotary meeting songfests, I was president of the Portia Society and Secretary of Phi Gamma Chi Sorority. (And, it was around this time that I decided that "Marilyn" needed a touch of sophistication and added the other "n." I was Marilynn Horne until I got to Germany and lopped off the extra consonant.) In June of 1950, I was chosen as one of the outstanding music students from Long Beach's three high schools. I received a season ticket to the Hollywood

Bowl Symphonies Under The Stars series.

Musically speaking, senior year at Polytechnic was a bit of a letdown. Royal Stanton had left and musicals were given in alternate years. Scholastically, though, all went well. I won a scholarship to the University of Southern California, and not only on musical ability, I also had an excellent academic record. Everything seemed to be looking up. Was there a fly in the ointment? Something that kept everything from being perfect? Well, I guess there was...is...and probably always will be—my weight. (The truth is, when I look at pictures from those days, I marvel at how thin I was.)

Someone once asked me what was the greatest struggle of my life and I'm sure anticipated a musical answer, a difficult role, or a song I couldn't master, something like that. My reply, however, was quick and sincere: "My greatest struggle is not to weigh three hundred pounds." Totie Fields, a wonderful comedienne, used to say she wasn't fat; she was the perfect weight, just the wrong height—me, too. I've fought the battle of the bulge all my life. Psychologically, I can understand my need for food—the travel, the loneliness, and the pressures—all those insidious incentives that propelled me into the cupboard. And I've tried everything.

In 1982, I began going to Structure House in Durham, North Carolina. It's been a haven for me for over twenty years. And boy, have I lost weight there. And man, have I gained it back. Structure House has one of the best programs for dealing with weight problems and severe obesity. You learn about foods and the psychology of eating. What it boils down to is, it's not what you're eating it's what's eating you. Although I'm living proof that it's no sure panacea, Structure House provides an incentive and a refuge and some people really do make life adjustments. I have resisted. Recently I went back for a three week stay. I was waiting to go into the dining room along with a trio of women. We started talking and one lady said to me, "Have you been here before?"

"Me? Why, I've been coming here off and on for twenty years."

A look of horror crossed their faces. I knew they wanted the quick fix. Forget it. It doesn't exist.

I know I'm too fat, and I'd strike a bargain with the devil for a permanent weight loss but "The Diet Secrets of Marilyn Horne" would not be a book destined for the best-seller lists. I'll let you in on a little secret, though. Excess pounds may drive me crazy but they never stopped me from enjoying life, especially the romantic life. Weight and all, I've gotten what I've wanted in music—many great singers are great in size, after all—and I've done all right in love, too. I always had plenty of men friends; I had the same beau in my freshman year at USC that I had in high school. We were still seeing each other when I met Henry Lewis.

I first saw Henry in 1951. I was on my way up the steps of the wide veranda that skirted the Victorian music building at USC and caught sight of this six-foot-one hunk talking to a group of friends.

"Wow," I thought to myself, "that guy's good-looking!"

As it turned out, Henry not only was good-looking, he was immensely talented and already a groundbreaker in his field—the Jackie Robinson of music. A double bass virtuoso, Henry went into the Los Angeles Philharmonic at the age of sixteen—the first black ever to join a major symphony or-chestra. Oh sure, there were other black musicians and con-ductors but—to continue the baseball analogy—they were all in the minors. Henry was a major leaguer. In 1955 he became conductor of the Seventh Army Symphony in Ger-many. Then, after his discharge in 1957, he went back to the bass section of the L.A. Philharmonic and from there he

44

went on to become the music director of the New Jersey Symphony. What happened to our marriage never changed my opinion of his musicianship; he was sensational.

Although I admired his looks, Henry had little impact on my life during the next couple of years. He was around, but so were others. Frankly, I was too busy with my music and classes to spend much time with any one man. The exceptions to that rule were my teachers. The way I selected them—one of them anyway—was typical Horne behavior.

I went to register for classes knowing nothing about the instructors. I was pondering over the choices when a student employee in the registrar's office, noticing my hesitation, asked me my course of study.

"Music," I said cheerfully, "I'm a singer."

"Who're you going to study singing with?

"Who's good?"

"Well, I'm studying with Bill Vennard and he's terrific. Why don't you go for him?"

"Okay, I'll put his name down."

I wrote down William Vennard on my form and because of my extensive research, I was fortunate enough to come under the wing of a remarkable teacher.

Although Bill modestly referred to himself as merely a "keeper" of my voice, he was a great deal more and, among other things, taught me exercises that I still use myself and in my teaching. At first, I wasn't as appreciative of him as I should have been; I wanted to sound like a combination of my opera heroines, Renata Tebaldi and Ebe Stignani. Tebaldi, the glorious Italian soprano, was very popular in the United States while Stignani, the mighty Italian mezzo, was more famous in her native land. I knew them both through their records and their appearances with the San Francisco Opera Company and I admired them to the point of imitation. Vennard's course of study was not turning me

45

into a Tebaldi-Stignani clone. So, exactly as I had done in high school when the choir director thwarted me, I bolted. I left Vennard and engaged two other teachers willing to do what I wanted. Neither of those instructors did me any good—worse, one caused real damage. After four lessons, the entire top of my voice, which had been so easy, disappeared. The feeling of how to go up the scale was gone. I couldn't sing an F top line, a cinch before my Vennard defection. I was scared stiff and penitently returned to him. Within a week, he had me soaring again.

I was very lucky this decisive moment came early. Anyone with a natural voice who doesn't understand the technical aspects of how that voice is produced eventually will get into trouble. The pressures of singing before the public, the traveling, the physical and vocal fatigue, all are important factors and heaven help the singer who doesn't know how to open up and when to shut up. The minor crisis I went through at age twenty made me want to learn everything about the technical aspects of my art. I made it my business to learn as much as I possibly could about the production of the singing voice and my erudition was a direct result of my association with Bill Vennard.

I also studied with Gwendolyn Williams Koldofsky, head of the Song Literature and Accompanying Department—a fortuitous association in every way. Gwen became my accompanist in 1953. (Fourteen years later, I asked her star pupil, Martin Katz, to take over, and Marty has been with me ever since.) While I was in school Gwen acted as my "social director" and also interceded for me in scholastic matters. At one point, I was up to my old tricks, especially in Harmony Class. I didn't think that the professor, the composer Leon Kirchner, was much of a teacher but, in all fairness, I couldn't stand the subject. Near the end of the semester, Professor Kirchner called me into his office and delivered an ultimatum.

"Miss Horne, you are capable of getting an A in this class and you are doing C work. I refuse to give you a C. You'll either get an A, which is what you can and should do, or I'll fail you."

"That's not fair," I protested. "You can't do that to me. I'll take the C!"

Kirchner was adamant, so naturally I went running to Gwen. She, in turn, pleaded my case.

"Marilyn is one of the great hopes for singing," she informed him, "and really is terribly sincere about her voice, even if she isn't so sincere about Harmony."

Thanks to her, Kirchner relented and I got the C.

Friends like Gwen, Dorothy DeCoudres, Dorothy Huttenback (who'll appear later), Bill Vennard, William Ripley Dorr, Roger Wagner, Jack Metz and my coach, Fritz Zweig, a great musician from the old German school, and so many others gave me the kind of encouragement I needed. Thanks to them, I got through some rough times—rough because I always was under financial strain. Consequently, I had to take on a lot of odd jobs—some very odd ones, indeed.

THE PIRATE QUEEN MEETS LOTTE LEHMANN

In the early fifties, a form of licensed larceny existed in the recording industry. In those pre-LP/CD days, popular songs came out on 78-rpm singles with an A and a B-side—the former was a possible hit, the latter, a filler. (Sometimes the tables were turned and the B became the hit like Gene Autry's "Rudolph the Red-Nosed Reindeer.") Frank Sinatra, Bing Crosby, Patti Page, Vaughn Monroe, Frankie Laine, Johnnie Ray, Rosemary Clooney and other popular artists, recorded songs that became anybody's property, which is very different from the present situation. In the popular field today, soloists and groups are so closely identified with their product, often written by them, that they beggar imitation. Fifty years ago, those restraints weren't there and "pirate" records, pure and simple imitations, became a thriving business. The process was simple: If a singer like Buddy Clark had a hit record with a major label, a pirate company would hire someone to mimic Clark's voice and delivery along with an orchestra to re-create the back-up sounds and, *voilà*, a pirate record—for far less money. Released under the "Varsity" label, pirates were distributed through nationwide chains, such as Sears Roebuck.

I got into pirate recordings through Charlie Scharbach, a fellow member of the Roger Wagner Chorale, and a fellow participant in the Madrigal Singers at USC. Charlie came to a rehearsal and announced that he'd been hired to do some background DooWahs on a pirate record.

48

"They need female voices, too, Jackie, and I gave them your name. They're holding auditions this afternoon."

It not only seemed like a good way to make money, it sounded like a lark. I went over to Garrison's recording studio in Long Beach, auditioned successfully, and soon was behind the mike doing my DooWahs. Within a few weeks, I let the powers that be know that I could do more than backup bellowing. Before long, I was given solo bits and made my first "gold record." Kay Starr, a headliner of the day, had a big hit called, "The Wheel of Fortune." The lyrics went something like, "the wheel of fortune goes spinning around... please don't pass me by, let me know the magic of a kiss and a sigh... while the wheel is turning, turning, turning, I'll be yearning, yearning, yearning," and so on. Ms. Starr had a distinctive delivery—a word like wheel came out "hu-wee-el" and fortune became "fah-hor-ti-yoon." Her multi-syllabic style was fun to recreate and though I made no personal fortune from it, this record did start me off on my new "ca-ree-ah."

Prep time was minimal. I'd go to Garrison's, listen to the original while following along with the sheet music and then, incorporating my skills as a trained classical musician and a born mimic, I was ready to roll. The producers were delighted with my fast work, but not elated enough to up the ante. I was paid forty dollars whether I sang as Kate Smith, Kay Starr or did my DooWahs.

After "The Wheel of Fortune," I did my take on Peggy Lee's fast-paced sexy version of the Rodgers and Hart waltz, "Lover." Here was the future Rosina and Tancredi spilling out at break-neck speed, "Lover, when I'm near you, and I hear you speak my name softly in my ear, you breathe a flame." I did a damn good job of approximating Miss Lee's sibilant, insinuative style, which was remarkably suited to Carmen's "*Habanera*." The next pirate was even more fun.

The guys at Garrison's called me into the office.

"We want you to record 'Bermuda,' you know: the one by the Bell Sisters," Hal Loman, the orchestra leader told me. "The only thing is, you're going to need a 'sister.'"

"I've got one!" I shouted, "And she's a singer, too."

I called Gloria. She came over, auditioned and before long both of us were pirates, DooWahing in the background and singing solos, too. Gloria did her version of Ella Mae Morse's "Blacksmith Blues," while I moved onto Jo Stafford's turf and recorded "Hambone." Miss Stafford's rendition included a syncopated pop every few bars, which sounded like a cork being pulled from a bottle. The studio had no bottle or cork and in order to recreate the sound, I puffed up my cheeks, stuck my finger in the side of my mouth and then pulled it forward quickly to get the "pop." Between playing my nose with Roger Wagner and popping my cheeks for Hal Loman, I was turning into a one-woman band.

I worked at Garrison's, on and off, for about two years and, though I thoroughly enjoyed myself, it made my schedule even more frenetic. Finally, I had to walk the plank as far as my pirate career. Sadly, I never thought to save any of the fifteen or twenty solo records I cut. A few became collector's items and are still around.

During my sophomore year, besides flourishing as a Pirate Queen, I also marked a watershed in my classical studies—I received a grant to study with the legendary soprano, Lotte Lehmann, who taught master classes at Cal Tech and the Music Academy of the West. Lotte Lehmann occupies a hallowed niche in the singers' pantheon. Critics and fans wax eloquent over her "human completeness," beauty of tone and technical sureness—and, like other titans of the past, she was elevated to sainthood. (I'm waiting; I'm waiting.)

Born in Perlberg, Germany, in 1888, Lehmann made her operatic debut in Hamburg in 1909 as the first or second boy (depending on which source you read) in Mozart's *Die Zauberflöte*. In 1916, she went to the Vienna Hofoper and until 1938, was that house's outstanding artist; she was most famous for her consummate portrayal of the Marschallin in Strauss's *Der Rosenkavalier*. Lehmann made her American debut in 1930 with the Chicago Opera Company as Sieglinde in Wagner's *Die Walküre* and in 1934, made her Metropolitan debut in the same role. Lehmann sang at the Met until 1945 and then spent the next six years on the concert stage. After a brief cinematic fling with MGM (which resulted in exactly one film, *The Big City*, in 1948), she retired to Santa Barbara where she taught at The Music Academy of the West. Occasionally, she sang in public and when the recitals were on the West Coast, her accompanist was Gwen Koldofsky. It was through Gwen that I got to Mme. Lehmann.

In 1951, Lehmann arrived at USC to conduct master classes for the Adolf Koldofsky Memorial Scholarship, which Gwen established in honor of her late husband. Adolf, concertmaster of the RKO orchestra in the glory days of film-studio symphonies, was not only an outstanding musician, but also a genuine humanist; he championed the music of Arnold Schönberg by playing the composer's sonatas and concertos whether or not the audiences were willing to listen. Lehmann's master classes were held in Bovard Auditorium and to my great delight, I was chosen as a participant.

At seventeen I learned my first "lied" or song, Schubert's *"Die Junge Nonne"* (The Young Nun). Mme. Lehmann was satisfied with my work and invited me to join her next series of classes at Cal Tech. I was thrilled but how was I going to afford it? Once again, I got lucky, this time thanks to Carolyn Scott. A true patron of the arts, Carolyn came by her philanthropy the hard way. Her only child, a daughter, died suddenly, and, barely two months later Carolyn's husband dropped dead in the street. Both Carolyn and her husband had been vitally interested in the arts, and with the money he left, she began to subsidize young people by sending promising students through Cal Tech. Although I was not on "full scholarship" with her, she helped me in many ways. Over the years she sent checks or clothes, both of which were welcome—thanks to her I was able to buy a car, an absolute necessity in California.

With Carolyn Scott's backing, I went to Cal Tech and the Music Academy of the West to work with Lotte Lehmann. I barreled in—chin held high, eyes sparkling—certain that I was going to knock 'em dead. I was in for a rude shock! Great artist that she was, Lotte Lehmann could be one very tough lady. Indeed, one of my classes with her proved to be one of the most upsetting episodes in my life. To this day, I cannot figure out what motivated her behavior. Here's what happened:

Before the classes themselves commenced, the participants were brought in to give a concert for students at the Lobero Theater. I sang German *lieder* and was applauded warmly. A few days later, in front of a select audience of friends and musicians, we performers met with Lehmann. We sat in a row near the stage and when my name was called, I got up and stepped forward to sing Brahms's "*Botschaft.*" Before I could open my mouth, the great Lehmann lit into me so heatedly I almost could feel the physical sting of her words.

"Your Cherman vas a disgrrrrace in ze Loberrro conzert," she began, and continued in her thick German accent. "You have no right to zing another language so poorly. A zinger must have command of the language. Not learning another tongue properly is a sign of laziness."

In the midst of my anguish and fear, I couldn't help noticing that my persecutor sounded like something out of the Katzenjammer Kids. The realization that she hadn't mastered my tongue didn't help my stomach—it was churning. I stood there as Lehmann continued her tirade. She didn't stop! The audience began to squirm and I looked over toward the piano where Gwen, the official accompanist, was seated. Gwen lowered her head in a feeble gesture of sympathy. Ironically, I had worked on my German with Gwen until we both considered it letter-perfect.

Lehmann raved on and on as the audience sat, aghast, wondering, I'm sure, not only what had gotten into the teacher but also how on earth this poor little student ever was going to be able to sing. At last, Lehmann stopped and, throwing me a look that could have destroyed Tebaldi, Stignani and Maria Callas combined, she commanded me to, "ZING."

I "zang" and I sang well. That special ability, the something in me, the "concentration," enabled me to block out everything that had gone before. I gave everything I had to "Botschaft." Gwen, caught up in the drama, accompanied superbly, as always. At the final note, the audience broke into cheers. I returned to my seat and sat through the rest of the class unable to hear another note that was sung. My mind was racing. One thing for sure, I would never, ever, sing for that woman again!

At the end of the class, it was Lehmann's custom to ask the participants what songs they'd present at the next meeting. In truth, I had a booking at the same time as the next session and hadn't planned to attend. Thus, when Lehmann reached me and posed the question, I answered,

"I won't be here, Madame. I have another engagement."

Dammed if she didn't get in a final lick.

"Well," Lehmann snorted curtly, "I hope you will be

studying your German."

The class was dismissed. Quickly, my friends surrounded me. They all expressed their admiration for my performance as well as outrage at Lehmann's behavior. I never went back and understandably assumed that my relationship with Lotte Lehmann was over. I was wrong.

In 1956 I was engaged to sing at the outdoor Ojai Festival near Santa Barbara. I was in my trailer making up my eyes—I'm very nearsighted and until contact lenses became a part of my wardrobe, I had a devil of a time making up. I heard a knock at the door, and with one eye painted and the other bare, I stumbled over and pushed open the door with my elbow. Standing there, a warm smile on her famous lips, was Lotte Lehmann. I couldn't believe my eyes.

"Come in, Madame," I stammered.

She walked in and cordially said that she'd heard I was going to study and audition in Germany, adding, "If there is anything I can do to help, please let me know."

My thoughts ran something like "Has she forgotten how hard she was on me in that public master class, or is it that she does remember and wants to bury the hatchet?"

I was a bit torn between wanting to tell her off and letting bygones be bygones. I decided to let it rest. We had a lovely conversation and parted on good terms.

Not long after, we happened to be in Vienna at the same time and Lehmann called to invite me to join her for a performance at the Staatsoper. I happily accepted thinking it would be quite an evening. I already had a sense of show-biz savvy, and the idea of walking into the Vienna Opera House for the very first time alongside the fabled Lehmann was delicious—a young singer's dream. Our entrance, however, was less than dramatic. For some reason, Lehmann arrived early; the only ones who spotted her as we walked to the box were the standees lined up for tickets. They burst into applause when they saw her, but by the time the rest of the audience filed in, she'd faded into the walls. No one knew that she was there! If she'd waited and come in right before the lights went down, the entire house would have been on its feet. Why did she go in unobtrusively? Why did she pick on me at the master class? Your guess is as good as mine.

From then on until her death, I was in touch with Lehmann, either in person or through the mail. If I were having difficulty with a song, she'd help me out and, even more, suggest songs suitable for my repertoire. I sought her advice when I began studying Schumann's "*Frauenliebe und Leben*" (A Woman in Love and Life), a cycle of eight songs in which Lehmann had excelled. (She made a fabulous recording with Bruno Walter at the piano.) I did a few performances before asking her counsel because I only wanted a bit of "pointing" from her; I didn't want to parrot her. The cycle is a little kitschy, but I love it. A woman sings of meeting a man, falling in love, getting engaged, getting married, giving birth and finally, of her husband's death. It's from the submissive school of female behavior, difficult to swallow in liberated times, but it does contain great music. I went to Santa Barbara and sang for Lehmann in her living room. She listened intently.

"There's nothing to add," she said, at the conclusion. "It's beautiful, Jackie. But, one little touch at the end, I think, would be goot. You should do something a bit more theatrical with your hands. Raise them and then let them fall slowly."

To demonstrate, she sang the end of the last song:

"The world is empty, empty. I have loved and I have lived; I do not live anymore. I silently withdraw into myself; the veil is falling. Then I have you and my lost happiness. You, my world!"

Lehmann raised her hands to her breast at the next-to-the-last line and dropped them on the final word.

I thought it was great, and I practiced doing it with her. With our arms moving up and down, up and down, it must have looked like a mother bird teaching her fledgling how to fly.

Shortly thereafter, armed with Lehmann's suggestion, I did the Schumann at my first Carnegie Hall recital. After the performance, Trude Rittman came to my dressing room. Trude, a German émigré was another marvelous person in my life. We met when I sang in the chorus of the "Small House of Uncle Thomas" ballet in the movie *The King and I*. Trude not only directed the musical sequences in that film, she composed the music for the big dance number based on a Siamese interpretation of Harriet Beecher Stowe's *Uncle Tom's Cabin*. I respected Trude's opinion and asked what she thought of the Schumann.

"It was fabulous, Jackie," she smiled, "just the right tone. Frankly, the only thing that didn't ring true was what you did with your hands at the end. It looked phony."

Realizing that what was good and true for Lotte Lehmann, wasn't necessarily good and true for Marilyn Horne, I dropped the gesture.

Although we had reached a détente, my relationship with Lotte Lehmann remained quirky. After all her cordiality, I didn't think she ever could upset me again. I was wrong. We had another encounter in 1964 when the *Los Angeles Times* gave her one of its ten prestigious Woman of the Year awards. I had received the award in 1960 for my appearance as Marie in Alban Berg's *Wozzeck* so, when the *Times* called and asked me to be part of the ceremony honoring Lehmann, I went.

During the reception, I was standing next to her when

an old friend from the DooWah years came over and greeted me.

"Jackie, I hear you're pregnant," she said. "Is it true?" I wasn't showing but answered happily, "Yes, I am."

"Wonderful! What do you want, a boy or a girl?"

"Listen," I answered, "I just hope it's a healthy baby."

At this Lehmann turned saying, "*Und ich hoffe es wird ein nul sein!*" ("And I hope it's a zero.")

Honest to God, that woman was something. What a thing to say to a woman pregnant for the first time.

"What do you mean?" I demanded.

"A singer has no business having children. You must concentrate on the career and only on the career."

I was shocked then but have learned since that there was an element of truth in her statement. (Sad to say, I'd heard that song before; I was still in my teens when my dad told me a singer shouldn't marry.) It is difficult to combine career and motherhood—it's difficult enough to be a mother—but why would she say such a thing when I already was pregnant!

Fair is fair. If I tell you of Lehmann's sternness, then I must also tell you that she opened the doors of singing *lieder* for me. Give or take a few arm motions, her instruction was inextricably woven into my own interpretations. As exponent and teacher, she was incomparable and inspirational. My late friend, the great American bass-baritone, Donald Gramm, was lucky enough to see her in performance and told me of her uniqueness.

"By God, when Lehmann sang Schubert's 'The Crow,' you really thought that bird was flying over her head! She made everything come alive."

In my early encounters with Lehmann, I was too green to cut through some of the flak and get to the greatness. I grew into her and am definitely of her school—as opposed to the Elisabeth Schwarzkopf method. Schwarzkopf was much more calculated in her approach, hugging and squeezing every note in order to reach the desired effect. Lehmann was innately theatrical; she used imagination to create an entire feeling or story, from the very opening of the piano chords to the final sounds—and beyond. Lehmann's approach had a residual effect; something remained with the listener even after the music was over. That "something" was sublime.

Schwarzkopf herself recognized the special ingredient in Lehmann's singing. Gwen Koldofsky told me that Lehmann once spoke of a visit Schwarzkopf made to Santa Barbara. The two singers were walking along the beach when Schwarzkopf said,

"You know, Lotte, I get the feeling from hearing your records that you really enjoyed singing."

Lehmann stopped in her tracks.

"Why, of course I enjoyed it!"

"I never have," Schwarzkopf responded.

"Well, it sounds it, Elisabeth," retorted Lehmann.

Except for what Donald Gramm and others told me, I never heard what Lehmann was like in an actual performance until 1961 when a friend played a tape of the historic 1936 San Francisco Opera broadcast of Wagner's *Die Walküre* for Henry and me. The cast included Kirsten Flagstad, Lauritz Melchior, Friedrich Schorr and Lotte Lehmann, a singing lineup comparable to the batting order of the 1929 New York Yankees. Oh, and Fritz Reiner was the conductor. If you don't know opera, let me tell you that those names represent the finest interpreters of the German repertoire—and Lehmann completely wiped out the others. How? By singing the music and words with such incredible intensity and conviction that the result was overwhelming. I was so thrilled I went home and wrote her a letter telling her that her performance was a revelation, a gift from God. She wrote back:

> Thank you for your wonderful words, my dear Jackie. It's just as the Marschallin says, *"Jedes Ding hat seine Zeit"* (Everything has its time). I had mine, and now Jackie, it's yours.

Lotte Lehmann was a true artist, susceptible at certain moments to the same petty jealousies and envious stabs ordinary people feel, but able to rise above them as a performer, and ultimately, as a person. Though I cite those momentary lapses in humanity, I really come to praise her.

KEEPING UP WITH THE CARMENS

Despite one master class fiasco, working with Lehmann showed me the way. I decided to pursue singing exclusively. After the fall semester of 1953, I withdrew from USC. As much as the University had given me, I couldn't get the things I needed as a professional singer—that is, voice lessons at least three times a week, coaching every day and extensive language study. All of which were available at the college but they came with excess baggage—namely, a required curriculum. I had no time for that anymore.

I didn't ask my parents for their approval, I simply told them my plan at dinner one evening.

"I'm leaving USC. I want to devote all my time to singing."

They barely blinked.

"Okay, whatever you think best, dear."

Why wouldn't they agree? The goal always had been for me to have a singing career and I already was making between ten and twelve thousand dollars a year as a solo performer. Also, I still lived at home, so our family routine wouldn't be changed. It didn't make sense to continue my education in a general way when I knew exactly where I was going. (I never did receive a degree and even though I've stockpiled a whole bunch of honors, including the French Legion of Honor, a Commendatore della Republica from Italy, and quite a few honorary Doctorates, to this day I regret not getting that Baccalaureate.)

In the ensuing months, I kept very busy, literally singing for my supper. You name it; I sang it! Besides engagements at prestigious places such as the Hollywood Bowl, I performed at weddings, funerals, and parties and only drew the line at appearing in nightclubs or bars.

Remember the movie *I Never Sang for My Father*? My life could be called, "I Always Sang for My Father." Musically, Dad continued to call the shots. For a long time he wouldn't allow me to take the big step and attempt an entire evening of opera. As professional as I was—I had a lot of weddings and funerals to prove it—Dad cautioned me not to try to sustain an operatic performance until I was physically and vocally mature. When I turned twenty, opportunity came knocking.

How's this for a role? You're married to a rich landlord and your stammering son, the laughingstock of the village, gets engaged to a pretty young thing because of your husband's wealth. Then, your husband's son by a previous marriage gets the girl and you wind up at the final curtain with your goofy son who's dressed up as a bear. The opera was Smetana's *The Bartered Bride* and the role was Hata (Agnes). Was this a way to begin an operatic career? It was for me. If I could play a merry widow at sixteen, at twenty, I could play the mother of a grown bear.

The Bartered Bride was a production of the Los Angeles Guild Opera, a professional group founded by the city to present opera to schoolchildren. Every year, the Guild put on a new production and gave around twenty performances. Kids were bussed to the Shrine Auditorium in Los Angeles, a huge sixty-eight-hundred-seat hall. Think of it, nearly seven thousand kids at an opera! The great Carl Ebert was the director and what an amazing personality. A Berliner trained in acting by Max Reinhardt, Ebert was a matinee idol in Germany, famous for his Hamlet. In 1927, he was appointed general director of the State Theater at Darmstadt and then became director general at the Stadtische Opera, Berlin. His productions were legendary. Unwilling to collaborate with the Nazis, he fled Germany in 1933 and began producing opera all over the world. Along with Conductor Fritz Busch, Ebert founded the Glyndebourne Festival in Great Britain and later organized the Turkish National Theatre and Opera. After the war, he returned to Berlin and brought the Stadtische Opera back to life. Besides producing and directing for the Los Angeles Opera Guild, Ebert also was the director of USC's opera department from 1948 to 1956, and that's when I met him.

Ebert's production of *The Bartered Bride* opened in the fall of 1954. How did I feel at my debut? How would you feel singing in front of sixty-eight hundred kids? Truthfully, I can't remember my debut state, other than that I was tremendously excited over having learned and performed an entire operatic role. Hata is a contralto, and though I still considered myself a soprano, I debuted in the range that became my home. I loved working with Carl Ebert and he must have been pleased with me because I was hired to appear the next year in *Hänsel und Gretel*. Despite these engagements, I still couldn't make a living singing opera, however, and had to continue working in other musical venues.

At this time, Otto Preminger, a renowned film director, decided to make a movie of Oscar Hammerstein's Broadway success, *Carmen Jones*, a re-creation of Bizet's *Carmen* in the black idiom. Hammerstein wrote a new book and lyrics for the opera in 1943 and it ran for 503 performances. In terms of employment *Carmen Jones* was a godsend because it gave blacks an opportunity to perform in something other than occasional character roles. The barring of blacks from the cultural world was an American tragedy. Impossible as it seems, though the New York City Opera presented black singers in leading roles in the late 1940's, it wasn't until 1955 that Marian Anderson broke the operatic color barrier at the Metropolitan Opera House. She sang Ulrica in Verdi's *Un Ballo in Maschera* but the voice, which Toscanini described as "one that comes once in a hundred years," was past its prime. Anderson's appearance was more a symbolic occasion than anything else. Until then, a young black with classical singing aspirations had no place to go except for the concert stage where Miss Anderson, Paul Robeson, Roland Hayes, Dorothy Maynor, and others, had found musical sanctuary. Even in the 1960's, a color barrier existed in opera although it affected men more than women. Black women were accepted as heroines but, with a few exceptions, audiences didn't readily embrace black men as heroes. Although things are much better now we can't pat ourselves on the back—there's still a ways to go.

Back to *Carmen Jones*. Oscar Hammerstein moved the action from nineteenth-century Spain to the twentieth-century American South. Don José became Joe, an Army corporal; Micaela, the sweet young thing in love with Joe, became Cindy Lou: Escamillo, the toreador, became Husky Miller, a heavyweight boxer; and Carmen, the gypsy, remained Carmen only now she was working in a parachute rather than a cigarette factory. Hammerstein also reworked the arias into songs to spectacular effect. Instead of singing the *"Habanera,"* ("Love's a rebellious bird no one can tame") Carmen oozes her way through "Dat's Love," ("Love's a baby dat grows up wild an' he don' do what you want him to"). In the *"Seguidilla," "Près des remparts de Séville, chez mon ami Lillas Pastia"* became "Dere's a café on de corner," a café run by Billy Pastor instead of Lillas Pastia. Carmen's "Card Song" flipped into "De Cards Don' Lie."

In the summer of 1954, John Noschese, a singer friend,

casually mentioned over lunch, that 20ᵗʰ Century Fox was hiring singers to record the chorus music in *Carmen Jones*. There was no color barrier either—whites could apply.

"What do you say; shall we audition and make a little money?" John asked.

"Sure," I said.

Off we went to the studio and what an incredible casting call it turned out to be! Hundreds of singers were waiting to "make a little money." I hadn't realized that the audition actually was for the soloists' soundtrack—not just the background music in which the chorus goes "ahhhh, ohhhhh, ahhhh, ohhhhh" while the credits flash by. Instead, everything was up for grabs, including the 'singing' voices of Harry Belafonte and Dorothy Dandridge. Pearl Bailey, the other star, was doing her own vocals.

Herschel Gilbert, the musical director, and his assistant Ted Low, were busily lining up singers when I arrived. Ted brought along his friend Henry Lewis. I hadn't seen Henry very much during the three years since we met; he was around and I did think he was gorgeous, but that was it. He'd played in the orchestra for *The Bartered Bride* although he was interested in the production's soprano, not the mezzo. A funny note—at one point in *The Bartered Bride*, after I sang a long low line, Henry turned to someone in the pit and, unable to see the stage, asked,

"Who's that terrific tenor?"

My turn came at the *Carmen Jones* audition and I sang Micaela's aria, "*Je dis que rien ne m'épouvante*," in French. ("I'se yo' gal, I was always yo' gal" in Mr. Hammerstein's English). Micaela is a soprano role.

"Nice, very nice, thank you," Mr. Gilbert said when I finished.

I was returning to my seat when I heard the next singer doing the "*Habanera*" with the Hammerstein lyrics. I got mad at myself for being Miss Purist and doing the original Bizet, so I turned to Mr. Gilbert and announced,

"You know, I can sing low, too!"

"Can you sing the 'Habanera?'" he asked, smiling.

"Sure!"

I was stretching it—like most people I knew the melody by ear but I'd never seen the music. The next thing I knew, Mr. Gilbert handed me a sheet of music and I was singing "You go for me an' I'm taboo, But if you're hard to get I go for you, An' if I do, den you are through, boy, my baby, dat's de end of you." I'm embarrassed to say I tore into those lyrics with the most blatant imitation of darky dialogue this side of Catfish Row. Of course, the score was written that way.

I finished, and Mr. Gilbert thanked me again adding that I could go, now. On my way out, Henry Lewis came over.

"Hi Jackie," he said amiably. "You know, I think they liked you. I'm sure you'll get something nice out of this. Do you want to have dinner?" I was excited and I wanted to talk about the audition. Henry knew music, plus he was good looking and lots of fun.

"Sure!" I said for the second time that evening.

We went off to a little restaurant on Santa Monica Boulevard and had a leisurely dinner and a lively conversation. Henry was wonderful to talk to and I lost track of time. It was late when we parted and I had a long way to go—there was no freeway to Long Beach in those days. I arrived home a little before midnight. Dad was sitting in the living room reading the paper. I'm sure he'd stayed up waiting for me.

"Jackie," he said as I came in the door, " a man named Gilbert called and left a number. He said to be sure and call when you came in."

"Gilbert?" I thought for a second. "GILBERT! You mean Herschel Gilbert, Dad?"

"That's it, that's his name," Dad replied casually. I was beginning to shake.

"I can't call him now, it's almost twelve."

"Honey, he said for you to call him whenever you got in. If I were you, I'd call him."

I did. Herschel Gilbert answered the phone and brushed aside my apologies for calling so late.

"We like what you did today, Miss Horne. We want you to come over tomorrow and test for Carmen."

What a stunner. I'd started out aiming for the chorus, and then made a stab at Micaela and here I was being given a chance for the leading role. I hung up the phone and started jumping around the room. Dad, caught up in the excitement, dropped his paper and his reserve and hopped around with me. Mother came in to see what the ruckus was, and when she found out, she began jumping, too. We hugged and kissed.

After my parents went to bed, I called Henry Lewis.

"Guess what, Henry?" I said with a new low lilt in my voice, "I'm going to audition for Carmen herself."

Then next day, I went to the studio, sang a few songs, and got the part.

In the three weeks that I worked on the dubbing, Henry Lewis and I began dating. The Hollywood Bowl season was on, and since Henry was in the orchestra, and since I was singing in the chorus at the Bowl, we saw each other fairly frequently. I didn't mention this to my parents for a very obvious reason. I didn't want to deal with it, so I didn't talk about it.

During the day, I was at the sound studio along with the other "voices." Pearl Bailey had slimmed down to pencil thinness for the film and showed up every day in a different, dazzling Don Loper dress. What style that lady had!

Marvin Hayes, a friend from U.S.C. sang the role of Husky Miller for the actor Joe Adams and LeVern Hutcherson and I sang for the two leads. LeVern really was a victim of those times. A lyrical spinto tenor who should have been on the operatic stage, he was forced to push his voice down so he could sing Porgy, the only role available to him.

I worked closely with Dorothy Dandridge, listening carefully to her speaking and singing voice in order to match the timbre and accent so that when I recorded the songs, I had a little bit of Dandridge in my throat. She sang in a register comfortable for her; then I mimicked her voice in the proper key. Later on, she filmed her scenes with my recorded voice blasting from huge loudspeakers. The tendency in dubbing is to overdo your mouth movements but Dandridge didn't—she was sensational. The sound technicians pieced music and film together and the result is a seamless performance by Dorothy Dandridge and (the voice of) "Marilynn" Horne.

Guess what? In typical Hollywood fashion, the final chords of the opera, the bone-chilling fate theme, was augmented at the end of the movie by—you guessed it—a full chorus wailing DOOWAH.

All told, I didn't make that much money doing *Carmen Jones*—around fifteen hundred dollars, I think. I'd have gotten a lot more if I hadn't sold the recording rights for a mere two hundred and fifty dollars. Damned if the record wasn't a best seller and it was re-released with my picture on the cover. On the other hand, what a great experience! I had learned, and had fun, and had a chance to meet, among others, Harry Belafonte, one really extraordinary man.

In 1979 I attended a roast for Tony Randall at Radio City Music Hall. Tony's an opera buff, consequently many people from the musical world were involved. We "roasters" were to take an elevator down to the basement and then go up on to the stage. I stepped into the elevator, and as the doors closed, a husky voice whispered in my ear, "I love you, Marilyn Horne." I turned and was face to face with Harry Belafonte, the first time I'd seen him since *Carmen Jones*. His hair was graying, but on him it looked good. I needed words fast but could only gulp, "Likewise!" Let me tell you, I'd sing for peanuts again just to hear and see him.

Carmen Jones did well both in the reviews and at the box office. *The Daily News* gave it four stars and the New Yorker critic praised "Dorothy Dandridge, whose configurations are remarkable and whose songs, rendered by Marilyn Horne, have a sultry effectiveness. I had no idea." added the reviewer, "that Miss Dandridge was not singing *in voce sua*, until I was given the news by a press agent." Twenty years later, when I recorded Bizet's *Carmen* (*in voce mia*) with Leonard Bernstein conducting the Metropolitan Opera, it was an all-time operatic best seller. In six months, it even outsold Maria Callas's classic *Tosca*. Not bad for a little girl from Bradford—with a lot of help from a certain conductor from Lawrence, Massachusetts.

I continued to work in films after *Carmen Jones* was over. Have you seen *The Rose Tattoo* with Anna Magnani and Burt Lancaster? Yours truly is warbling the song behind the opening credits. I also did a lot of television shows, such as the monthly "Shower of Stars," which included a musical version of Dickens's *A Christmas Carol*, with Fredric March as Scrooge. Maxwell Anderson did the libretto and Bernard Herrmann wrote the music. Benny Herrmann was another special person in my life. He's probably best known for his brilliant score for *Citizen Kane* and all those Hitchcock films, but what isn't as well known is, Benny was crazy about 18th century music. He used to go burrowing in places like the British Museum to unearth original manuscripts. I did a lot of concerts with him. On one occasion at the L.A. County Museum, I sang a backbreaking program—three Handel arias, plus "*Che faro*" from Gluck's *Orfeo*, and Arne's "Water parted from the sea." Moreover, because of Hermann's total immersion in the 18th century style, I had to sing each aria twice—*da capo* really meant *da capo* to him. And now, if I may, a little digression:

I first sang those arias straight, as they were written, and then with a famous castrato's elaborate embellishments. The embellishments were so florid the critics kind of stuck up their noses—something I had to deal with throughout my career. "*Che faro*" is one of those glorious arias that has been sung a certain way for so long, there's no room for interpretation. It's usually done s-l-o-w-l-y. Henry and I discussed the piece and both agreed that since Orfeo is distraught, the music should be agitated. The tempo is marked *alla breve*, two beats to the bar, but that can mean a fast two as well as a slow two. It makes more sense to take it fairly fast so that it can be slowed up in the places Gluck marked *lento* and *adagio*. The Horne version of "*Che faro senza Euridice*" went quite quickly, and every time I sang it, the critics said I was wrong. However, the French baritone, Martial Singher, a great male Orfeo and a consummate musician, said it was right and his opinion meant a lot more to me than what the critics had to say. (Singher, by the way, took over Lehmann's position at the Music Academy of the West.) Embellishments disappeared because they went out of fashion and most singers no longer attempted them. I had to argue with a lot of conductors before I could sing the music as it was originally conceived.

In 1955, I appeared in front of the camera instead of singing behind the scenes when I got on "Arthur Godfrey's Talent Scouts," a popular television show. Years ago, amateur nights and talent shows constituted an important aspect of American life, providing not only entertainment but also the opportunity to socialize for a purpose. The big talent showcases started on radio with "The Original Amateur Hour." Major Edward Bowes turned a small-town phenomenon into a national pastime; every musical-saw player, spoon slapper, accordion squeezer and coloratura in the country wanted to get on the "Amateur Hour" and take his/her chances with the gong. (A cymbal crashed if an act wasn't up to snuff.) Bowes was a tough man with the gong and the program was punctuated with ear-splitting cymbal crashes. His affable assistant, Ted Mack, eventually replaced Bowes after which, the cymbal rarely was heard. In 1949, "The Original Amateur Hour" premiered on TV and was a big hit. So was Arthur Godfrey's show, which featured fewer amateurs—and no gong. Whatever else, the programs provided a showcase for talent. By the 1960's, we became too sophisticated or maybe too critical and the talent shows died out. (They're back again in the form of programs like "American Idol" and "Star Search.")

Actually, there's no such thing as "amateur" anymore; everyone is an immediate professional. When performers in their early and mid-twenties make debuts before their techniques and skills are ready in blockbuster roles and in blockbuster houses, it shocks and saddens me. I was thirty-six years old at my Metropolitan Opera debut, sixteen years after my debut in *The Bartered Bride*, and I knew what I had, what I wanted and where I was going. There is no substitute for training and experience—and both take years and years of old-fashioned work. The voice is only the starting point in opera; then comes determination, brains, acting ability, knowledge of languages and business acumen, not necessarily in that order. You must come up the hard way; shortcuts at the beginning of a career will only shorten that career's span. Unfortunately, singers often are not guided intelligently. Teachers, coaches, managers, agents, etc., take promising raw material and do little or nothing to refine it. If, by some miracle, they do try to hold the singer back, the singer bristles and insists on jumping, willy-nilly, into the big roles—wholesale hubris! Bellini's *Norma* provides a good illustration.

Norma is impossibly demanding and for decades only appeared when a qualified singer could do it. In America, while *Norma* was seen in Philadelphia in 1841 and in New York in 1843, the first major production occurred at the inaugural of the Academy of Music in New York City on October 2, 1854 with Giulia Grisi in the title role. The Metropolitan Opera staged the work on February 27, 1890, with Walter Damrosch conducting a German-language version. Lilli Lehmann (no relation to Lotte), an outstanding 19th century Wagnerian soprano, sang the title role. Lehmann, in an often-quoted statement, declared that it was "easier to sing all three Brunnhildes than one Norma."

"When you sing Wagner," wrote Lilli Lehmann, "you are so carried away by the dramatic emotion, the action, and the scene that you do not have to think how to sing the words. That comes of itself. But in Bellini, you must always have a care for beauty of tone and correct emission."

After two more performances by Lehmann in the 1891-82 season, *Norma* did not appear on the Met stage until November 16, 1927, when it was revived for Rosa Ponselle who had worked her way up to it gradually. Gina Cigna sang Norma in 1937, Zinka Milanov in 1943, and in 1956, Maria Callas opened the season as the Druid priestess. That was it, until Joan Sutherland brought *Norma* back to the Met on March 3, 1970. Things really have changed. Honestly, it seems as though anyone who has a hankering to

71

sing it, does, whether or not she's up to it or even suited for it. Believe me, some wonderful artists have come close to committing vocal suicide by doing it. I guess, if I have any advice to give young singers on the subject, it's this: Don't push, don't rush, and remember, you've got resources we older singers never had. There are more opera companies in the United States than ever before. Use them!

In 1955, regional opera companies were scarce, so I used the "Arthur Godfrey Talent Show."

Godfrey was at the height of his TV fame and his scouts were all over the country—Ace Goodman was the Los Angeles representative. Someone told me that Mr. Goodman was holding auditions and once again, I was off and running.

Goodman, a brusque, Runyonesque, heart-of-gold character, had had a bellyful of talent by the time I got to him.

"Okay, kid, whatcha gonna do?" he queried disinterestedly.

"I'm going to sing an operatic aria."

"Esshhh," sighed Mr. Goodman, obviously not bowled over by my announcement. He sat back with his eyes closed as I sang *"Ritorna vincitor,"* from *Aida*. When I finished, his eyes were wide open.

"What else can you do, kid?" he asked enthusiastically.

This time I sang a popular song of the day, and when I finished, Mr. Goodman blasted me.

"Are you crazy to sing junk like that with a voice like yours!"

"Listen," I shot back, "I'll sing anything!"

"That's the most ridiculous thing I've ever heard. You stick to opera, kid."

Ace Goodman arranged for me to go to New York and appear on the Godfrey program and Dorothy DeCoudres came along to present me. I was excited for two reasons:

First, I'd get to be on national television, and secondly, I'd get the chance to see the Metropolitan Opera House, which I yearned to do.

We arrived in New York, and after registering at the Taft Hotel at Seventh Avenue and 50th Street I raced over to Broadway and down to 39th Street. Imagine my disappointment when I discovered that the opera house was officially closed for the summer. I begged a custodian to let me look inside for one lousy little minute. He wouldn't. I had to return to the hotel without accomplishing my goal. As it turned out, I never saw Arthur Godfrey, either—he was on vacation. Jack Paar was the substitute host.

When I stepped into the television spotlight that Monday evening, Paar chatted with me.

"I understand that your heart's desire was to get inside the Metropolitan Opera House, Miss Horne."

Obviously, someone had done a bit of research.

"Oh yes, Mr. Paar," I cried. "It means so much to me to see it."

"Well, Miss Horne," Paar responded avuncularly, "if you win, we've arranged for you to be given a tour of the Met. Maybe that'll give you an added incentive."

It did. I sang the hell out of *"Un bel dì"* from *Madama Butterfly* and won. Not only would I get to see the Met, the winner also got to appear on Arthur Godfrey's morning radio show for the week.

Dorothy and I settled in at the Taft and I went out each day to the studio. Peter Lind Hayes and Mary Healy, a popular husband-and-wife talk team of the fifties, were hosting in Godfrey's absence and among the other guests were Jerry Vale and Rosalind Russell, then appearing in *Auntie Mame* on Broadway. Everyone was wonderful to me—and I was in pretty rough shape. Still on California time, unable to get a good night's sleep, I had to get up early every morning and sing an aria. It was killing. Sometimes I didn't know where the voice was going to come from. I guess it came, because on Friday, Mr. Hayes asked me to stay on for another week.

"Gee, Mr. Hayes, I'd love to," I said, "but I've got to get back to Hollywood. I'm singing in *Carmina Burana* with Leopold Stokowski at the Hollywood Bowl." I sort of bowled them over with that excuse.

While being on the Godfrey show was fabulous, I did not get to the Met—for some reason, the personal tour never materialized. In fact, I didn't get inside until several years later when I attended a performance. I was lucky to get that opportunity, too—the building was demolished in 1966. I still don't get it. Italy, France or Germany would have bought the next block in order to preserve the place, but we tore it down and built a new one at Lincoln Center. I know that Montserrat Caballé debuted in the old house in a third-rate production, simply because she wanted to appear on that hallowed stage. I wouldn't do that. I wanted to come in with style and that's why I never appeared in the legendary "Yellow Brick Brewery." To this day, not having sung at the original Met is one of my deepest regrets.

EUROPE BECKONS

In 1955, simply being near the Metropolitan Opera House lit a fire under me. I returned to California more determined that ever to make it operatically. The *Carmina Burana* at the Hollywood Bowl was terrific and the opportunity to work with Leopold Stokowski was well worth sacrificing another week with the Arthur Godfrey Show. (Talk about showmen! Whenever Stokowski conducted at the Bowl, a huge searchlight flashed a silhouette of his distinctive profile up into the sky.) I also appeared in the Los Angeles Guild Opera's *Hänsel und Gretel*—first, as the Sandman (soprano) and then, as Hänsel (mezzo). Professionally, I continued to work as a soloist and in small groups. Meanwhile, the situation at home changed—our ranks had thinned. By the midfiifties, Gloria had married and moved to Hawaii; Dick and Joanne married and were out on their own, which left Jay, Grandma Horne, Mom and Dad, and me in residence. I may have taken some solo flights but I remained very much part of the nest and our family life continued strong. Whatever came along, we were a unit just as we'd been in Bradford.

Sometimes I think how difficult it must have been for my parents to relocate, especially my father. He loved California's climate, as any sane person would, but Bradford was in his soul. Back East, he'd been a prominent person, involved in all facets of city life, hobnobbing with the political elite as well as everyday citizens. When anything needed doing, Bentz Horne was either on the committee or heading it up. He had a quiet charisma and was smart about so many things. Self-educated, a voracious reader and far more intellectual in his thinking than the rest of his family, he was a dreamer in many ways but a dreamer willing to accept his role as head of a family. Above all, he was a great talker. As kids, we had to wait around while Dad discussed politics with his cronies and I'm sure my inclination to gab was another legacy from him. Dad took many jobs in California, including a stint as a shoe salesman in a store where he eventually became manager. He also was employed as a county assessor, a seasonal venture. By 1955, he was a traveling salesman for the "Invalid Walker and Wheelchair Company;" Mom worked there too, as an executive secretary. Dad wasn't satisfied and I can't help thinking he must have been a bit chagrined because Mother held a higher position. I saw a letter my Dad wrote in March of 1955 in which he actively sought other employment. He cited his dislike of travel as the reason he wanted to change jobs. That letter tore me apart. At forty-eight years of age, unfulfilled in his work, my dad was trying to find his niche.

If Dad gave me the desire, incentive and discipline to succeed, Mom gave me the strength. She tended to stay in the background, but Berneice Horne was the rock of the family, a constant wellspring of resourcefulness. Because she kept quiet, Mom's opinion, whenever she expressed it, counted for a lot. I like to think I inherited Mother's "spine" and Dad's "spirit." I also flatter myself in thinking I look like her—Mother was a beauty. Dad, well, he was clean-favored, with a grin that lit up his whole face, but handsome—no. Although she never went past the eleventh grade—Dick was born when she was seventeen—Mom rose from bookkeeper to executive vice president in her company. Eighteen years later, when she died, her estate was considerable: twenty-five thousand dollars for each of her four children and one thousand dollars for each of her grandchildren. She'd earned it all herself.

I was a dutiful daughter, free-spirited yet obedient. True, I'd been seeing a man of whom neither parent would have approved, but before it became too serious, my romance with Henry petered out. I can't say why, we simply drifted apart just as we had drifted together. My mind was on other projects and I literally was too busy for a serious commitment. In addition, Henry was drafted into the army in 1955. We corresponded briefly—very briefly, he never wrote—after he was sent to Germany. I did see him once when he came home on furlough, but we were no longer a twosome.

In the mid-fifties, I met Robert Craft. Bob, a fabulous musician, became my very close friend; through him I met the musical genius of the twentieth century, Igor Stravinsky. Stravinsky had arrived on the scene around 1910 when everyone was either rehashing Wagner or, in limited numbers, doing quasi-atonal compositions. Stravinsky went back to primitive rhythms and combined them with modified atonal music. The result was something completely new or "renewed." Bob Craft assisted the Maestro and became his right arm. One of Bob's pet projects was the music of Carlo Gesualdo, (c.1560-1613) an Italian gentleman whose life and work were equally tempestuous. According to the Larousse Encyclopedia of Music, Gesualdo's "music displays most openly his ardent southern temperament; he pushes to extreme lengths the most daring contrapuntal and chromatic harmonies." "Ardent southern temperament" is putting it mildly. Gesualdo murdered his wife, her lover and a child he did not accept as his own. As they lay in bed, hired assassins stabbed the spouse and her boyfriend. The child then was placed in a cradle suspended from the ceiling by four ropes and, in a scene worthy of Jacobean drama, rocked to death. Gesualdo's uncle, Pope San Carlo Borromeo, was canonized—proving that even saints have skeletons in the closet.

Bob Craft loved Gesualdo's madrigals and motets and enlisted a group of singers to perform the "ardent" musician's works. I was one of the five chosen. Charlie Scharbach was our bass; Grace-Lynne Martin, the soprano, I was second soprano, Cora Lauridsen was alto and Richard Robinson, tenor. Charlie and Grace-Lynne each had absolute pitch and they waged "pitched" battles about the pitch. (As I remember, Grace-Lynne always yielded to Charlie.) Among other places, we performed at the Monday Evening Concerts sponsored by the Southern California Chamber Music Society. The concerts, a vital part of the musical scene, took place in Los Angeles County Auditorium. (The list of artists in the Monday Night Series, featured the cream of the young musicians' crop, and included a pianist named Andre Previn and a certain contrabassist by the name of Henry Lewis.) In one memorable program we did five madrigals and premiered Stravinsky's, "In Memoriam, Dylan Thomas." Bob arranged for us to record the madrigals, and Stravinsky was in on the sessions—in fact, he actually "composed" portions of the works which had been lost. David Raksin, the film composer—he wrote "Laura"–was the backer of these recordings. And, we were most fortunate to have Aldous Huxley, a Gesualdo enthusiast, join us as a commentator.

Our contrapuntal group traveled around performing music interspersed and illuminated by Huxley's commentary on "The Court of Ferrara and Gesualdo." Huxley gave incredibly brilliant lectures. He loved the word "extraordinary," and we singers made a game of counting the number of times he uttered that word in a single lecture. The record? Fifty! The lanky, aquiline Englishman and the gnomish, balding Russian (Huxley was at least six feet, three inches tall, while Stravinsky was my height) were an extraordinary duo—a psychedelic Mutt and Jeff. Poor Huxley had terrible cataracts and though he got partial sight back through the Bates exercise method, his vision was minimal. Stravinsky's eyesight wasn't great, either. In fact, the Maestro always wore three pairs of glasses, one on his head, and another on his forehead and the last over his eyes. Depending upon what he wanted to see he'd flip down the required pair and flip up the other two.

One time in the midst of a session at Capitol Records, I sat in the control room while Huxley and the Maestro worked in the recording room. Through the window, I could see them hunched over the piano, staring intently at something. Suddenly, Stravinsky's voice came over the intercom.

"Let's get Jackie," he said, "she knows these things."

"Jackie!" Huxley's clipped English tones came over the mike, "could you come here and tell us what this extraordinary sign means."

I couldn't believe it! Igor Stravinsky and Aldous Huxley wanted to check something with me.

I went into the studio and over to the two men. Huxley pointed to a hand-lettered sign on the piano.

"What is this?" he asked, pointing to the sign reading: NO COTTON-PICKIN' DRINKS ON THIS INSTRUMENT.

Neither Igor Stravinsky nor Aldous Huxley could figure out what "cotton-pickin" meant.

Whenever East Coast friends refer to the Atlantic States as the cultural center of the world, I love to remind them that my Southern California circle included, among others, Bob Craft, Igor Stravinsky, Aldous Huxley, Jascha Heifetz and Gregor Piatigorsky. To use Mr. Huxley's word, my brushes with greatness were "extraordinary." I was also very fortunate in meeting people willing and able to help me in my career.

Dad set things in motion and Gwen Koldofsky helped keep things going. Through her I made essential professional contacts: Lotte Lehmann, Marty Katz—and around this time, Dorothy Huttenback. Dorothy was an artists' representative and manager, but oh so much more. It's one thing to represent an artist, and quite another to believe in, encourage, and counsel that person, especially a raw recruit, which I sure was. How lucky I was to have her both as an adviser and as a friend. Dorothy managed my early West Coast career and got me local bookings. Then, she introduced me to Martin Taubman, an impresario from Vienna and New York. Taubman offered to manage my career—only if I would prepare in Europe and give him a couple of thousand dollars for a retainer. He could as easily have asked for a million.

"Some people have money, and some people have talent," Dorothy told Taubman. He took the hint and waived the retainer.

"Get yourself over to Europe, and I'll arrange for auditions, he growled.

"Okay," I replied. "I'll be there."

Dorothy DeCoudres decided I should give a benefit concert to raise money for my European sojourn. All my mentors agreed with this plan—save one. The most influential person in my life, the overseer of my career, the man who had taught me, guided me, located the right opportunities for me and never allowed me to be exploited or pushed, thought I should stay in the United States. My dad opposed Taubman's plan. I was determined to go and the conflict with my father was a turning point in my professional and personal life.

From the beginning, my parents recognized my free spirit

and catered to it, allowing me to believe I was a willing servant of my voice and not its slave. I had plenty of opportunity to fool around, after which I'd buckle down to practice. No matter how much Dad wanted me to work, he rarely interfered with my play, wisely allowing me to feel I was doing my own thing even though he was pulling the strings. Consequently, we rarely had been at odds concerning my professional life. Now, for the first time, I was arguing about my career with its master builder. Privately, Mother told me I should take the chance and go to Europe, but she wouldn't say that to Dad. He told me I was crazy to go overseas without a booking, let alone a contract. What's more, he argued, why should I desert a burgeoning American career? My domestic career indeed was taking off. Thanks to Dorothy Huttenback, I was working steadily and receiving excellent notices—with a bit of confusion thrown in. A soprano named Marilynn Hall was performing at the same time and I cannot tell you the number of times she got credit for my singing, and vice versa. Fortunately, she was a good singer, too. Eventually she changed her name to Maria Hall to avoid confusion.

Meanwhile, the controversy continued non-stop at the Horne's. Meals were spent discussing America versus Europe with Dad and me as the protagonists; Mom, Jay and Nanny just listened. Then, one evening, after a particularly fierce discussion, I stood up and announced, "I'm going to bed and think this over for the last time. Tomorrow, I'll tell you what I'm going to do."

The next morning, when I came to breakfast, Dad looked searchingly at me while Mother pretended to be engrossed in her coffee cup. I took my place at the table, reached for the orange juice, looked Dad squarely in the face and said softy, "I'm going."

I'd made up my mind, now I had to get the financing.

Dorothy DeCoudres, Gwen and I immediately went to work on the Marilynn Horne Benefit Concert. I wrote to the board of the California Heights Methodist Church and received permission to use their social hall. Gwen and I planned the program while Dorothy literally forced people to buy tickets and/or become patrons. She unearthed one purportedly wealthy man and arranged for him to hear me sing at a concert. She told me Mr. Big Bucks was impressed with my voice but wouldn't give me any money.

"He said you were too fat." (I wonder whether the story was true or if Dorothy was trying to get me to lose weight.)

We continued to sell, advertise, and promote The Marilynn Horne Benefit. Then, Bentz Horne got into the act. Dad still was convinced I should stay in America but after my declaration of independence, he got on my bandwagon—big time.

"Peanut, you're going to do a second benefit—" he announced one morning, "—in Bradford! After all, you're a hometown girl and I've got clout back there. We'll have a fabulous turnout."

Dad wrote to Will Davis, the church organist who had discovered Dad's voice many years before. When Will asked some prominent citizens associated with the arts for support, he was told that I was not up to the level of talent brought to Bradford. That hurt. The putdown did not come from the town but Dad felt his beloved Bradford let him down. I wish he had lived long enough to see Bradford declare a Marilyn Horne Day in 1979 and name a street in the public square after me in 2000.

The Long Beach concert raised about a thousand dollars, and by scrimping and saving, I managed to come up with an additional two thousand. People rallied round; I was overcome by the generosity of friends and strangers. Burton Chace, Supervisor of the Fourth District Los Angeles County Board, was one of the contributors—like all the others, he got his money back. I'm proud that I paid off every single loan. (Mr. Chace was doubly generous; he returned my check, saying that he and his wife thought it might come in handy.) While all the fund-raising was going on, Bob Craft made his own contribution by arranging for me to appear with him—and Stravinsky—at an International Music Festival in Venice in September. I purchased a round-trip ticket for a boat sailing on July 31, with an open return date. I had no idea when I'd be back but I wanted to make damn sure I could get back.

By the summer of 1956, with their adult children settled, for the first time in their lives my parents saw a glimmer of financial security. Immediately, they decided to return east and give me a bang-up send off. Dad was going on a sales trip anyway, and arranged to stop in Bradford where Mom, Jay, Nanny and I would join him. We'd visit with family and friends and then I'd go on to New York. I had a huge steamer trunk, and because I was concerned about its arriving when I did—as well as the cost of the trip, we traveled by train instead of plane. The journey from Long Beach was dreadful; sitting up for three days in a railroad car was not my idea of heaven. To top it off, there was a mix-up with the luggage and our bags went on a separate train.

We arrived in Buffalo at six a.m. and Grandpa Hokanson and my Uncle Kenny picked us up. On the drive to Bradford, I asked my uncle where my dad was. My uncle hemmed and hawed. Finally, he said,

"Your father's sick."

"Sick? You mean he's in bed?" No answer.

"He's not in the hospital is he?"

"Ah, I think he is, Jackie. But you'll have to ask your Aunt Adelaide for details."

"Stop the car, here," said my Mom, speaking for the first time. Kenny pulled over. Mom got out and went to a phone booth. She called Adelaide who told her to come by the house first so we could all go to the hospital together. Adelaide was trying to cushion things but Mom really wasn't listening. She got back into the car and told Kenny to go directly to the hospital.

It was early, the staff was skeletal and typically clinical—no one seemed to know about my father's case. Mom telephoned our old family doctor, the attending physician, and asked for the straight story. She got it.

Mom turned ashen, and hung up the phone.

"What is it?" I cried, "What's the matter with Dad."

"He's got acute leukemia," Mother said with disbelief. The minute I heard that, I began to scream. I screamed and screamed until the nurses rushed over and told me to get a hold of myself.

"Get a hold of myself! What are you talking about! This is my father!"

The doctor came right over to the hospital, sat Mom and me down, and related the grim facts.

"Bentz's condition is hopeless. He's got two days to two weeks to live. We can give him cortisone to keep him going for the two weeks but the treatment causes blood cells to build-up. He'll strangle on his own blood."

"Is there any chance he might live beyond two weeks?" Mother asked quietly.

"No," answered the doctor.

"Well, sighed Mother, "forget the cortisone. Give him the painkillers."

I called Dick in California.

"Hey, Jackie, how are you? What's doing? Did you have a good trip?"

"Dick, Dick . . . something awful's happened. You bet-

84

ter sit down."

There was a long silence after I finished explaining. I wondered if the connection had broken until I realized Dick couldn't talk. He was crying. My brother, the Rock of Gibraltar to his kid sister, was weeping uncontrollably. I wept, too.

Dad lingered on for two days, during which time the other members of the family flew out to join us. We all took turns staying in the hospital room because we didn't want him to be alone. On the second night, after Mom had gone to get some rest, Gloria and I sat by the bed watching him. His color was awful and his breathing laborious.

My thoughts were of the past: the voice lessons, the grandstands with Gloria and me standing in front of the band and Dad smiling in the background, the concerts, the recitals, Sunday mornings in church with Dad singing gloriously in the choir. I could not imagine a world without his familiar presence. I thought of all he had done for me—and was overcome with guilt. Although he'd come around, my final act had been one of rebellion.

As though he had read my thoughts, Dad opened his eyes and looked lovingly at us. In a little while, he spoke, first to Gloria, then to me.

"Well, Peanut," he whispered slowly, "I've been doing a lot of thinking. You know, up to now I didn't know if you really had it in you. I couldn't be sure. But now, I think you do. You are right to go to Europe and you've got to go on from there. I know you'll make it, I know it." He closed his eyes and lapsed back into sleep. Those were his last words to me. The next day, he was dead.

After the funeral and burial, I told Mom I'd cancel Europe and come home with her.

"Nothing doing! You're going."

We said our goodbyes on a sunlit street in Bradford in

front of my grandfather's house. I wore a white Lanz dress covered with tiny red rosebuds; I loved that dress because it seemed so "European." Dick was the last to enter the car that would take the family back to California. Before getting into the driver's seat, he gave me a hug. That day, my big brother took over the dominant male role in the family and his words, like my Dad's last words, will be with me forever. He put his hands on my shoulders and looked into my eyes.

"Jackie, I just want you to remember it's okay for you to fail. If things don't work out, you'll still be our daughter and sister. You can come home. We'll love you."

He kissed me on the cheek, hugged me again, then got into the car and drove off. I waved until the car turned the corner, then I began to cry.

My father was gone for good, the rest of the family was on the way home and I was headed for the other side of the world. A moment before, I almost wavered in my resolve. I wanted to be with them, not alone in a strange country. Then my dear brother said what no one ever had said before—not Dad, not Mom, not anyone. Dick told me it was okay to fail. He assured me that I was loved whether or not I succeeded. That assurance not only helped me to leave my family, it gave me the strength to face the next four years.

THE GALLEY YEARS

My father died in Bradford on July 11, 1956. Three weeks later, I set sail on the Dutch ship Maasdam from Hoboken, New Jersey, to Rotterdam, Holland. I was twenty-two years old, suddenly half-orphaned, on my way to a strange continent, most of whose languages I did not speak and where, aside from my engagement in Venice, not one bona fide job awaited me.

I was no sailor. The ocean filled me with apprehension and it loomed endless, dark, and terrifying. The situation wasn't helped any when, on the overnight sleeper from Buffalo to Newark, the conductor greeted me at breakfast.

"Boy, how about that ship going down? Wasn't that something?"

I heard about the sinking of the Andrea Doria on the morning I was to set sail.

The Maasdam was full of young people like me on their way to Europe for experience or training. While I was still reeling from the loss of my father, I was young and on a big adventure and the Maasdam turned out to be a mini-Love Boat. During the crossing, I participated in shipboard talent shows *and* romances. (A young painter zealously pursued me. He even turned up on my doorstep in Germany and asked me to marry him!)

Despite my sadness over Dad's passing, the voyage went quickly and for the most part pleasantly.

John Meadows, an old school friend, met the boat in

Rotterdam and drove me to Salzburg to see Martin Taubman. On the way, I asked John to stop in Stuttgart where the Seventh Army was stationed. I wanted to see a particular Specialist Second Class. Henry Lewis, now the conductor of the Seventh Army Symphony, would lead more than one hundred concerts in Germany, France, Holland, Luxembourg and Greece as well as record over fifty concerts for the Armed Forces Network and the German radio. I hadn't heard from Henry in many months but I had a yen to see him. Once again, as she had at the *Carmen Jones* audition, Fate stepped in.

At the main gate of the Seventh Army compound, an obliging sentry called Henry's barracks. Henry got on the phone and I kidded around, telling him to come out to the gate for a big surprise. He didn't even recognize my voice! When he walked over to the gate and saw me, Henry roared with delight.

"You're not going to believe this, Jackie," he said, "I'm leaving on vacation. I only went back to the barracks because I forgot something. If you'd called a few minutes earlier or later, you'd have missed me."

Henry, John, and I went out for dinner. Henry and I rattled on and on; poor John must have felt like a fifth wheel. After dinner, we parted. Henry went on to Italy and John and I drove to Salzburg.

I studied in Salzburg for a month and then went on to Vienna. Martin Taubman had reserved a room for me in the Pension Schneider, a residence that made Mrs. Loma Murphy's house look like the Beverly Wilshire Hotel. I found the Pension gloomy and depressing although I'm sure my feelings were colored by my situation. I know other singers who found it a perfectly pleasant to stay. (Why do I remember an overbearing maid named Fritzi who leaped around the room in high-top shoes, cleaning and chattering like a character from an operetta?)

Within the month, I was on an overnight sleeper to Venice for the International Festival of Contemporary Music. Bob Craft and Stravinsky's wife, Vera, met me at the train. I was ushered out of the station and into a gondola and we were on our way to St. Mark's Square. Bob was excited about showing me the city. He wanted to make sure I got the right view of St. Marks and made me promise not to look up until he said so. We got out of the gondola and with my head bowed down I clutched Bob's hand and scrambled onto the quay.

"Don't look up. Don't look up," he kept admonishing as he led me through a narrow alley of tiny shops until we reached an arcade.

"Shut your eyes, Jackie!" said Bob.

I did as he asked as he led me on.

"Okay, now open them!"

Bob barely could contain his enthusiasm—and no wonder. There, glittering before me was the most beautiful sight in the world, the Piazza San Marco. To this day I thank Bob for orchestrating my first view of that incredible scene.

Venice was awesome, but the festival had fallen on hard times. A government austerity rule cut funds, so the city administration had to cancel plans for costly operatic premieres. (*The Rake's Progress* premiered at the 1951 festival.) Instead, they commissioned a choral piece from Stravinsky. His "*Canticum Sacrum ad Honorem Sancti Marci Nominis*" (A Canticle to Honor the Name of Saint Mark) was only seventeen minutes long and comprised the second half of the program. The first half featured music of Monteverdi and Schutz conducted by Bob Craft and sung by Richard Lewis, Gérard Souzay, Magda Laszlo, Petre Munteanu, and me. For the second half, Stravinsky was going to take the podium. The Maestro had been asked to lengthen the Canticle to fill out the program. He wouldn't— he told them he'd conduct the piece twice. And that's exactly what he did. The audience was enjoined from applauding because we were inside a church and the effect really was eerie. To hear it played, then to have complete silence, then to have it played again, and once more to have silence.

Digression: Applause.

Convention says that you don't applaud until the end of a piece. I find that disconcerting—there's nothing better than hearing applause after you've done your work. As a performer, I wanted to know that listeners were reacting. (I took my cue from Artur Rubinstein. He once said that if he didn't get applause after the first movement of the Tchaikovsky Piano Concerto, he knew something was wrong.) I don't agree with purist nonsense about not clapping, particularly in opera when applause often erupts between the cavatina and cabaletta, interrupting the complete aria. And don't forget the opening section, the recitative. When I poured everything I had into a terrific recitative, I wanted to hear the reaction before I launched into the cavatina.

End of digression.

Back to Venice. I thought the "Canticle" was great but Stravinsky's twelve-tone experiment was not a smashing success. What's more, the maestro already had run into trouble at the festival. He wrote a note for an instrument— the bass clarinet, I think—which was too low to play. The cognoscenti were agog—imagine Stravinsky making such an error.

Whatever happened musically, seeing Venice was thrill enough for me. When I wasn't rehearsing, I spent long hours exploring the city with Bob Craft, soaking up everything. I'll never forget some special moments on that initial visit.

Stravinsky was an indefatigable worker, always busy at something, whether composing, arranging, writing or discoursing. That September, the climate was not conducive to work. The sirocco was up, and anyone who's ever lived through this thick, warm, damp wind knows how debilitating it is and how badly it affects people. The density and humidity is crushing; you simply cannot move let alone work. One miserably humid day, late in the afternoon, Mme. Stravinsky, Bob and I were sitting in the Stravinsky's suite in the Bauer-Grunwald Hotel when the Maestro walked into the room. He had been working in the bar, which was closed during the day. He shook his head—the three pairs of glasses moved with each nod—and groaned.

"It is impossible!" he moaned. "I cannot compose my dry music in this damp weather!"

While in Venice preparing a concert with Gérard Souzay and his accompanist, Dalton Baldwin, I talked to them about my father—about how I had no choice other than to go on because that's what my dad and mother wanted. I often got tearful and found it difficult to work. Whenever that happened, Gérard and Dalton sustained me, praising me for my courage in staying the course. I bonded with those two men and still count them among my dearest friends. I also had the privilege of meeting the redoubtable Nadia Boulanger, a great musician and teacher and a gentle, wise and darling woman. One evening as Stravinsky and the orchestra rehearsed, she and I sat together in St Mark's Basilica. At the end, Boulanger turned to me and said, "He's always twenty-five years ahead of everyone."

(A footnote: The San Marco performance was attended by the Cardinal of Venice who became Pope John XXIII.)

Twenty-five years later, I stood at Stravinsky's grave in Venice's San Michele cemetery and thought of all our times together, especially the last time I sang for him. We were in

Toronto, in 1968, for a broadcast of *Oedipus Rex*. Despite his failing health, Stravinsky still kept up his work. I was in his dressing room, along with him, his wife and a few others. Someone asked me if I ever had sung a particular work.

"Oh, I've already forgotten that," I replied.

Stravinsky reflected a bit and then spoke.

"Ah yes, the things we have forgotten," he said. "But, my dear Jackie, one thing I will never forget—your beautiful voice."

Much later, Bob Craft told me that the Maestro dedicated his last work to me. How I cherish that honor!

After the festival, I returned to Vienna and began studying with Heinrich Schmidt, head of musical preparation at the Vienna State Opera. Meanwhile, Martin Taubman arranged for me to audition with a well-known German agent. I forget his name but I remember that he was one of the biggest guns in the industry and a real stickler. Taubman urged me to be on top of everything. I was on top of everything, including German pastries. Since the day Dad died, I'd been on an eating rampage and my weight was up, up, up.

I went to Frankfurt to meet the agent. I walked into his office and introduced myself to Herr Richard Mohr, who was seated on the sofa. The minute he saw me, Herr Mohr rose and began shaking his finger in my face.

"*Sie sind zu dick!*" (You're too fat!)

What's the phrase, "fight or flight?" Well, I wasn't going to run. I planted my two feet on the floor, put one arm on my hip and raising the other, pointed my finger right at the Junker's nose.

"*Warten und hören!*" (Wait and listen!)

Herr Mohr fell back on the sofa and I sang "*Ritorna vincitor.*" When he called Taubman later he said:

"*Die kleine dicke wird etwas sein!*" (That little fat one

is going to be something!)

Where did I go? Of all places, I wound up in the boonies of West Germany. Herr Mohr arranged for me to audition at the local opera company in Gelsenkirchen, a city in the Ruhr Valley. I was hired immediately even though there wasn't a place for me—wasn't that nice? I was excited about my appointment and eager to be part of a working repertory company.

The Gelsenkirchen Opera is part of a long and noble German tradition. For centuries, the government has supported the arts by patronizing artists and establishing theatres. In 1956, the country boasted nearly 200 subsidized theatres including over fifty opera companies—small wonder Mr. Taubman wanted me over there.

Giuseppe Verdi often spoke of his "*anni di galera,*" his "galley years"—the early days when he worked non-stop under less than ideal conditions. Now, I entered my "*anni di galera*" and slaved for the next three years. While my contract specified time off for summers and home and concerts in other European cities, 95% of my time was spent in the Ruhr Valley. Don't be misled by the lovely sound of the words "Ruhr Valley"—Gelsenkirchen was the pits, literally, since it was in the middle of Germany's coal and steel area. The climate ranged from fog to rain to snow and a film of just plain dirt hung like a mantle over the town. The winters were frightfully frigid; I had colds, colds, and more colds, plus bronchitis. I was lonely and not only plain old sick, I was homesick, too.

Post-war Germany was a complicated community and when I lived there, I learned a lot about people, not all of it pleasant. Still, I appreciated some of the ironies I encountered. The *Intendant* (or Director) of the Opera was a former Nazi who'd been given a lifetime contract at the Stuttgart theatre by Adolf Hitler. After the war, he was removed from Stuttgart and jailed as a war criminal. Upon his release, he was appointed to Gelsenkirchen, Siberia for the Germans. I was prepared to hate this man, yet I grew to love and admire him. He was a marvelous director, a papa who ran the theatre with an iron hand but also looked after his opera family. When he retired, his replacement, a Jewish guy, proved to be somewhat of an SOB. Go figure.

Our company did a few out-of-town performances. On one bus trip to small opera house miles from our home base, someone picked up a newspaper filled with news about the devaluation of the British pound. A German singer laughingly commented,

"So the English have devalued the pound—and we're the ones who were supposed to have lost the war."

"I'm sure in 1945 there was no doubt in your minds who lost!" I snorted.

Quite a few Americans were in Gelsenkirchen, including a guest baritone who happened to be black. One evening, a bunch of us were in the local café when a group of townsfolk came in and drank themselves into advanced loutishness. One walked over to our table and, weaving from side-to-side, stood behind the baritone. The drunken oaf flopped his arms around the singer, gave him a bear hug, and announced loudly, "You are a black man, but we don't mind you or your color. It's the Jews we don't like!"

"Well, I'm Jewish!" I jumped up and shouted, "So you get the hell out of here." Without another word, the drunk returned to his companions. They threw some dirty looks our way and then left. I sat down and reached for a glass of water; the baritone took my outstretched hand in his.

"Gee, Jackie," he said sympathetically, I'm really sorry that happened"—adding, "I didn't know you were Jewish."

My philosophy? At times like that, everybody's Jewish,

or black or whatever!

The nadir of my German years came on Christmas Eve, 1958. Christmas has got to be the hardest holiday to spend alone, especially if, like me, your memories are full of family gatherings right out of Dickens. I wasn't scheduled to perform for a few days during the holiday week; I had no place to go on December 25th and was relieved and grateful when a friend, Karol Lorraine, invited me to join her in Heidelberg. I took a train, arrived late on the 24th and joined Karol and others for dinner. After the meal, we parted for the evening and I returned to the sparse room she'd reserved for me in a nearby pension. I appreciated all Karol had done, still I could not stop thinking of my family. I missed them so much.

I began to undress and was overcome with a terrific itch in my groin. I inspected and, without going into the gory details, discovered I was hosting lice. I let out a shriek that must have reached C above high C. I couldn't imagine why I was infested. I've always been fastidious about personal hygiene; moreover I'd been celibate in Gelsenkirchen. Martin Taubman's parting words to me had been, "Don't sleep around, Jackie." Not that I needed him to tell me—that was not the way I intended to get ahead. Still, there was no denying the state I was in. What to do? No drugstore was open, and I had no phone in my room in case I could find a doctor willing to come out on Christmas Eve. I thought of taking a hot bath yet that didn't seem right. And then I got an idea. I took a razor out of my cosmetics case and used it. Next, I rummaged through my overnight case for some sort of antiseptic. All I could find was a bottle of Arpège cologne. I splashed it on expecting it might smart but, God, I wasn't prepared for the intense burning. It was killing! Sobbing, I crawled into the bed and lay there whimpering. I thought of home and all the Christmases with Dad, Mom, Dick, Gloria, Jay and Nanny. I thought of the holiday music that had filled our house and the love, warmth and joy we had shared. Now, I was completely and utterly alone. Stung with pain and filled with shame, I was able to imagine how it had happened. I had rented a room in Gelsenkirchen and my landlady's boyfriend, a grubby, unkempt slob, was always hanging around. There was only one bathroom. That had to be it. The day after Christmas, Karol took me to her doctor. After examining me, the doctor said I'd administered the best possible treatment by applying the cologne—a hot bath would have been exactly the thing not to do. I'd actually cured myself.

In retelling this story, comical aspects emerge, but there was nothing funny about it at the time. I was miserable in every way. And they call a diva's life "glamorous."

A few things kept me going during those Gelsenkirchen years. First, I performed constantly—for the most part in soprano roles: Mimi in *La Bohème*, Giulietta in *The Tales of Hoffmann*, Minnie in *The Girl of the Golden West*, Amelia in *Simon Boccanegra* and Tatiana in *Eugene Onegin*. For many years, much of the soprano repertoire remained good for me—I could have sung Mimi during my prime, although the high C might not have come quite as easily. My growing fluency in the language was another plus. In Germany, operas were done in the native tongue. I became proficient in speaking, reading and writing German. Later I learned French and Italian—my fluency in the latter came through Nico Zaccaria. (I'm not sure Berlitz would admit it, but the best way to learn another language is in bed.) The dreariness of Gelsenkirchen also was relieved by the Monday-evening short-wave broadcasts of the "Martini and Rossi Hour." This Italian version of America's Bell Tele-

phone or Firestone Hours presented concerts by outstanding singers of the day. I listened entranced to artist such as
Renata Tebaldi, Giulietta Simionato and Maria Callas. And,
in 1959, for the first time, I heard the Australian wonder,
Joan Sutherland, on the West Deutsche Rundfunk.

Summers I returned home to my family. Jay was blasé
about my comings and goings and it drove me wild. I ached
to see him and he was so casual, I'd want to wring his neck.
Once, when he was sixteen, I made a transatlantic phone
call. Jay answered and I began shouting,

"Jay, Jay! It's me. It's Jackie!"

"Wanna talk to Mom?" he asked.

That's a kid brother for you.

In 1957, Carl Ebert called me back to Los Angeles to repeat
my first starring mezzo role, Cinderella in the Guild's En-
glish-language version of Rossini's *Cenerentola*. (I first did
the part for him in March of 1956.) Ebert offered a great
deal to a singer, not only in the staging but also in his interpretation of the Rossini style. It was heady stuff for a twenty-
two-year old—and made all the more bubbly by the presence of a certain handsome baritone who will remain name-
less. From the very beginning of rehearsals, Mr. Big and I
felt a strong attraction, an immediate empathy perhaps because we were the youngest members of the cast. Although
we spoke to each other only on a professional level, I felt a
"tug" throughout the preliminary run-throughs. Then, it
happened.

Ebert stood in front of the stage directing a walk-through;
I was standing, center stage, listening to his instructions;
the rest of the cast was positioned around the set. Suddenly,
without a word, the baritone walked over, took me in his
arms and kissed me like I'd never been kissed before—right
in the middle of a rehearsal in the Shrine Auditorium. I

dropped my score, wrapped my arms around him and kissed him right back! I'll never forget the look on Ebert's face when I came out of the clinch. His blue eyes widened and he grinned from ear-to-ear.

"I would like to get kissed like that, too!" he laughed.

After that, the baritone and mezzo embarked on a long, wonderful love affair. It wasn't perfect bliss. My friend was married, and though the marriage was an unhappy one, he adored his children. I didn't want a backstairs relationship and eventually gave him the classic "either/or" speech. He couldn't leave his family, thus the affair ended. A few years later, when he did divorce his wife, Henry Lewis was back in the picture.

While I was indentured at Gelsenkirchen, Henry was back with the L.A. Philharmonic. I renewed my correspondence with him and as usual wrote the lion's share of letters. Henry didn't feel the need to write when he could phone and he kept the wires buzzing. At last, we arranged to meet in Vienna. I really was eager to see him. He arrived on the appointed day and near the appointed hour...with another woman—his mother. Good old Henry neglected to inform either his parent visiting from the States or his girlfriend that the other would be there. I'm sure Mrs. Lewis was as delighted to share her son with me as I was having her along as a chaperone.

I guess it's time to fill in a bit more about Henry Lewis.

He was born October 16, 1932, in Los Angeles, the only child of Mary Josephine Turnham Lewis, (always called, Jo) a registered nurse, and Henry Lewis, Sr., an automobile dealer. Although neither of his parents was musical, he began playing the piano at age 5. Henry was enrolled at the Holy Name School—the only black kid. During recess, taunted by the jeers of his classmates, he ran inside to the

Sister in charge. Tearfully, he told her the kids were calling him a "nigger."

"Well, you are one, aren't you?" responded the Sister. "Go back out there and play."

Other nuns encouraged Henry, particularly one Sister who knew music. Henry gave piano recitals and during one, he played a Handel piece from memory. Halfway through he drew a blank. Quickly, he began improvising Handel-sounding music at the keyboard and finished with a flourish.

"I'll never forget the look on the Sister's face as I walked off the stage," he told me. "She knew something was wrong, but couldn't quite put her finger on it."

Eventually, Henry persuaded his parents to enroll him in public school. He became interested first in band instruments and then took up the double bass. At the same time, at his father's insistence, Henry went out for the football team. He made it, and soon quit.

"I wasn't interested," said Henry, "but I wanted to show my dad I could do it."

After finishing Dorsey High School, Henry received a scholarship to the University of Southern California. The senior Lewises divorced when their son was twenty years old, and from then on Henry had to divide his loyalties although he always was closer to his mother. From the beginning, I was embraced with open arms by both Lewises.

For four years, I continued to shuttle back and forth between Europe and the United States. I had quite a few engagements. During Henry's time with the Seventh Army Symphony, we did a radio broadcast recording in Stuttgart of *Cavalleria rusticana*. I learned the role of Santuzza in two days.

In addition, Dorothy Huttenback got me summer bookings in America, which barely paid my fare, but gave me the opportunity to go home. Martin Taubman arranged engagements on the Continent and through him I made a memorable appearance at the San Carlo Opera in Naples. I was engaged to sing in *Die Walküre*.

Besides Brünnhilde, there are eight Valkyries in Wagner's opera—four sopranos, and four mezzos and contraltos— and they all appear in Act III. (By the way, I sang Gerhilde, a high soprano.) The Naples Valkyries resembled a Las Vegas chorus line; each was a statuesque five feet, seven inches tall (or more) and each had been issued a long blond wig and platform shoes. The shoes raised them another three inches off the ground. I should say that everyone but Gerhilde got the blonde hair and the platform shoes. I was presented with a long black wig and a pair of flat sandals. Since we were warriors, we wore coats of mail. My sisters' mail hung neatly below their rear ends; mine dangled somewhere around mid-calf. You can imagine what I looked like on stage. And that's not all. In *Die Walküre*, one of the Valkyries is the designated "runner," required to dash to and fro carrying messages. Seven leggy sprinters and one runt to choose from and guess who got the job? The stagehands got a kick out of me. I was called "*La Valkieretta*" (The Little Valkyrie) and as I raced in and out of the wings, they would hold my spear and shield while I straightened the wig, which threatened to fly off my head. I lost weight chasing around that stage. As ridiculous as the situation was, I was so happy to be in sunny Italy after somber Gelsenkirchen that I didn't care how stupid I looked. Not to have black coal dust in my nose was a joy!

During my San Carlo stint, I lived in a hotel overlooking the Bay of Naples and struck up an acquaintance with a well-mannered, swarthy man also staying at the hotel. He'd stop me in the lobby to ask how things were going and offered to help in any way he could. One day the concierge called me over.

"You know, Signorina, this man you are talking to, I think maybe you don't want to get too friendly. He is named Lucky Luciano."

Luciano, the Mafia kingpin, had been deported to Italy by the U.S. government and was living in exile. Thereafter, whenever a certain expatriate was around, the Valkirietta avoided the lobby.

In Naples, a filling in my front tooth started acting up. I was in pain but not keen on seeking professional aid. As far as I was concerned, Naples' many natural splendors did not include medical excellence. Alas, the tooth would not wait until I returned to Germany. It got so bad I had to call the hotel doctor. He gave me a shot of codeine and sent me to a dentist. I went to the address and walked into the most modern, well-equipped office this side of Central Park South. The dentist, a double for Rosanno Brazzi, had studied in the United States and imported every new dental device on the market.

"The nerve must come out, Signora," he told me, adding, "The tooth probably will turn black in about six months because of exposure to the air."

Thereupon, he whipped that nerve out and plugged my tooth so fast that air barely had a chance to get into the shell. Moreover, it took five years for that tooth to blacken. You'll never hear a disparaging word from me about the practice of dentistry in Naples.

I still was writing to Henry Lewis. He'd returned to his position as bass player in the Los Angeles Philharmonic, and though he was hardly an assiduous pen pal, our correspondence was steady and full of allusions to mutual affection and musical happenings. I guess you could call them love letters with a downbeat, or should I say upbeat. They also served to chronicle events.

I wrote one letter from Vienna where I was appearing in the Vienna Festival. At the same time, Leontyne Price, Birgit Nilsson, Cesare Valletti and Cesare Siepi were recording *Don Giovanni* with Erich Leinsdorf, and Martin Taubman took me to one session. It was amazing. All my life, exceptional artistry has knocked me out. I don't care if the artist is my biggest rival; I adore great singing. For one singer to be moved to tears by another is very rare; Leontyne Price touched me that deeply. After she finished singing in the "balcony trio," I turned to Martin and said, "I quit."

"This is great, great singing of the first rank," I wrote to Henry. "Leontyne was fabulous."

Price always was a favorite of the general, not just the operatic, public. She could make a charm bracelet out of her Grammy awards—no matter what she recorded, she won. Once, I was asked to sing at the Grammy presentations.

"Why bother with me?" I said. "Why don't you ask Leontyne to sing so she can be there to pick up her Grammy?"

I was privileged to appear with Leontyne Price on several occasions, and each time she revealed her greatness as a person as well as an artist. In February of 1976, after we barged down the Nile together as Aida and Amneris, I received a note from my co-star. In the letter she said that I was "the greatest singer alive" and the "greatest female colleague" she'd ever worked with. Me? The greatest? I'm still speechless.

In February 1982, at a rehearsal for a special performance of the *Verdi Requiem* at the Metropolitan Opera, Leontyne spun out a high B flat at the end of the "*Libera me*" that could have melted steel. I told her afterward that she'd done me in.

"How do you do it? How do you get those high notes?"
I asked.

"How?" answered the Diva, tucking a wisp of hair under her turban, "Why, I've been listening to your records, honey, that's how."

I was supposed to be singing in that *Requiem*, too, but I became ill and had to cancel—the first of only two Met performances I ever missed. I desperately wanted to sing because the broadcast was a memorial tribute to Francis Robinson. Francis, Assistant General Manager of the Metropolitan, was a dear, dear friend. Unfortunately, I had major throat problems and the doctor told me to keep my mouth shut. The minute my cancellation was announced, Leontyne called to see how I was doing. She wouldn't listen to my apologies for dropping out.

"Don't you worry about the Requiem," she said firmly. "You just take care of you, honey."

What a thrill when we finally did appear together in a joint concert in March of 1982, at Lincoln Center. For me the shining moment came in rehearsal. We sang the "*Mira, o Norma*" duet and at the end of the opening cavatina, we embraced. I could feel her trembling. Leontyne was in tears, unable, for the moment, to continue. Tears are a luxury singers rarely allow themselves in actual performance yet there are times when the glory of the music simply overwhelms you. Leontyne Price never sang *Norma*, that most challenging and glorious of operatic roles, and perhaps the realization that she never would be performing it, got to her. Or, perhaps it was simply the sheer beauty of the moment.

"Oh rats," she muttered as we moved apart. She dabbed at her eyes with the back of her hand. "Forgive me, Jackie, I'm so silly."

Silly? Splendid is more like it.

After the concert, Leontyne once again gave me one of my highest compliments.

"Working with you has been beautiful," she wrote in a brief note. "You give so much. I just never expected to get these things back from another singer."

Ditto, dear Leontyne, and I'm so happy I was witness to your splendor all those decades ago in Vienna.

In the letter to Henry praising Price, I also wrote about my own status.

> I definitely am staying lyric for at least another five years; this is where I belong! Natch, I'm no light lyric and lean towards spinto but I'm going to stick to it with a vehemence.

Okay, I got vengeance and vehemence mixed up, but I was sure about my voice. And I was right, too—it would be years before I turned mezzo.

TRIUMPHS AND DISASTERS

I tried to make the best of every situation in Germany yet I fought an uphill battle, not only emotionally but physically. My Gelsenkirchen days were filled with upper respiratory disease. Early in 1959, I developed a breathiness that made it difficult for me to make the passage of air smooth and supportive. In Vienna, I'd already experienced minor troubles and consulted with Dr. Kriso, a well-known throat specialist with a reputation for helping singers. An excellent diagnostician, Dr. Kriso knew vocal problems first-hand—he was married to Emmy Loose, a soprano with the Vienna State Opera. I revisited the good doctor to find out why I was taking two or three breaths instead of one. Dr. Kriso examined me and was loath to say what was wrong. Later, he confessed that he felt singers were not models of stability about voice-related problems and feared I'd be too rattled by the truth. Bentz Horne's daughter insisted on knowing the facts.

The vocal cords, the lower of two pairs of folds in the larynx, vibrate when pulled together; air, passing up from the lungs, produces vocal sound. Dr. Kriso found a swollen spot on one of my cords and when the vocal cords closed, the lump got hit first. Thus, more air was needed to stretch out and shut the cord. The swelling was in a very precarious place and, untreated, might have led to a rupture or a node.

"What do I have to do to get rid of it?" I asked Dr. Kriso

the minute he finished his explanation. No way would I sit around and let this go on.

Immediately, he began a treatment program that ran concurrently with my rehearsals for the Vienna Festival. In the morning, I went to the theatre and rehearsed. That over, I walked to the doctor's office where he applied deep heat or ultra short waves on the outside of my throat for a few minutes. After that, I wouldn't speak for the rest of the day. The next day, I followed the same routine. In only two days, the swelling went away. Dr. Kriso determined the cause; he was sure that I must have sung a performance on a dreadful cold. The minute he said it, I pinpointed the exact moment. I did a *Girl of the Golden West* in Frankfurt and, indeed, had sung over one mother of a cold. The doctor advised that if I was careful for a year and did not overtire myself, the cord would strengthen and all would be well.

Dr. Kriso told me that, many years before, his mentor and teacher discovered nodes on Lotte Lehmann's vocal cords. The surgeon wanted to remove them, but Lehmann said no; she was convinced that the tiny calluses gave her voice a special quality which she did not want to lose. Lehmann, the doctor told me, made her entire career with nodes on her vocal cords. When he told me this, a bell went off in my head. No wonder Lehmann took two or three breaths to other singers' one; she was always short of breath but she made it effective—God, she made it effective! Indeed, one of her oft quoted statements was, "Don't sacrifice your expression on the altar of breath."

Unlike my erstwhile teacher, I wouldn't go through life with anything less than perfect vocal cords.

"By the way," Dr. Kriso added, "you should have your adenoids removed."

"What? I've already had them out."

Guess what? The adenoids excised in childhood had

106

made a return visit. Within a few weeks, I sat in a chair in Dr. Kriso's office and he cut away the tissue. A friend of mine waited in the outer office and heard the doctor and me mumbling and conversing in German for a half-hour as he prepped me for the minor surgery. Then, after a short silence, my German gave way to English.

"Ow! That hurts!" I cried. Forty-five minutes later, I drove myself home. No nonsense, that's me.

My experience with Dr. Kriso reconfirmed what my father had said about proper training and care of the vocal equipment. The vocal cords and the retina of the eye are the only tissues in the human body which, when damaged, do not come back with full elasticity. After damage, the muscular membrane of the vocal cord, originally yellow in color, turns almost black. I suspect that's what might have happened to Maria Callas and probably to Ljuba Welitsch. Welitsch, a red haired, dynamic soprano, was a sensation in Richard Strauss's *Salome*, the one-act opera based on Oscar Wilde's play. Dr. Kriso advised her not to do the wickedly demanding role more than six or seven times a year. Mme. Welitsch didn't heed his warning and sang *Salome* often and everywhere. Tragically, by her mid-thirties, Ljuba Welitsch's prima donna days were over; thereafter she sang character parts. According to Dr. Kriso, *Salome* wasn't her only problem.

"She lived her life *gespannt* (intensely) and that, too, was dangerous. Remember," he cautioned me, "in order to continue singing, a singer must try to create an atmosphere of calm."

Truer words were never spoken and harder advice to follow was never given! Prima donnas can become highstrung trying to be calm. I must also add that Dr. Kriso told me he only would discuss singers no longer performing. The Doctor's medical skill and personal attention greatly impressed me. He didn't have to counsel me; I was just another young singer with an undetermined future, but this man really cared about the "instrument." I'm so thankful I listened to him.

Vocal troubles weren't all that bedeviled me; all sorts of minor crises arose. One was a hair-raising experience on the highway. I'd bought a car, a little Renault Dauphine, and, after a trip to Vienna, was returning to Gelsenkirchen via Salzburg. My friend Uta Wagner came along with me. It was January of a very severe winter with record-breaking snows and the trip was miserable in every way. The Autobahn is a highway with no speed limit—big Mercedes cars usually whiz by at Mach 1. We were traveling at a reasonable pace on a bright, sunny, day when, suddenly we found ourselves on a sheet of ice—*glatteis*, the Germans call it. I felt the car skidding and took my foot off the accelerator—not smart, I know now—and the car went into a long slide. We spun around for three complete revolutions and then flipped over onto the snow piled in the center of the highway. If it hadn't been for the snow cushioning the impact, the car roof would have caved in more than it did.

Uta and I were wedged in upside down, and remained so till some truck drivers stopped and pulled us out. They turned the Renault right side up and told us to get back in the car and sit there while they went for a tow truck. We did as they said and huddled together in the tiny front seat. I took a look in the rearview mirror at the approaching cars when it dawned on me that we were sitting ducks. Sure enough, a car came up behind us, hit the *glatteis* and crashed right into the back of the Renault practically embedding it in the snow. The car backed off, the tow truck arrived and we were hooked up. They towed us to a garage in nearby Munich. I called Martin Taubman and asked him to wire money for repairs and the return fare to Gelsenkirchen.

Martin came through. Uta and I took the first train back.

I'd been a model of decorum through the whole ordeal, talking, arranging, and discussing what had to be done without a hint of panic. The minute we reached Gelsenkirchen, I went into shock. I crawled into bed and slept for one solid week, rising only to eat and use the bathroom. When I returned to the opera house, my makeup lady was *gespannt*. Rumors had been flying and according to all reports, my face was severely gashed.

"Ach, ach," moaned the makeup lady, "When I thought that beautiful face was ruined, ach, ach."

As it happened, my face wasn't ruined—my figure was! I did a lot of compensatory eating and I didn't get back into shape until March. Dorothy Huttenback and Martin Taubman kept writing letters of encouragement exhorting me to keep slimming—I didn't mention any of this to Henry.

In April, I wrote Martin Taubman and told him that the loneliness was getting to me; I wanted to take a quick visit home. He advised me to stay put, adding that travel would be bad for my health. So I stayed—and got the grippe and bronchitis. Gelsenkirchen was one big Petri dish where germ after germ was cultivated for my benefit. The coldness and dampness were excruciating and my bones were permanently chilled. Why, oh why hadn't some Caribbean government subsidized the arts?

Meanwhile, Gwen Koldofsky had been working on a tour idea for my next visit home, a month-long series of concerts. Where do you think Miss Horne and Mrs. Koldofsky were scheduled to appear—London? Paris? Rome? Montego Bay? Not quite. She'd booked us into Canada and Alaska! Here I was miserable from the cold in Germany and Gwen put me into the tundra. She thought it was an excellent training ground to prepare recital programs, and she was right. What's more, Alaska actually seemed warmer than Gelsenkirchen. The tour was called The Alaska Music Trail.

Kitimat, Ketchikan, Wrangell, Petersburg, Sitka, Juneau, Cordova, Kodiak, Anchorage, Seward, Fairbanks and Grand Prairie—from October 31 to December 2, 1959, I played them all to appreciative and hospitable audiences. Television hadn't yet replaced live concertgoing and the houses were packed. One of my favorite reviews appeared in the Petticoat Gazette, published by the Women's Club of Seward:

> Miss Marilyn Horne came to sing for us and Mrs. Gwendolyn Koldofsky play piano. All of us enjoying your song, what you sing for us and Mrs. Gwendolyn.

Don't be misled by the ingenuousness of the Petticoat Gazette's reporter—the Alaskan critics knew their stuff. One had this to say:

> Miss Horne does not seek to overpower an audience with her voice as some vocalists do, but has excellent dynamic control. She has the best diction many of us have heard in a vocalist.

Lest you think I received nothing but praise, another erudite reviewer wrote that I sang okay, but that my German diction was poor. I called up the newspaper and, without identifying myself, asked to speak to the critic. When he got on the phone, I began to chatter non-stop—in German.

"Excuse me, excuse me," he interrupted. "I don't speak German."

"Oh," I replied sweetly. "Well, this is Marilyn Horne, and I do!"

We packed nineteen full recitals and thirty-three half-hour children's concerts into those five weeks. The only way we didn't travel was by dog sled. Almost as soon as we started out, poor Gwen sprained her ankle. A doctor taped it up before we took off on a prop plane to Kodiak. I sat in the cockpit gabbing with the pilot while Gwen huddled in the back; she almost passed out during the bouncy ride. Gwen played that whole trip with her pedal foot strapped.

During this "have lungs, will travel" tour, we performed in any available arena, mostly high-school auditoriums. In one, the only room available between numbers was the girls' lavatory. Off I'd trot after each section to get myself a drink of water or wipe my brow. At the end of the performance, Gwen overheard a kid say to her mother,

"I like that lady's singing, but why does she always go to the bathroom?"

Our appearance in Sitka was special. I was used to looking out and seeing a variety of people in the audience; in Sitka, for the first time in my life, I looked out at an audience composed entirely of Eskimos.

While I toured, my correspondence with Henry boomed. I wrote almost daily, about everything that was happening. I could tell him things I'd never mention to my parents. For one thing, until this trip, I'd never indulged in "extras"—how could I when I had to use every cent towards my upkeep. In Alaska, I saw a lovely watercolor by an artist named Claire Fejes. I had to have it! So I bought it. I wrote Henry but cautioned him not to tell my mother or anyone else in my family. Unlike him, they wouldn't understand. I could just hear it…. "You spent your money on WHAT?" This was the first time I'd ever spent money on a "what," the first time I'd ever indulged myself in something other than the mundane or the practical. I've never regretted it.

On Thanksgiving Day, Henry mailed a three-page typewritten letter, a record length. He told of visiting my mother in Long Beach to discuss our plans for the future—a future that included marriage. Before he left for Europe, Henry

111

and I decided it was time to do something permanent about our relationship. We set a date for the summer of 1960. My mother was not happy. She liked Henry very much, admired his intelligence and his character, but he was a Negro. Henry believed that her stand on our marriage was based on a purely social perspective. According to him, she was interested in our mutual welfare and because we lived our lives with such intensity, she doubted that we could be happy as a couple. Furthermore, our careers might suffer because of bigoted people in high places or not so high places. Apparently my mother also believed that while Henry had examined the situation, I hadn't. What nonsense! I'd thought long, hard, and in excruciating detail about what my marriage might mean in terms of my career. I was used to thinking for myself, and Mother didn't appreciate my independent status. She really thought I wasn't capable of decision-making and up until the last minute she tried to forestall our wedding.

"What do you have to marry him for?" she pleaded with me. "Why can't you just live with him? Be his mistress, for God's sake, not his wife!"

I couldn't believe my ears. This was 1960, long before live-in relationships became commonplace and my mother was telling me to "live in sin." Her avant-garde suggestion was not the solution for me; I was determined to marry Henry Lewis.

I returned to Gelsenkirchen for my final season and for the next six months well-meaning friends sent "subtle" messages cautioning against marriage. The admonitions came every way but Pony Express. Right before I left for Germany on Christmas Eve, 1959, Roger Wagner telephoned.

"If you marry Henry, Jackie, you're finished in America. You can carry it off in Europe, but you'll never have a career in your own country. Americans won't tolerate it."

112

"Do you really know what you're doing?" my brother Dick wrote.

And so it went—letter after letter, phone call after phone call. I'm sure my mother put many of my friends up to it. She pulled out all the stops but it didn't work. I was engaged to Henry Lewis and we would be married.

From January to July, I was in such a state I picked up every malady under the sun. For a brief scary time I had a pulse rate of 110. My agitation over my impending marriage and the running battle I was having with my family and some of my friends accounted for it. But, simultaneously another crisis arose. I was preparing a Mimi in *La Bohème* when the Intendant called me into his office and announced that my next role would be Marie in Alban Berg's *Wozzeck*.

Mimi and Marie are polar opposites. *Wozzeck*, a twentieth century masterpiece is based on Georg Büchner's play about a poor, simple-minded soldier who murders his prostitute mistress. It's full of lung-busting twelve-tone music and frankly the idea of learning the part did not appeal to me. I'd sung enough modern music to know it requires a great deal of energy and stretching. Berg's music, murderous for the voice, lay halfway between speech and song, with so many leaps, jumps, and skips you have to be a vocal acrobat to get through a measure. I was concerned that I'd be too busy thinking about the notes and the rhythm to even consider my voice. Immediately, I called Martin Taubman. He about forbade me to attempt Marie and for a while I seriously considered refusing. However, the Intendant needed me and I knew that singers who didn't fuss about assignments received greater consideration when they wanted favors. Consequently, I said I'd learn the first scene and see how it felt. In the process I had to give up Maddalena in *Andrea Chénier*, a role I really wanted. At my request, Henry Lewis mailed a copy of Dmitri Mitropoulos's recording of *Wozzeck*. As a rule, I didn't listen to other interpretations—I was too good a mimic and thought it would interfere with my musical freedom. This time I felt I needed all the help I could get. I played the Mitropoulos recording for guidance and discovered so many errors in the first scene alone I realized I could never use it. In those days, nobody knew *Wozzeck* well, so mistakes went practically unnoticed unless, like me, you followed along with the score. I decided to throw in the towel. Who needs favors, anyway?

"I cannot sing Marie," I protested to the Intendant. "It will hinder my vocal progress."

"You will sing Marie," he answered. "Look, this is a formidable acting as well as singing part. You could really sink your teeth into it."

He had a point.

At that time, maybe five other women in the whole world knew the role—Eleanor Steber was the Metropolitan's Marie in 1959—so I'd be in exclusive company. What's more, *Wozzeck* was scheduled for the inaugural of Gelsenkirchen's new opera house; critics would be coming from all over. I had to do it.

I began to study the part and gradually made myself comfortable. It was grueling, though, and not only vocally. Performing Marie is like going through an emotional wringer, especially in the haunting scene where *Wozzeck* goes mad and slits her throat. You can't help being overcome by the sadness and nihilism pervading the work. Nevertheless, the years with Bob Craft and Stravinsky proved to be excellent preparation for the modern musical idiom. In a few months, I was ready to roll.

Wozzeck opened on May 22, 1960, to complete acclaim. According to the renowned Berlin critic H.H. Stuckenschmidt, I was the greatest Marie he'd ever seen, and he'd seen them all. Even the United States sent press representatives; Irving Kolodin gave me a rave in the Saturday Review of Literature. I sent my reviews to Henry. He showed them to Dorothy Huttenback and she passed them on to Kurt Herbert Adler, Director of the San Francisco Opera, where *Wozzeck* was scheduled for a fall premiere.

Once again, Fate stepped in.

Brenda Lewis, engaged to sing Marie, took ill and dropped out. The next thing I knew, I had an audition with Mr. Adler on Monday, the Fourth of July. If my pulse had been a mere 110 before, it must have raced to 210 that Independence Day weekend.

On Friday, I flew from Düsseldorf to Los Angeles and arrived at two a.m. At two p.m. on Saturday, in the presence of Henry's mother, father and stepmother; my sister, Gloria and her husband, Jack; Gwen Koldofsky; Dorothy Huttenback; Bill and Leona Vennard; and our witnesses, Poldi and Susie Engleman, Henry Lewis and I were married by Dr. Stephen Fritchman, a Unitarian minister. That evening, Henry and I flew to San Francisco and on Monday I auditioned for Kurt Adler. He later told me, mine was one of the greatest auditions he'd ever witnessed in all his years at the San Francisco Opera.

And so, my galley years in Gelsenkirchen came to a close. In terms of my career, I had a fantastic opportunity to appear in the great roles. Funny, the only composer whose work I didn't get a chance to perform was one of my favorites... Mozart. I came to Gelsenkirchen the year after the bicentennial celebration of his birth and they'd done so many of his operas, they called a moratorium while I was there. Besides the opportunity to learn and perform in a professional opera company, Gelsenkirchen provided me with many lessons in humanity. Post-war Germany hardly loomed as Xanadu for a liberal Democrat from California but like anywhere else in the world, I found good and bad among the people. I could not have survived without the help of individuals such as the Molwitz family, who always had a place for me at their table. The members of the company, from artists to stagehands, were true cohorts. Generous with praise, they could criticize, too, and their standards were high. Once, I was appearing as Amelia in Verdi's *Simon Boccanegra* and had finished singing the gorgeous trio which ends with two treacherous high C's. I flatted the first, doggedly scrambled up for the second, nailed it, and then walked off into the wings.

"*Das war kein 'hohes C,'*" (That wasn't a high C) a stagehand sneered.

"*Scheisse!*" I muttered to myself and kept moving.

His words got to me, though, and when the recording of *Simon Boccanegra* with Victoria de los Angeles was released, I bought it to hear how the high C's should sound. You know what? They cut the first one! I didn't know it at the time, but it's so damn hard, they always cut it.

At my last performance in Gelsenkirchen, I sang Marie. To my complete surprise, I was brought back onstage for a farewell. Flowers and gifts were piled around me, and the audience rose, cheering. The stagehands gave me a huge picture of myself as Marie and I stood next to my cardboard counterfeit and bawled. Ruth, my makeup lady, told me it was the first such demonstration ever held for anyone in the history of the Gelsenkirchen Opera. To this day, I look back on the German experience with mixed emotions. That *kohlenpot* (coalpot), a place a California kid could only loathe, has stayed in my heart. While they were often painful to get through, those years made my future achievements possible; I literally paid my dues.

Thank God singers don't have to go to Europe anymore—careers certainly can be made right here at home.

But for my money, performers never can get the flavor of the languages as they're used in opera or song unless they experience it over there. When I went to Europe in 1956, many of my colleagues were more mature than I and yet a lot of them couldn't take it. The loneliness, hard work, lack of success and sheer boredom drove them out. I suffered too, but my suffering had to do with my incredible drive to succeed. Bentz Horne's daughter had to stay on track and everything else had to be set aside. Like Scarlett O'Hara, I forced myself to think about other things "tomorrow." The career didn't suffer—but I did. I should have dealt directly, on its own terms, with the trauma of losing my father and of going alone to a foreign country. I didn't. I forced myself to make the best of the situation and to get the best out of it. I shelved my fears and my feelings and put all my energies into my singing.

RITORNA VINCITOR

Now Henry Lewis and I were together as man and wife. We were delighted but also a little nervous. Our wedding ceremony was one example of what we'd been through. You'll notice that in my brief description of that ceremony, the only member of my immediate family to attend was Gloria—out of respect for Mother everyone else stayed away. On the morning of my wedding day, I telephoned Mom from Dorothy's house and pleaded with her to come. She refused. Her absence weighed heavily. It took all my courage to marry without her being present. Years later, Dick admitted that he'd felt terrible boycotting my wedding.

"I knew I was letting you down, Jackie, but I felt that Mom needed me more than you did."

Two weeks after the wedding, Mother called and declared a truce. She'd made her point by doing what she as a parent had felt was right, but now that the marriage had taken place, she had the grace to accept the change. It takes a big person to concede, and Berneice Hokanson Horne was a very big person. Sometimes I miss her so much it hurts, but the memory of her courage and her love helps ease the pain. She was forty-seven years old when dad died and left her with no support. Jay was only six and I wasn't yet the Miss Independence I thought I was. She missed Dad terribly yet she kept on going because we needed her. I remember her with adoration, and she was never more wonderful than when she finally embraced Henry as one of her children. Years later, she told me how much she loved Henry, adding, "You know, Jackie, not being at your wedding was the biggest mistake of my life."

Dick, Gloria, and Jay rallied around too, and forever after provided the necessary family support for me, Henry, and later, Angela. Even after Henry and I went our separate ways, my family still considered him one of us. In October of 1982, my sister-in-law Joanne and I went to hear Henry conduct *Dialogues of the Carmelites* at the San Francisco Opera. Henry was staying with friends, and when he told them Joanne and I were going to the opera, and then celebrating his birthday with him, their comment was, "Didn't you divorce that family?" The truth is, he never did.

My rehearsals for *Wozzeck* were due to begin in September and there were other engagements to fulfill. Henry was caught up in his work with the Los Angeles Philharmonic, as well as a number of splinter organizations he'd formed, including chamber music and opera groups. We both were terribly busy. The only difference? We were together—a big difference indeed.

Wozzeck proved to be a perfect choice for my re-entry into the American operatic orbit. The West Coast premiere on October 4, 1960, was a smash. The critics and the public hailed me as a new star. To think, this was the role I hadn't wanted. One of the most enthusiastic members of the premiere audience was Dorothy Huttenback. She continued to promote my career by bringing me to the attention of Colbert Artists Management. Anne Colbert and her husband, Henry, ran a successful New York agency and Dorothy handled some of their West Coast business. Now that I'd returned as a "discovery," the Colberts were willing to take me on as a client.

Henry wasn't sitting idly by, either. Newspapers all over

the country carried the story on February 10, 1961, and though the race issue was the headline, the news still was thrilling. "NEGRO CONDUCTS COAST *SYMPHONY*: Henry Lewis, First of Race to Lead Major Orchestra in Regular Concert" wrote *The New York Times*. The key words are "major" and "regular." Henry had led the L.A. Philharmonic before, but outside L.A. And, there were other black conductors—but not with major orchestras. (Dean Dixon appeared with the New York Philharmonic as a guest conductor and led a radio concert with the NBC Symphony, but as a substitute. Eventually, Dixon moved to Europe.) The L.A. Philharmonic was Henry's home base; he'd been in the bass section since 1951 and briefly studied conducting with the orchestra's onetime director, Eduard von Beinum. George Kuyper, the Philharmonic's manager was instrumental in giving Henry the opportunity with the approval of Dorothy Chandler and the Board of Trustees. Henry scored an enormous hit that night and received a rousing ovation. Oh, *The New York Times* also pointed out that the soloist that evening, Marilyn Horne, was Mrs. Henry Lewis.

Mr. and Mrs. Henry Lewis now lived in a modest aerie overlooking the Golden Gate Freeway. Although I had little time for steady domesticity, I loved "playing house." Concerts, appearances with Henry and his Chamber Orchestra and with other groups came almost faster than I could cope with them. Early in 1961, my next big break arrived and again, another artist's indisposition paved the way.

Joan Sutherland was about to make her first New York appearance in Bellini's *Beatrice di Tenda*, a bel canto opera. Bel canto literally means "beautiful singing," and fifty years ago Maria Callas brought back this eighteenth-century Italian vocal style and technique. Bel canto emphasizes beauty of sound as well as ease, flexibility and brilliance of performance and until the Callas revolution—except for surefire hits such as *Lucia di Lammermoor* and *Il Barbiere di Siviglia*—the operas of Donizetti, Rossini and Bellini had been put aside. Sporadically, a particular work was dusted off, usually because a superstar wanted to do it. (Someone like Lily Pons had enough clout at the box office to make it worthwhile for the management to present her in *The Daughter of the Regiment*.) Callas became interested in the repertoire and one by one, resuscitated lost masterworks such as *Anna Bolena, Medea, La Sonnambula* and *I Puritani*. What's more, Callas added dramatic and emotional expression previously thought incompatible with the bel canto, and the combination was electric. Instinctively, Maria Callas plumbed the depths of music, infusing understanding, passion and meaning into her interpretations, most notably in the recitatives. Recitative is the declamatory portion of opera in which, generally speaking, the plot is advanced as opposed to the more static or reflective lyrical settings in the arias. It's one thing to sing a beautiful aria and quite another to present a beautifully conceived recitative.

When Callas tragically lost her agility and ability, Joan Sutherland carried on the tradition. Joan was leaning toward the Wagnerian repertoire until her husband, Richard Bonynge, recognized her singular gifts. Together, they were largely responsible for the re-emergence of bel canto operas. Bottom line? Maria Callas started the renaissance, Sutherland furthered it, and then I came along. Like an Olympic torch of song, the light was passed and through Joan's generosity, I became part of the great chain of beautiful singing.

Back to my big break.

The American Opera Society was presenting a concert version of *Beatrice di Tenda* in Town Hall. Giulietta Simionato was scheduled to sing the mezzo role of Agnese, but had to withdraw. Anne Colbert, Sutherland's agent as well as mine, called and asked me if I could do it. Could I do it? Nothing on earth could have stopped me. I learned that part during a heavy concert schedule with Henry and the L.A. Chamber Orchestra. Three weeks from the day I received Colbert's call, I arrived in New York City for the audition—so did a major snowstorm. I auditioned, got the part and had three weeks to learn my first Bellini opera. The idea of appearing with Joan Sutherland was enough to constrict anyone's vocal cords. Joan made her Covent Garden debut in 1952, as the First Lady in *Die Zauberflöte*, and eleven days later, appeared as the handmaiden Clotilde in *Norma*. Maria Callas sang the title role. Then, in 1959, after a triumphant *Lucia*, Joan was dubbed Callas's successor. To say that Sutherland's New York debut was eagerly awaited doesn't capture the attendant frenzy—the New York music world was at fever pitch at the prospect of hearing her in person. Basically, I was along for the ride.

At our first session, Joan, Richard Cassilly and Enzo Sordello were warm and welcoming—heartening for me because I was the unknown quantity. I had to prove myself. After that first rehearsal, Ricky Bonynge went to a telephone in Town Hall and called Terry McEwen, then director of London Records.

"Get over here, quick," urged Bonynge. "We've got a girl who sounds like Rosa Ponselle!"

Me? Ponselle? Wow. What a thrill to be compared to one of the greatest singers in the history of the Metropolitan. Years later, I met Ponselle and she commented on our similarities both in singing and appearance. She gave me a picture of herself as Carmen, and wrote, "To Jackie, Does the face look familiar? Sisters under the Skin, Love Rosa." According to her, our faces were constructed along the same lines [wide!] and that's why we sounded alike. Such a

122

comparison was very flattering, since her own face had been compared to Caruso's by the great tenor himself. Skull cavities, in fact, constitute an important part of the singer's equipment. Air is something we learn to control, but bones are bones: if you've got 'em, you're lucky.

Terry McEwen did come over, heard me for the first time and became not only an enthusiastic champion of my voice but a true and beloved friend until his untimely death.

Beatrice di Tenda had all the ingredients of a smash hit. Briefly, it's the story of Beatrice (soprano) wife of the Duke of Milan. The Duke is in love with (mezzo) Agnese. However Agnese is secretly in love with Orombello. You guessed it. Orombello is in love with Beatrice. In the course of two acts, the Duke tries to dump his wife and to make an involved story a little less so, Beatrice is falsely accused and executed. On her way to the executioner's block, she pauses to forgive Agnese. As Beatrice is led away, Agnese faints dead away. What takes this material out of the realm of 19th century soap opera is some of the loveliest music Bellini ever wrote.

I needed to do a lot of preparation for my initiation into the bel canto style. I had done Rossini's *Cenerentola* in Los Angeles, but in English, which is very different from the true bel canto. I worked like a dog on the score. My husband was my coach and Henry provided lots of insights and counsel. He, however, was skeptical of what I was doing. You see, I'd become increasingly comfortable in the mezzo range and occasionally mentioned the possibility of concentrating there.

"Mezzo–soprano means half a soprano," warned Henry, who thought the switch a bad idea.

He had a point.

Look at it this way, operas have been composed since 1597, and in almost every one of them the leading female role has been written for the soprano voice. As a result, sopranos are content to stay put, while mezzos are always on the lookout for ways to move up. Except for a handful of parts, mezzos stand around and watch the soprano get the big arias and the hero. Even Amneris, a top mezzo role, got a raw deal from Verdi: he was going to name his opera after her, but at the last minute gave the title to the soprano, Aida. All told, I would alternate between soprano and mezzo roles right through to the early 70's.

Henry and I worked unceasingly on the fine points of bel canto. Intense concentration is required particularly to get the rubati, and the shape of the recitatives. In Italian, "*rubato*" comes from "*rubare*," "to rob" and literally means "stolen." In music the term denotes liberty or freedom in tempo—you rob from one note to give to another. Jazz musicians take liberties, too but opera is stricter. We have to stick to the printed music; the most we can do is embellish and ornament around it.

I went crazy trying to learn Agnese. After one harrowing session, in which Henry kept interrupting and correcting, I threw the music across the room at him and screamed.

"I cannot sing this shit!" (I don't think the bel canto is usually described with that term.)

It took years and years of study to reach the "perfection" later attributed to me. The key was, is and always will be, concentration. By marshalling all my forces to get the technique down pat, I could work on the "beauty of tone and correct emission"—the hallmark of bel canto.

On February 21, 1961, Joan Sutherland as *Beatrice di Tenda* completely conquered New York. I can't recall anyone giving her less than a rave. I picked up a few raves in six of the seven daily papers, although Harold Schonberg's *New York Times* review didn't mention me at all! This was definitely Miss Sutherland's evening and how lucky I was to be part of it! Both personally and professionally, we proved to be completely compatible.

I believe the incredible blending of our voices had a lot to do with my ability as a mimic and all those years of singing duets with Gloria. My desire to form a united singing front had its roots way back in Bradford. I never "imitated" the sound; I was just totally attuned to my colleague. Terry McEwen commented that while many mezzos want to do this, few can. I'm so happy I could. If you're determined to outsing, outshine, or outdo everyone else, you don't belong on an opera stage. In my experience, the greater the cast, the greater the result.

Nicola Rescigno conducted the Beatrice, which may come as a surprise to some Sutherland/Bonynge aficionados. Most assume that Ricky always conducted her performances. The truth is, for a long time Ricky was a musicologist, teacher and pianist rather than a conductor. Furthermore, I can tell you exactly when and how Ricky got into the podium business. It was at the Lewis home Los Angeles.

The Bonynges were in California for a Hollywood Bowl appearance. Ricky was scheduled to lead an orchestra for the second time in his life. Terry McEwen was around, too, and one day we all got together at my house. The five of us were gathered around the pool, swimming, cavorting and taking pictures, acting as goofy as most friends do when they get together around water. At one point, Ricky started questioning Henry about conducting and Henry began giving him tips. Terry, who thought Henry could have been the greatest teacher of conducting in the world, called it your basic "fifteen-minute conducting course." I swear that Ricky began to take himself seriously as a conductor from that day on. Eventually, he conducted all Joan's performances and conducts to this very day—long after his wife's retirement.

That afternoon was significant for music in another way. Following the session at poolside, Ricky took me into the living room. He sat at the piano and asked me to sing some selections from *Cenerentola*. That night, he told Henry and me, flat out, that I was a bel canto singer.

"Chuck the *Wozzeck*s, *Fanciulla*s, and the rest of that stuff and concentrate on a repertoire that suits you!" he advised.

Ricky Bonynge put me on the road to the Rossini medal that day. Actually, the successful combination of Sutherland and Horne had much to do with both Joan and Ricky's unbelievable generosity. They allowed me to share not only in their limelight but also in their musical knowledge. Although Henry knew a lot about the style, it was Ricky who taught us how bel canto worked. With a dramatic composer like Verdi, you need support to carry the full weight of the sound all the way up; it's like a column of sound moving from the basement to the penthouse of the voice. In Donizetti, Rossini, and Bellini roles, the orchestration usually is lighter. Thus, you don't have to worry about being drowned out. You don't have to sing an incredibly big middle register; you can open up on the top and let the coloratura fly. I actually "moved the center of my voice" (Ricky's term) for certain roles: up for Adalgisa, down for Arsace. Since that "center" was positioned differently, I had to alternate my roles carefully in order to preserve my voice and thus spaced my appearances in vehicles that called for a lightening or darkening of the voice. For example, during one four-month span, I sang Handel's *Rinaldo*, returned to *Carmen* for the first time in seven years, performed *Norma* after a twelve-year layoff and then went waltzing into *Cererentola* after a twenty-five year hiatus. It might have been easier to sing roles that lay in the same range, but a lot less fun and fulfilling.

Ricky Bonynge taught me a lot about ornamentation and I also must mention Fritz Zweig, my coach in Los Angeles. Zweig taught me style and did ornamentations for me as well. Of course, all those years, I had my in-house coach, Henry Lewis—my real teacher.

I wasn't the only beneficiary of the Sutherland/Bonynge largesse. Joan pulled another colleague right into the spotlight—a tenor of hearty proportions whom Joan dubbed "The Big P." Way before the public fell in love with him, Luciano Pavarotti sang in performances and on records with Joan. His career took off like a rocket. Luciano's very bright and had a positive genius for salesmanship as well as music. He came to this country, saw it was good for him, and learned English immediately. Foreign singers don't always master the language—they usually squeak by—but somewhere in that big, wide, wonderful Pavarotti, a little voice said, "You've got to make contact, and in order to do that, you've got to speak the language." Luciano's special ingredient, that vocal beauty and "ping," produced goose bumps on listeners, especially women. Our mutual history probably accounts for the special alchemy when Joan appeared with him, or me, or most magical of all, when the three of us were onstage together. Luciano and I became stars, but in the beginning, Joan Sutherland was our fairy godmother—a wave of her wand, and we were performing. She was the sun and we reflected her glory.

In October 1979, Joan and I gave a televised joint concert at Lincoln Center after which we went to a fancy Upper East Side Chinese restaurant. I know it was fancy because the waiter had never heard of duck sauce. I was very happy that evening, not only at being reunited with Joan and singing well, but because I'd lost a great deal of weight. I looked and felt good. Not long after we sat down to moo sho pork without duck sauce, Joan was called to the telephone.

She returned in a few minutes and said, "Jackie, it's Luciano. He wants to talk to you, too." I went to the phone and picked up the receiver.

"Jackeee," boomed the big boy. "Jackeee, I saw on the television Joan an' you. Oh Jackee, you were so wonderful, you sang so beeyootiful, you look so beeyootiful, and you look so fuckable!"

Yes, Luciano Pavarotti had definitely mastered the language.

1. Grandmother Ada Prunkard Horn(e). My beloved "Nanny."

2. Paternal Great-grandmother Elizabeth Foringer Prunkard.

3. Great-grandfather David Horn, Civil War veteran and York, Pa., councilman.

4. My mother in 1923.

5. Mom.

6. *(above) Dad.*

7. *(opposite, above left) At age one. Mom said I wouldn't go anywhere without my beads.*

8. *(opposite, above right) With cousin Charles Wynkoop, Jr.*

9. *(opposite, below) Jolly Molly front and center. Fifth Ward School, Bradford, Pennsylvania. I'm singing "Up in Santa Land." My dad added a high C—which I cracked, then immediately re-attacked.*

10. Bobby-soxer. George Washington Junior High School, Long Beach, California.

11. The California beach bunny, age 13.

12. Off to the Senior Prom.

13. *(below) An early fifties glamour shot.*

14. Brothers: Dick and Jay (1978).

15. Sisters: Gloria and I (1978).

16. *My first trip to Paris. I climbed to the top—no kidding!*

17. *(below) The Gesualdo Madrigal Singers on Stravinsky's lawn. Robert Craft is the man to my immediate left (1954).*

18. At Toscanini's home in Milano. Angela and I at one of Wally's famous luncheons.

19. Andre, Angela, Daisy and Henry Houle at my home in Santa Barbara.

20. Glamour shot from the 1980s.

21. *(above left) Angela and I in Bora-Bora (1992).*

22. *(above right) After my retirement gala at the San Francisco Opera. My sister-in-law Joanne, Jim Nabors, my niece Marisa with Angela and me (1999).*

23. *(left) Heaven, I'm in heaven! Cheek to cheek with Henry and Daisy.*

24. *(opposite, above) Gloria and I belting out "You're a Grand Old Flag," sixty years on. Bradford notable Jim Guelfi looks on (2000).*

25. *(opposite, below) Bradford's public square, 2000. (A great way to start the millenium!)*

Extended Family...

26. *My rock and my salvation. The Marilyn Horne Foundation staff: Heidi Franksen, Barbara Hocher (Executive Director) and Jaime Solano in the foundation office, New York City.*

27. *(from left) Warren Jones, Bruce Ford, Renée Fleming, Thomas Hampson and Chris Merritt at a benefit for my foundation at the home of my dear friends Barrie and Ada Regan in Hillsborough, California.*

PHOTO: ROBERT CAHEN

Performing...

PHOTO: JIM CALDWELL

28. La Donna del lago *(Rossini), as Malcolm; this time in a kilt.* Dano Raffanti, Nicola Zaccaria, Frederica von Stade. Houston Opera, 1981.

29. Cenerentola *(Rossini), San Francisco, 1989; (from left)* John DelCarlo, Paolo Montarsolo, Sesto Bruscantini, Francisco Araiza.

PHOTO: ROBERT CAHEN

30. *(above) Rossini's* Maometto II *at the San Francisco Opera in 1988. Simone Alaimo is singing to me.*

31. Cenerentola *at the Met (1972; not to be confused with* Carmen).

32. Tancredi *in Los Angeles (1989).*

33. Cenerentola *in San Francisco (1982).*

34. The Merry Wives of Windsor plotting in Verdi's Falstaff; *(from left) Ruth Ann Swenson, Pilar Lorengar, Kathryn Cowdrick and I (San Francisco, 1988).*

35. (left) Marie in Alban Berg's Wozzeck. *San Francisco Opera, 1960.*

36. Handel's Orlando; *San Francisco Opera.*

37. Mignon. *Dallas Opera, 1974.*

PHOTO: BOB SMITH/
      LAURA GARZA

38. (below) Orfeo; *Santa Fe, 1990. With the wonderful Benita Valente, an old friend from California.*

PHOTO: MURRAE HAYNES

39. *My last Rosina at the Met.*

40. *(below)* Rinaldo *(Handel). Venice, 1989.*

41. (above) The Harvest *of Vittorio Giannini, with Barry Morrell and Geraint Evans.*

42. (left) My first Marie in Wozzeck. *Gelsenkirchen, 1960.*

43. Cinderella, *later* La Cenerentola. *Los Angeles Guild Opera, 1956.*

PHOTO: ALBERT DUVAL

44. Rossini's La Cenerentola; *San Francisco Opera, 1982.*

PHOTO: BETTY GUY

45. *My Metropolitan debut as Adalgisa in Bellini's* Norma *(1970). Joan Sutherlan Norma.*

46. I Capuleti e i Montecchi. *I'm Romeo in Bellini's version of* Romeo *and* Juliet. *Dallas Opera, 1977.*

47. *(above)* Orlando Furioso *in Paris. I'm going mad—or should I say "folle."*

48. *(left)* Semiramide, *Aix-en-Provence with Montserrat Caballé. For the reason Montsy and I sometimes had trouble keeping a straight face at this point in the opera, see pp. 136-7.*

Photo: Agence de Presse Bernand

49. Tancredi. *Chicago; 1989.*

50. *(opposite, above) Justino Diaz, Beverly Sills, Thomas Schippers and I at*
The Siege of Corinth. *My first Rossini opera at La Scala, 1969.*

51. *(opposite, below) My Italian debut:* Il Barbiere *in Firenze, 1968. I'm surrounded by Alfredo Kraus, Sesto Bruscantini to my right, and (among others)
Nino Sanzogno (conductor), Fernando Corena and Paolo Washington on my
left.*

50.   PHOTO: E. PICCAGLIANI

51.   PHOTO: LEVI

52. As Eboli in Verdi's Don Carlo at the Metropolitan Opera, 1978.

53. As Andromaca in Rossini's Ermione. Pesaro, 1986

54. *(Above)* Carmen. *The Met opening in 1972.*

55. In Gelsenkirchen (1957). Verdi's Simon Boccanegra *with Gert Niensted. I'm singing Amelia.*

56. (below) Pagliacci *(San Francisco, 1962). With Mario Del Monaco as Canio, what Nedda would go for Silvio?*

PHOTO: ROBERT CAHEN

57. Aida in Dallas, 1979. I felt really good about the Amneris I did there.

PHOTO:
PHIL SCHEXNYDER

58. Samira in The Ghosts of Versailles *at the Met. I literally was on my last legs, but I managed to dance.*

'HOTO: THE METROPOLITAN
)PERA ARCHIVES

59. Dame Quickly and Falstaff (Paul Plishka), 1992.

60. Tancredi. *Barcelona, 1989.*

61. Norma. *San
Francisco Opera,
1982. A pensive
Adalgisa.*

62. Dalila, getting ready to clip Samson. The Met production.

63. L'Italiana in Algeri *at the Met.*

64. *(below)*Bianca e Falliero. *With Katia Ricciarelli in Pesaro, 1986.*

65. *My gala in San Francisco.*

66. *Farewell to Rossini.* L'Italiana *at Covent Garden, 1993.*

On the world stage...

67. The Parthenon...

68. Igor Stravinsky's grave in Venice.

69. That's not an opera house behind us. India, 1998.

70. Luciano, Joan and I after our joint concert at Avery Fisher Hall (1981).

71. Emily and Doc Severinsen's. Emily is in the kitchen preparing one of her fantastic meals.

72. *Sara and Ronald Wilford, Seiji Ozawa and I having lunch at the Schloss Fuschl, Austria.*

73. *Villecroze, France, 2003. Christa Ludwig and her husband Paul Émile Deiber with Orhan Memed, director of l'Académie Musicale. (I taught master classes.)*

74. *My dear friends Farol Seretean and Jihan Sadat—two terrific ladies.*

75. *The Hornes—Lena and Marilyn (1988).*

76. Dorothy Huttenback: so important in my life, and an hysterically funny lady.

77. The late Arthur Sackler and his wife, Jill. She's been a stalwart of the Marilyn Horne Foundation since its inception.

78. *Nico and I in Australia.*

79. *With Prince Rainier and Princess Caroline in Monaco. Larry Foster is on the other side of the prince.*

80. *Rehearsing my first* Semiramide. *With Joan, Henry, Ricky (the conductor) and Dick Cross. Los Angeles, 1964.*

81.*The gang's all here: Lotfi Mansouri, Joan, Ricky and Sally Billinghurst are in the crowd.* Norma *in San Francisco, 1982.*

82. *Pinky (Zukerman) and Jackie in St. Paul.*

83. *Rehearsing* Falstaff *at the Met with Mirella Freni and Susan Graham. After 26 years, my Met swan song (1996).*

84. *Recording with Nicolai Gedda in Toulouse.*

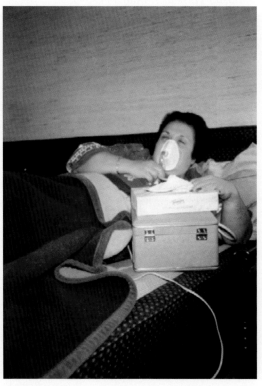

85. *This Aerosol inhaler was recommended by a doctor. I used it and lost my voice (temporarily) during a performance of* Samson and Delilah.

86. Warming up, yet again.
L'Italiana in Venice.

87. The song continues... Teaching a master class at Juilliard (1997).

38. *The incomparable Gwen Koldofsky—teacher, mentor, accompanist and dear, dear friend.*

89. *Enjoying the company of Matthew Epstein and Mike Wallace.*

90. Il Barbiere *in Macerata, 1980. That's the fabulous Cesare Siepi as Don Basilio.*

91. *With my dear friend, Lotfi Mansouri, General Director of the San Francisco Opera, in 1990. I was presented with a medal for my thirtieth anniversary with the SFO (which was extended for almost another decade!).*

92. *Opening night,* The Ghosts of Versailles: *(left to right) John Corigliano, Bill Hoffman and Jim Levine.*

93. *I would like to think I did as much for him as he did for me, but I doubt it. Pesaro, 1986.*

94. PHOTO BELOW: GLORIA GOTTSCHA

A Rossini 200th Birthday Gift from Marilyn Horne

As a special gift on Rossini's 200th Birthday, Marilyn Horne will give a free one-hour recital of Rossini songs with pianist Martin Katz on Saturday, February 29th at 12 Noon in Alice Tully Hall

Any seats not occupied by 11:45am will be made available to the public.

95.

OPERA

TUESDAY, DECEMBER 6 AT 8:0

SOLD OUT

CARMEN

Conductor: Placido Domingo
Staged by: Paul Mills
Set and Costume Designer: John ˮury
Lighting Designer: Gil Wechsler
Choreographer: Maria Benitez

CARMEN   Marilyn Horne
MICAELA   Ilona Tokody
DON JOSÉ   Veriano Luchetti
ESCAMILLO   Jean-Philippe Lafo
FRASQUITA   Myra Merritt
MERCÉDÈS   Diane Kesling
LE REMENDADO   Anthony Laciur
LE DANCAIRE   Russell Christo
MORALÈS   Erich Parce
ZUNIGA   James Courtn
LILLAS PASTIA   Nico Castel

96. *Honorary doctorate at Juilliard—1994. President Joe Pelisi, Garth Fagin, Jane Alexander and Andre Watts standing behind June Noble Larkin and me.*

97. *Me and my pals at the inauguration of the Marilyn Horne Foundation (and number 60 for me).*

Special Performances

98. With Marty in Salzburg. A triumphant recital following a disappointing Aida.

99. My dear friend Robert Cahen took this picture during a San Francisco recital.

PHOTO: ROBERT CAHEN

100. *A private recital at Weill Recital Hall (at Carnegie Hall) with Marty Katz. Twenty-seven years of music-making.*

101. *(below) Brian Zeger and I accepting applause.*

Conductors

102. L.A. Philharmonic, 1960. The newlyweds: Marilyn Horne and Henry Lewis.

03. At the Vier Jahreszeiten in Hamburg with Georg Solti (early 1980s).

04. Jimmy Levine: a dear friend. What more can I say?

105. *Lenny—the last time I saw him. He had just conducted the Vienna Philharmonic at Carnegie Hall.* <small>Photo: Ralph Gabriner</small>

106. *Opera in the park: Montserrat and I with Kurt Herbert Adler in San Francisco, 19*

107. *Concert with Nicola Rescigno in Dallas.*

Presidents

108. President Gerald Ford, Mrs. Betty Ford, Don Pippin and I after a Palm Beac recital.
109. Receiving the National Medal for the Arts in 1992. I like President and Mr. Bush enormously. (This from a lifelong Democrat.)

10. Hail to the Chief: Inauguration Day, 1993. (I had just sung.)

11. The Kennedy Center honors. At the White House with the President, a future Senator and a future son-in-law.

Special Appearances

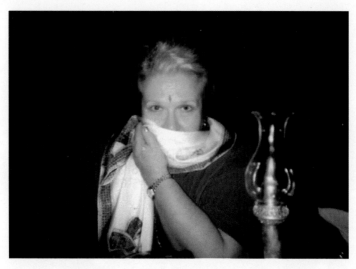

112. *Trip to India.*

113. *I finally made it: singing an opera based on Cleopatra with the Muppets. (Miss Piggy was furious—she wanted to be the star.)*

114. Eileen Farrell, Carol Burnett and I on Carol's TV show (1971).

115. Winning $35,000 on the Wheel of Fortune (for the Marilyn Horne Foundation, of course), 1994.

116. The magnificent Leontyne Price.

117. (below) Sharing the stage at Carnegie Hall with Lenny. (My hand is blocking my friend Toni Zavistovski).

PHOTO: STEVE J. SHERMAN

118. Having a go at "Bridge over Troubled Water." With Don Pippin at the St. Louis Art Museum (September, 2003).

HENRY, ANGELA, AND JUDY, JUDY, JUDY

From the day of our marriage, Henry and I had been happy together. Our first years were good; we worked, played, fought and loved together. In direct contrast to what had been predicted, both our careers were advancing, in many instances side by side. In the fall of 1963, the Los Angeles Chamber Orchestra went on a tour of Western Europe sponsored by the State Department. Thanks to Henry, I got to go along as a soloist. The trip was memorable because I had my first success in Italy. In Milan, I sang a show-stopping, "*Superbo di me stesso*" from *Meraspe*, a pastiche by Lampugnani. Next day the headline in the *Corriere della Sera* read, "Three thousand were on their feet yelling *Bis! Bis!* (Again! Again!) at the end!" Very heady stuff, indeed! And only the beginning of the career that flourished in the land of opera's birth.

In Los Angeles, Henry and I became part of the Hollywood scene and from those giddy years came everlasting friendships. I worked with a vocal coach named Jack Metz, and kept seeing a tall, shy Alabama boy at Jack's studio. I thought the fellow was studying to be an opera singer—until I turned on the television one evening and saw him on his own TV show. In person, Jim Nabors was a far cry from the doltish "Gomer Pyle" he portrayed on the screen—and he possessed a marvelous, rich baritone voice! After "Gomer Pyle," when Jim starred in variety shows that gave him an opportunity to display his singing talents, people were amazed. We appeared together on TV specials and had a wonderful time singing duets and doing skits. For years, Jim has lived in a beautiful Oceanside house in Honolulu. In 1981, while he was filming a "Love Boat" episode in Australia, Jim generously turned his home over to me. In that incredibly lovely setting I began work on my book.

Through Jim, I met another superstar, Carol Burnett, on whose variety show I also appeared. With Eileen Farrell rounding out a "trio," we dressed up like three Mae Wests, three little pigs, the Andrew Sisters and Cinderella and her two stepsisters, and performed skits and songs. In later years, Carol transcended her great gift for comedy to become a powerful dramatic actress.

I displayed my own histrionic abilities in an "Odd Couple" episode with Tony Randall and Jack Klugman. I came on the set with one aria to sing and one line to say and by the time we finished filming, I'd worked myself into a featured part! People still tell me they've just seen me on TV. I never underestimate the power of television, not with all the re-runs.

I was seriously and studiously at work on my music yet the Hollywood scene was captivating and for a while I succumbed; a bit of hedonism trickled into the mainstream of my life and the little girl from Bradford, the one who bottled her ebullience, pulled out a few stops. I went to parties and ate, and worse, drank. Don't misunderstand—I never was a serious drinker. First and foremost I was a singer, and every singer knows alcohol is bad for the voice. Still, going to social events meant social drinking and, without realizing it, in a low-key sort of way, I was becoming a bit of a party girl. It remained for a very special star to set me straight. I learned my booze lesson at a party Rock Hudson gave for Princess Grace and Prince Rainier of Monaco.

Rock Hudson was another dear friend, very dear. He

was the most gorgeous hunk of man I've ever seen, and as kind and good and funny as he was handsome. The gathering that night was a typical intimate Hollywood soiree of around four hundred people—a galaxy of stars and a number of assorted meteors, celebrities who shoot by fast and burn themselves up. Dazzled, I whirled from star to star. Princess Grace was utterly beautiful, although much shorter than I'd expected. Prince Rainier, a soft-spoken, serious man, discussed the Monte Carlo Opera and impressed me with his astute and informed commentary on opera and artists. I stood next to Henry Fonda and couldn't resist telling him he was one of my favorites. He, a perfect gentleman, responded graciously to my gaucherie. I said the same thing to Rex Harrison and he too affably accepted my praise. Of all the people there, however, I was most thrilled at seeing Judy Garland and anyone from my generation of moviegoers would understand why.

It grieves me when people equate the Judy of the drink-and-drug-ridden last years with the lovely, lively girl and woman I saw on the screen. She was a main reason why I spent those Bradford Saturday afternoons at the movies. Judy Garland was a great entertainer, as unique in the popular field as Lotte Lehmann was in the classical. Like Lehmann, Judy sang words with such meaning and coloring that you had to be moved—and she was a damn good actress, too. I adored her. Judy had so many ups and downs in weight, mood, and career, you never knew how she was going to appear. At Rock's house, she was radiant. She wore a red velvet dress with a mink trim on a curving décolletage and at the end of the sleeves. I wanted to talk to her but in the crush I never got near her.

That evening, Henry and I were in the throes of our first real marital squabble. He was completely captivated by the Gabor sisters. While I was thoroughly involved in disparate stargazing, my husband was lost in a sea of goulash. I continued to whirl like a top around the celebrity maze and every time I stopped, I found a drink in my hand. Eventually, I wandered off into Rock's red-walled guest bedroom. I closed the door behind me, and enveloped in a boozy miasma, I sat on the floor in the middle of the room, swaying back and forth, humming to myself, and feeling no pain.

The door opened, and in walked Judy Garland.

"Hi," she said, "You're the opera singer aren't you?"

"Yes."

"Well, I'm a singer, too."

She came over and sat down next to me and said, "So, why don't we sing?"

We did. We put our arms around each other and began belting out medley after medley of popular songs. Gershwin, Porter, Kern, Youmans—we sang them all; Judy wasn't surprised in the least that I knew all the lyrics. Every so often, she'd put her finger to her lips and shush me. Then, she'd then sing a refrain that went, "Louis A., Louis B., Louis C., Louis D., Louis E., Louis F." Then, she'd switch the words and growl, "F. you Louis!"

She was singing about Louis B. Mayer, head of MGM, who'd made her a star, but at tremendous cost. Judy had been groomed as another Deanna Durbin, the pretty teenage singing queen of Universal Pictures, but Mayer thought Judy was homely and poured thousands of dollars into recreating her. Later, he'd point her out to others as an example of his ability to create stars. "What do you think of my little hunchback?" he'd crow. "Look where she is, thanks to me."

Judy had a weight problem and MGM gave her pills to reduce. She also took pills to stay awake and then to go to sleep. It's common knowledge that drugs along with alcohol finally did her in. That's sad, but only part of the story—

she was fabulous, an irreplaceable artist, and that's how she should be remembered.

So Garland and Horne crooned together for a long, long time—and in the bass clef—until my husband extricated himself from the Paprika sisters and came to get me. What a sight I was! Mascara dribbled down my cheeks and I'd lost one of my false eyelashes. Henry pulled me to my feet and after Judy and I swore eternal friendship, he took me home.

The next morning, I had a classic hangover. Worse—a raw throat. When I thought of what happened the previous evening, how I'd overindulged and how I was suffering the consequences, I felt even sicker. A performing artist has to be in control of herself; my controls, on automatic pilot since childhood, needed a permanent resetting. I vowed then and there to stay away from liquor, a vow I've kept. You may see me with a glass of wine at dinner, but that's it. That party in Hollywood remained my one and only "lost weekend."

Beatrice di Tenda proved that Joan Sutherland, Ricky Bonynge and I were a fabulous combination; it only remained for us to find other operas calling for a bel canto one-two punch. In 1963, we found one, again from Bellini's pen—his masterpiece, *Norma*. Asked by the Vancouver Opera to mount the opera, the Bonynges agreed but told them to hire me, too. Thus did Sutherland and Horne begin their partnership as the Druid duo, in the vehicle that eventually brought the latter to the Metropolitan Opera. But before that auspicious moment occurred, I had some "field work" to do.

On Tuesday, February 18, 1964, after highly successful performances in Los Angeles and Boston, Joan, Ricky and I returned to New York for a concert performance of

Semiramide in Carnegie Hall. At that time *Semiramide* was a virtually unknown *opera seria* by Gioacchino Rossini. Rossini's comic operas were fixed in everybody's repertory, but the many serious works he produced only began to be resurrected A.C. (After Callas). Premiered in 1823, *Semiramide* was an immensely popular work and for a time was performed all over the Continent. The Metropolitan Opera put it into the 1893-94 season where it remained until 1904. After that, it virtually disappeared in the United States and only rarely was revived in Europe.

In the opera, Semiramide, the Queen of Babylon, aided by Prince Assur, murders her husband. Assur has his eye on the throne and the Queen, while she is attracted to the young commander of her armies, Arsace. Natch, he's in love with Princess Azema and a lucky thing, too. Semiramide is his mother! In the middle of the opera, the ghost of the King appears and tells an assembled crowd that Arsace will be his successor. Assur tries to prevent that eventuality and goes after Arsace. When the young commander moves to stab Assur, Semiramide throws herself between the two men and receives the fatal thrust. Arsace is proclaimed King and whoever is left lives happily ever after. Joan sang Semiramide, I sang Arsace and, with Ricky on the podium, the Trylon and Perisphere of bel canto triumphed once again.

The great English conductor John Pritchard came to my dressing room following the performance. I had met him the previous summer when I auditioned for the Glyndebourne Opera. I was not hired. Even so, I greeted Pritchard cordially. He took my hand and kissed it.

"It appears we made a mistake at Glyndebourne," he said smilingly.

Although my success that evening was fantastic and although my association with Sutherland brought me worldwide recognition, it would be another six years before I realized my operatic goal. Rudolf Bing, the Metropolitan Opera's general director, made offers but none were acceptable. I didn't want to debut in a ragbag production or in an unsuitable part simply to get on the Metropolitan stage—I wouldn't do that to get in the old house—I wanted something special, and for that I had to wait. At the time, I didn't mind that much—I was awaiting something else, something even more wonderful than my Metropolitan debut.

In October 1964, at the time of my Covent Garden *Wozzeck* debut, conducted by John Pritchard, I learned that I was pregnant. The difficulty of playing Marie was aggravated by my condition, which was further aggravated by the weather. London was in the midst of a major pea-soup fog, the kind Jack the Ripper used to pick his way through. I had morning sickness all day. There are fifteen scenes in *Wozzeck* and after each one I went into the wings to throw up. By the time my throat was slit onstage, it was a relief! Between my personal nausea and the heavy weight of *Wozzeck*'s message, I was a wreck! The doctor prescribed some pills which he thought might clear up the nausea. The pills sat on my dresser. I never took one. I didn't like the idea of taking medicine while I was carrying a child. The medicine was Thalidomide.

In the spring of 1965, Joan and I did *Semiramide* in Boston. I waddled around the sets looking more like a Sherman tank than a conquering hero. I wore a funny little beard, and at the curtain call Joan looked over, started giggling and tugged at my Assyrian Vandyke. Singing to a pregnant bearded lady was too much even for Joan. Come to think of it, I may have been the first pregnant general since the Amazons.

After Boston, I sang *L'Italiana* in Vancouver, and though I expected to stop and wait at least two months for the birth, I felt great. I sang several concerts, too. At this point

I could do concerts, not operas, and then finally I had to stop. I was scheduled to appear in Donizetti's *Lucrezia Borgia* in New York City and bowed out. To replace me, the American Opera Society plucked a Spanish girl from the Bremen Opera House and put her on the world stage— and that is why Montserrat Caballé always had a special feeling for my daughter.

I didn't meet Montserrat until 1976 and after that we appeared together on many grand occasions. I loved working with her, not only because of her great singing but because I could make her laugh onstage. It's bliss to have a colleague of the highest artistry, but absolute heaven to know you've got a stooge. Montserrat had a built-in comic shtick; in the course of an opera, she sometimes got lazy with her Italian "v's" and "Spanishized" them to "b's." We were doing a visually stunning production of *Semiramide* in San Francisco and wore elaborate baroque costumes with huge white powdered wigs. One evening we finished the grand duet and embraced each other as the auditorium rang with applause. We stood on a ramp spanning the orchestra pit with our heads buried in each other's necks, our arms around each other, for what seemed like an eternity. In fact it went on for so long, Montserrat became confused and lost her place. She was supposed to say, "I vostri voti omai" but she forgot.

"What are my first words?" she hissed in my ear.

"I *bostri boti* omai," I shot back.

If anyone present at that particular performance wondered why Arsace and Semiramide were locked together for an inordinate amount of time, the answer is, Montserrat and I were hysterical with laughter and could not move apart until she got enough control to sing out her first words. By that time, the ramp was bobbing up and down.

On another occasion, we did *Semiramide* at the Paris

Opera House and because the stage got slippery, the crew poured Coca Cola all over the floorboards to keep the singers from sliding around. Caballé and I finished our *scena* and stood arm-in-arm taking our bows. I was supposed to walk away first (you know, the mezzo yielding to the soprano thing). I turned and tried to lift my foot; it was stuck to the floor. All that Coke had turned to glue!

"Montsy," I whispered, "I can't move. I'm stuck."

"Don' worry, Jackee," Montsy answered. "I'm strong, I pull you with me!"

Montsy made her turn, tugged on my arm, but neither of us went anywhere. Sure enough, she was mired in the Coke and couldn't move either! Imagine, we were bonded to the floor! No wonder I loved appearing with Montserrat. Not only did we make beautiful music together, we had the best time doing it.

Three weeks before Angela arrived I gave my last concert at USC. My dressmaker made two gowns with big darts to let out along the way—I was at the outermost dart when I stopped. On June 14, 1965, Angela was born at the Cedars of Lebanon Hospital. She came along as my career was beginning to skyrocket—and for a while it looked as though I might be shot down. I was given a caudal block for the delivery and, according to the anesthetist, the contours of my spine weren't right; consequently, I went into paralysis. The pain was excruciating. I couldn't move. I couldn't even give my baby her bottle. Henry panicked and raised hell with the obstetrician. I was put on saline solutions and immediately developed a bladder infection. Meanwhile, concerned with my inability to move, the doctors put me in traction and began a physical therapy program. Thank God, my mother-in-law came to the hospital to look after me. One week after the delivery I was back to normal. By the time we took Angela home, everything was wonderful.

Ten weeks later, Henry and I had a recording session in Europe. Leaving Angela caused me more pain than I'd experienced in the hospital. Torn between wanting to be with her and the legitimate demands of my profession, I felt that I had to fulfill my career commitments. At such times, I was never sure where the drive came from—was it all mine or was it a residual fear of disappointing my father? I've never figured it out. Put it this way, I was thirty-one years old and had been singing all my life when Angela came. Her birth was the most important moment of my life, and she became the most important thing in my life. Still, singing was my life and that sometimes made motherhood very difficult. I wasn't the first and I won't be the last to deal with the problem.

I once saw Alexandra Danilova, former prima ballerina of the Ballet Russe de Monte Carlo, interviewed on television. After she recounted the her life story, the interviewer, Mike Wallace, said,

"Madame Danilova, you've been a very successful woman."

"No, no," she replied shaking her head. "I am not a successful woman. A woman's success is in marriage and children. I wasn't successful in marriage and I have no children. I have never known of a dancer who combined motherhood and career. You can't have both. I am a successful creature, not a successful woman."

That's a hard line point of view, similar to the one that Lotte Lehmann expressed about singers. I'm not so sure it's correct. Yes, my marriage failed, but it wasn't a mistake, Henry and I had some fabulously productive years together, and we had Angela. Angela certainly had her cross to bear. Being the child of career parents, especially a mother, is notoriously difficult—the stuff of sensational biographies, but one thing I swear, I did my best. Combining mezzohood and motherhood was one hard business and guilt became one of my vital signs. I learned to live with it, though, as I'm sure all caring parents do. Berneice and Bentz did what they thought was right and so did Henry and I.

We left Angela with Henry's mother and flew to Switzerland for that recording session and I cried almost the entire flight. I should have saved some tears for the next crisis.

Immediately after our arrival, we received news that Henry's mother had been hospitalized with a heart attack—for a while we had no idea what had happened to Angela. Friends of ours, Barbara and Bill Kraft, had taken her in and through a torrent of transcontinental calls we finally located our daughter. I called my mother and she got Angela and brought her home with her. Mom was ecstatic; I was frantic with worry and guilt. Mom had a full time job so she had to get a baby sitter but she came home for lunch every day. Angela stayed for a month and my mother said it was one of the happiest times of her life. I'm glad someone enjoyed it. Happily, Jo Lewis recovered, although she did have a heart condition for the rest of her life.

My afterbirth experiences were pretty scary. My throat muscles didn't come back until about six weeks from the delivery. I was recording an album, "Souvenir of a Golden Era," which was full of bel canto excursions, and I kept cracking on the high notes. "This is it," I thought—"curtains!" I didn't feel ready to support my voice. Eventually, the muscles did come back and I was able to continue. I wish I'd known then that nursing helps to tighten the muscles. Where are the doctors when you could use information like that?

My postpartum misadventures continued. Henry and I had a charming room on the top floor of a chic hostelry in

Geneva. I especially loved the mansard roof in which we were housed, that is until I discovered that the roof also was home for an army of squealing rats. The minute he hit the pillow, good old Henry went out like a light. I lay there listening to the rodents running in the roof. The next morning, we moved down three floors. I was so tired I spent the afternoon in bed, dozing and going over music scores. I ordered a steak from room service and a side dish of spaghetti Bolognese. A waiter brought in the meal and, smiling and bowing, exited.

I took a bite of the pasta. It tasted funny. The impulse to make sure that what you tasted is what you tasted made me take another mouthful. Still awful! I put the dish aside, figuring the Swiss didn't know what to do with Italian food. That evening, I developed the worst case of ptomaine poisoning you can imagine, and all from two lousy bites. If I'd eaten the whole thing, I swear I'd have died. I threw up everything. Acid bile passed over my vocal cords all night. The next morning, Sunday, I had no voice. A doctor came and wrote a prescription for suppositories because I couldn't keep anything down. Mind you, all this happened in one of Geneva's most celebrated boutique hotels.

If I had thought my voice was in trouble before, now I was certain. I was convinced those high notes were gone for good. B is the money note in Rossini arias and all the ones I sang were in the key of E, ergo, all the high notes are B. Henry re-arraigned cadenzas like crazy and the B's were out of my repertoire for six months. To this day, I find it difficult to listen to some of the records made during those sessions following Angela's birth and my food poisoning.

When we returned to Los Angeles, I'd made up my mind how I was going to greet my daughter. I knew she was too little to actually remember us, so I determined to approach her calmly, without pushing. Sure enough, Angela didn't know me. I'd go to pick her up and she'd start to bawl. "Just grab her and hug her," Henry said.

I played Mother Courage and remained casual. I wanted to scoop her up and smother her with hugs and kisses. I didn't. I smiled and cooed to my own flesh and blood as though she was an adorable stranger. At last, Nature triumphed. Something clicked and Angela stretched out her arms to me. I cried with relief and happiness and held her in my arms for the rest of the day.

Looking back, I have very few complaints about the sixties. Besides the joy of having Angela, my career steadily moved forward. I was appearing with major symphonies as well as opera companies from coast to coast. In 1967, for example, to commemorate the hundredth anniversary of Toscanini's birth, I sang the Verdi *Requiem* with Leonard Bernstein and the New York Philharmonic. Home life was good, too. Angela was young and mobile, and we took her everywhere. Troubles with her wouldn't start until she began school and the flexibility ended. I often wished I had those early years on videotape to show my daughter how much her dad and I were around. It would have been easier if she'd had brothers and sisters, but it wasn't to be. Not that I didn't want more kids. Angela was no vanity child, conceived and produced to prove my total womanhood. I really believe we're here to procreate—it just never happened again.

Henry's career was advancing, too. After his Los Angeles Philharmonic conducting debut, he took over all the orchestra's youth concerts. In 1967, he was offered the position of assistant conductor to Zubin Mehta, the music director. Henry really didn't want the job and asked for what he thought was an impossible salary figuring they'd reject his asking price and leave him alone. They agreed. Henry spent the next year as Mehta's assistant. At the end

141

of that year, Henry's agent, Ronald Wilford, called to tell him that the New Jersey Symphony needed a conductor.

"You're nuts," said Henry.

The New Jersey Symphony was strictly bush-league, a community ensemble that gave about fifteen concerts a year—hardly an organization Henry Lewis wanted to front. There were some selling points, though—most important, Henry would be in the driver's seat and could fashion his own orchestra. We talked an awful lot about it, with friends, agents, and between the two of us. In the end, the idea of building an orchestra intrigued him. In February of 1968, he accepted the appointment. Of course, I had to go with him. I was happy in Los Angeles and had no yen to return East, but I did. We bought a home in Orange, New Jersey, a large brick Tudor mansion on two woody acres where we lived for the next nine years.

Angela's odyssey, from west to east was the reverse of her mother's two decades before. She was a lot younger and accustomed to travel, and her adjustment went smoothly. She was enrolled in the best school around, the Temple Israel Nursery School. That it was affiliated with a Jewish temple was no problem for me, but what about my daughter? Angela hadn't been baptized but was raised in a Christmas/Easter way. Could she cope with Rosh Hashanah and Hanukah? I worried for nothing. Angela adjusted to school without a hitch. She never asked me why she was in a Jewish temple—I guess she assumed that was the way you started school. Every Friday, one little student was appointed Shabbos (Shabbat, nowadays) girl or boy and whoever was chosen invited his or her parent to be Shabbos mother. I had that honor, one of my greatest roles. As Shabbos mother, I brought challah bread to Angela's school where we celebrated with candle lighting and prayers.

I'd spent my DooWah Years in Hollywood, my Galley

142

Years in Gelsenkirchen, and now began my Mother/Diva Years in Orange, New Jersey. It was the best of times and we were in the best of places: 273 Elmwynd Drive was a sylvan paradise, rife with incredible azaleas, dogwood trees, pines and an apple orchard. Angela was settled at school, my husband soon would pull the New Jersey Symphony up to a Class A rating, and my debuts at La Scala and the Met would take place within the next two years. Most important, I was in love with Henry Lewis, and was so happy...for a time.

LA SCALA

Designed and erected in 1778 by the architect Piermarini, Milan's Teatro alla Scala (Theatre of the Stairs) replaced the burnt-down Royal Ducal Theatre, and was named in honor of Duke Barnabo Visconti's wife, Regina della Scala, who founded a church on the same site in the fourteenth century. The first performance was Salieri's *Europa riconosciuta*; thereafter, La Scala was opening-night headquarters for scores of new works, many of which still are performed. All the great Italian composers wrote for this venerable house, among them: Verdi, Rossini, Bellini, Donizetti and Puccini. Arturo Toscanini reigned as director for two glorious eras, 1898-1908(except for 1904-05) and 1921-1929 when he left because of his opposition to the Fascist government; Toscanini refused to play the Fascist anthem before performances. Mussolini attempted to turn the Rome Opera into the premiere company of Italy but the Italians ignored Il Duce's mandate and La Scala held sway. Heavily damaged by bombs in 1943, the theatre was completely restored in 1946. Toscanini returned to conduct a reopening concert on May 11, 1946 and one of the soloists on that memorable occasion was Renata Tebaldi. Although the Metropolitan was my goal, La Scala beckoned first.

I made my Scala debut not, as many people think, in April of 1969 in the widely publicized revival of Rossini's *L'Assedio di Corinto* (The Siege of Corinth), but one month earlier, in Stravinsky's *Oedipus Rex*. The huge success of the Rossini opus somewhat obscured the Stravinsky evening. I had signed my contract with La Scala to appear in *L'Assedio* and was working in Canada when I received an emergency phone call from the La Scala management. They asked me to make my debut as Jocasta in *Oedipus* rather than in the Rossini. Because of my feelings for Stravinsky, I agreed. It seemed only fitting that my debut should come in a work by a man who'd so enriched my musical life.

I was studying both *L'Assedio* and *Oedipus* and singing *Il Barbiere* at the Vancouver Opera, when I received another phone call from Milan; they were having casting difficulties with the Rossini. Originally Montserrat Caballé had been mentioned for the soprano heroine, Pamira, then Renata Scotto replaced her. Now, Scotto was pregnant and had to step down. La Scala suggested that, since I still was singing soprano and mezzo roles, I should take over the role of Pamira, and they'd get a tenor to step into the trouser role of Neocle. (Rossini wrote two versions, one for mezzo and one for tenor.)

I declined. I'd been learning Neocle's part and was very comfortable in the range. I refused to go up to Pamira.

"Who can we get? Do you know Teresa Zylis-Gara?"

"I know her name, "I answered, "and I understand she's a fine singer, but I've never heard her sing."

We batted around a few names for a while until I had a brainstorm.

"What about Beverly Sills?" I asked.

"Who?"

"Beverly Sills. She's a fabulous American singer who's had a great success with Handel's *Julius Caesar* at the New York City Opera. I think she could sing it. Why don't you ask Tommy Schippers?"

Schippers, the fine young American conductor was scheduled to conduct *The Seige*. La Scala thanked me and hung

145

up. Afterward I called Bev, whom I knew professionally. I told her to alert her agent that La Scala might be calling. I'll never forget her excitement at the news.

"La Scala! La Scala!" she cried.

The next time we spoke was over lunch at the Beverly Hills Hotel. Beverly practically was airborne with delight and kept saying. "I'm going to La Scala; I'm going to La Scala!" I, too, was looking forward to appearing there and eagerly anticipated working with Bev, a fellow American and a woman of intelligence and humor. (Bev said at the time that she thought debuting in *Oedipus* wasn't such a smart move. The opera was obscure and my premiere appearance might be smothered in a lot of criticism of the work. She had a point. Still, I felt I owed it to Stravinsky.)

I arrived in Milan along with Angela and her nanny and we settled in for a three-month stay. I began rehearsing with time out to explore the city. Onstage, I was busy giving my son an Oedipus complex, but offstage, I was enjoying the company of my little girl.

Oedipus Rex, a fifty-two minute opera-oratorio with Latin text based on Sophocles's *Oedipus Tyrannos*, had its world premiere in Paris on May 30, 1927, in oratorio form and on February 23, 1928 was given as an opera in Vienna. Stravinsky all along envisioned his work as a static stage piece. He wanted as little movement as possible with the chief characters standing like figures in a frieze, moving only their arms and heads. "They should give the impression of living statues," said the Maestro. On the occasion of my La Scala debut, Stravinsky got his wish.

Giorgio de Lullo directed the Pier Luigi Pizzi production. "Pigi" Pizzi was in forefront of the avant-garde and this production was avant avant-garde. We voyaged deep into Freudian territory—eggs became the production's motif. As Jocasta, I was encased in a purple plastic egg with little plastic eggs attached in strategic spots around my plastic shell—fortunately not that strategic or I'd have resembled a high-tech Gypsy Rose Lee. The first time I tried on the costume, I made Humpty Dumpty look like Calista Flockhart. When I thought of the lovely classic Grecian costumes Jocasta usually wore, and how I was got up like a hard-boiled lavender balloon, my blood curdled. Surrounded by this plastic prison, with only my head visible, I had no choice but to be static. I could barely move my arms and legs and, what's worse, I couldn't hear. The conductor, Claudio Abbado, stopped me in the middle of one solo.

"Can't you hear what your music is?" he demanded.

I rolled down to the front of the stage and shot back,

"My music? I can't even hear what this opera is!"

My ears were covered with plastic and everything sounded as though it were coming through glass. I made them alter the costume by cutting away the headgear to expose my ears—at least I could hear my cues. In the center of the stage stood a huge prop egg—Jocasta's home base. Antaeus-like, I had to clutch this gigantic ovian replica at all times. I'm sure you get the symbolism.

Oedipus, played by the Hungarian tenor, Lajos Kozma, also had some wild costume effects. After the eye gouging, two huge red beads dangled from a golden blindfold wrapped around his head. Again, I'm sure you get the symbolism. The production was further enhanced by the use of conveyer belts and elevators upon which Oedipus and I were lifted on stage. One critic called the production "*Oedipus in ascensore*" (Oedipus in the Elevator). We opened on March 13, 1969; the production was fairly well received and despite the fact that my purple egg suit was a veritable incubator, I received fine notices.

One note of sadness, my mother wasn't there. Shortly before my departure, she'd been operated on for cancer, and though she came through the surgery okay, the recovery was rough and she was too weak to travel. She sent me a telegram on opening night:

SOCK IT TO THEM BABY, WITH YOU ALL THE WAY.

After the opening, the Countess Castelbarco (a.k.a. Wally Toscanini, daughter of the late conductor and reigning queen of Milan social life) threw a gala fête for Italian opera society. She neglected to invite the stage queen, Jocasta or indeed King Oedipus himself. Even though we were the stars of the opera, Mr. Kozma and I weren't well known enough to warrant inclusion. The slight didn't bother me. I don't like big parties. If I was in the least miffed at being left out, I certainly got my revenge four weeks later—thanks to Gioacchino Rossini.

My *Oedipus* debut, as Beverly Sills had warned, was overshadowed by the upcoming revival of *L'Assedio di Corinto*. With Beverly, Justino Diaz, and me in the leads, and Tommy Schippers on the podium, it was All-American night at La Scala. The *Siege* is a complicated story about Pamira, daughter of Cleomene, governor of Corinth. He wants her to marry Neocle, a young Greek officer. Need I tell you that Pamira is in love with someone else? She's crazy about Almanzor who turns out to be Maometto, leader of the invading Turks. The Turks conquer and Maometto offers to marry Pamira and make peace with the Greeks. Cleomene insists that she marry Neocle. Neocle comes to claim her and Pamira saves his life by telling the Turkish leader that Neocle is her brother. The Greeks and the Turks have another big battle and the Turks win again. Maometto comes to get Pamira but she has killed herself. Don't ask about Neocle and Cleomene, they've been killed in battle. Justino was Maometto; Beverly was Pamira and I was Neocle.

As I've said, it's necessary to hire others to look out for you. I wanted press coverage for my La Scala debut and there's a lengthy correspondence between my then publicist and me, in which I was told there was little or no interest in the *Oedipus* back home. Newsweek was considering a cover on Sills, which about wrapped up the space they'd give to opera, and other periodicals and newspapers followed suit. With its Yankee Doodle cast, *L'Assedio* was far more newsworthy than the Stravinsky.

L'Assedio triumphed. I had a seven minute ovation following my third act *scena*. The success stunned the Milanese including a certain Countess Castelbarco. She quickly sent the cast invitations to her *Siege* soiree. Beverly went, I couldn't. Jim Nabors had come over for the opening and arranged a party at Biffi Scala, the restaurant adjoining the theatre. I told the Countess I was unable to come because too many friends were with me.

"Bring them all," she said.

Again I demurred. I didn't bear any grudges from my *Oedipus* treatment and sent her a magnificent spray of flowers along with a note explaining how sorry I was that I couldn't join her. She must have been stunned that a "star" sent her flowers, or maybe it was the first time anyone had bothered to thank her—anyway, from then on Wally Toscanini was on the phone with me every day and inviting me to lunch. I went many times along with Angela, and grew very fond of La Scala's doyenne. The luncheons were like nothing I'd ever experienced. Eight to ten intelligent people, sophisticated as all get out, yet the main topic, the only topic was plain old gossip. (Incidental intelligence: Wally and I were born on January 16 and her father died on that date.)

Jim's opening night party was terrific, the kind I like, full of people I knew and loved and vice versa. Angela was in her element. My daughter has a great ear and memory for music and even at that age knew entire scores. She used to go to sleep listening to tapes of *L'Assedio* and could sing all the parts herself. Like her mother, she is a mimic and you can believe me that Sills never sounded more like Sills than when she came out of my daughter's mouth. Rossini's one thing but Stravinsky's quite another; Angela also could hum Oedipus!

In general, I had a happy time in Milan. Aside from my mother's absence, the only unhappy part of my stay came when Gloria called me at four a.m. after the opening of *L'Assedio* and told me that Nanny Horne had died in her sleep. I cried for the rest of the night. It's odd but I'd had some kind of premonition about this. I called to say goodbye to Nanny before I left and she sounded so weak over the phone, I immediately thought this might really be goodbye. She was some wonderful lady, Ada Mae Horne, right out of Central Casting under the heading, "Grandmother." Her life was long, ninety-plus years and full of love generously distributed to her family. She never asked anything for herself and only was interested in giving. Intensely proud of my achievements, she often mentioned how pleased my dad would have been at what I'd accomplished.

Soon my siege of La Scala came to an end. Shortly before I left Milan, I was introduced to a distinguished member of the La Scala company. I'd heard him on records and seen him on stage in Vienna and Salzburg and told him how much I admired his artistry. He smiled, kissed my hand and was off to Africa for a singing engagement. It would be two years before I realized the significance of that meeting with Nicola Zaccaria.

AMERICA'S OPERA HOUSE

The Metropolitan Opera House is one hundred and twenty years old—not such a long time for opera houses when you consider that the temples of music in Milan, Naples, Venice, Paris, and Vienna were standing a century before the Metropolitan opened its doors. The story of the Met's founding is typically American; unable to buy their way into the boxes at the Academy of Music, a group of wealthy New York businessmen got together, put up $800,000 to finance their own opera house, and launched it on October 22, 1883 with Gounod's *Faust*. Today, the Metropolitan's reach far exceeds the grasp of its founders. The company travels around the world and the Saturday afternoon broadcasts are aired over the Internet as well as the radio to remote corners of the planet. For an American intent upon a classical music career, where else was there to go? The Metropolitan was the pinnacle and to appear on its stage was my goal. But before I reached my goal, progress reared its ugly head.

The old house on West 39th Street had many problems including inadequate backstage space—sets could be propped up on the sidewalk in back of the building on Seventh Avenue. I've often said that another country would have bought the next block and annexed it to the old house, whereas we tore it down, and with scarcely a backward glance, moved to Lincoln Center. The new Met opened in September 1966 with a premiere: Samuel Barber's *Antony*

151

and Cleopatra. That I never appeared at the old Met still hurts but the operas offered to my manager ranged from silly to insulting. As I recall, they proposed supporting leads like Teresa in Bellini's *La Sonnambula.* Teresa is the mother of Amina, the lead soprano. I didn't mind playing Mom on stage—I'd done Hata at twenty—but there wasn't enough in that mother part. I had a certain feeling about myself. I wanted the Met debut more than anything in the world but I wouldn't go in with a second-class production or in a secondary part. Moreover, since I'd declared myself a mezzo, the problem of finding a proper vehicle was intensified.

Mezzos always are on the lookout for interesting roles because, compared to sopranos, relatively few are in the standard repertoire. Eventually, I solved that problem by specializing in the bel canto and baroque. You don't have to delve too deeply into Rossini, Handel and Vivaldi to come up with fabulous mezzo roles. True, many are pants parts, but the opportunity to sing works hand-tailored for a particular artist by the composer himself makes what you wear unimportant. Whether you're in knickers or a fancy ball gown, it's heaven to sing music of the kind Rossini wrote for his favorite artists. I helped unearth many of those operas and as a result, mezzos have more choices today.

During the old Met's pursuit of my services, the only Rossini opera in its repertoire was *Il Barbiere di Siviglia* and it was never offered to me. What I did best was unavailable. To some extent the Met-Horne situation reminded me of the old Borscht Circuit joke about the resort-hotel mixer. A gentleman approaches a lady and the following dialogue ensues:

MAN: You dancing?
GIRL: You asking?
MAN: I'm asking.
GIRL: I'm dancing.

The Met couldn't simply ask me and expect me to leap to my feet. Even though it was risky to play such games with a musical monolith like the Metropolitan Opera, I was determined to go in through the front door or, as in this instance, the stage door. And, for a while it appeared that it might not happen; then, the redhead from Australia got on my case.

Originally, Joan Sutherland was to have opened the 1964-65 season as Norma. According to the Met's General Manager, Rudolf Bing, Joan decided "rather late in the game that she was not quite ready for the part." Mr. Bing chose not to mention that Miss Sutherland was ready and willing but only able to do Norma at the Met if I was her Adalgisa. (When apprised of this Bing answered, "Miss Sutherland is not in charge of casting.") Not even Rudolf Bing could say no to Joan Sutherland; he had to capitulate. In 1968, I signed a contract to appear with the Met during the 1970 season—in the right vehicle.

Joan and I had smashing successes with *Norma* in Vancouver and at Covent Garden. The opera was perfectly suited to us, a stately and beautiful study of love and sacrifice with roots in classical tragedy set to a magnificent score. Even Richard Wagner liked *Norma,* and he hated almost everything he didn't write, particularly Italian melodramas. Bellini was a supreme melodist and a wonderful story illustrates his supremacy. At a soiree, the hostess handed manuscript paper to two of her guests, Gioacchino Rossini and Gaetano Donizetti. She asked each of them to write a beautiful melody. They did, and when the manuscripts were compared, the composers each had written the same thing.

"You see," gloated the hostess, "two creative talents can arrive independently at the same result."

"Oh no," protested Donizetti. "We both stole the melody from Bellini."

Norma, Bellini's masterpiece, takes place in ancient Gaul, during the Roman occupation. Norma, the high priestess, is the daughter of Oroveso, the chief Druid. Adalgisa is a virgin of the temple and Norma's handmaiden. Pollione is the Roman Proconsul and unbeknownst to the Druids, he and Norma have been lovers; in fact, Norma, the virgin priestess, has two children hidden away. Pollione becomes infatuated with Adalgisa who confesses to Norma that she loves the Roman. Norma is furious, and contemplates killing her children. She can't do it and instead decides that Adalgisa must marry Pollione and take the children with them. Adalgisa learns of the liaison, and tells Pollione he must stand by Norma. Pollione says no and threatens to abduct Adalgisa. Norma decides to declare war on the Romans. Pollione is captured and in a heart-wrenching finale, Norma undergoes a change of heart and offers herself in place of the Roman, telling her people that she's broken her vow of chastity big-time. She turns her children over to Oroveso and mounts the funeral pyre. When she reaches the top, she finds Pollione. Deeply moved by her majestic dignity, he's fallen in love with her again and chooses to join Norma in death as the opera ends—proving yet again that the mezzo isn't going to get the guy.

(In case you're wondering what Adalgisa is doing during that last emotionally charged scene, I can tell you from experience that she's in her dressing room removing her makeup and preparing to beat the traffic back home.)

Ricky Bonynge has wisely said:

> The singer who can be a complete Norma probably never has existed—maybe never will exist. The opera requires almost too much of one soprano—the greatest dramatic ability, superhuman emotional response, the greatest bel canto technique, and a voice of quality and size.

Giuditta Pasta created the role of Norma at La Scala on December 26, 1831 and sang it very little thereafter. The first Adalgisa, Giulia Grisi, eventually took on the title role. She probably fared better than Pasta who had great difficulty with the part. According to contemporary accounts, Pasta's pitch wavered so dramatically the violins had to play out of tune to accompany her. The dominant roles in Pasta's career were Rossini's Rosina and Cenerentola, and one truly has to wonder how she sang Norma. I was asked to do it several times. I wouldn't touch it!

[Apocrypha cling to *Norma* like a barnacle. One story tells of a performance in which Mme. Barili-Patti sang the lead while her little daughter Adelina portrayed one of the children. During the *"Mira, o Norma"* duet, little Adelina got carried away and began singing along. Her mother stopped the show and administered a sound spanking. Discipline paid off—Adelina Patti became one of the greatest prima donnas of all time. On another occasion, the two little ones, tired by sitting still so long, answered the call of nature. Norma fainted and Adalgisa had to be carried into the wings as the curtain dropped. Legend also has it that on her death bed, the great 19th century singer Pauline Viardot-Garcia gasped the word "Norma" and expired. In her lifetime, the role had eluded her.]

Once I'd been offered Adalgisa, Henry and I got together and discussed whether it was the right role for my debut. Although Adalgisa plays a secondary part, she has some glorious and powerful music to sing, moreover, I liked the "woman." Adalgisa represents pure lyric innocence; she's a real believer and, in the end, her purity of thought triumphs as she sides with Norma and takes her stand against Pollione. I sympathized with her conflicts and her feelings, and reveled in her melodies. Henry also pointed out that Adalgisa is an ideal debut role—while she's in every sense a star, the burden really falls on the Norma. If for any reason an Adalgisa should fade—or faint from nerves—Norma can pick up the evening with her immolation scene. Bottom line? With Joan Sutherland as The High Priestess, I couldn't lose.

I'd been living the suburban housewife role in New Jersey but when the time came for the first *Norma* rehearsal, Henry stepped in. With typical Lewis largesse, my husband pulled me out of the kitchen in style.

"Jackie, this is a very special day in your life," he said on that first rehearsal morning. "You're making your debut at the Metropolitan Opera, so I'm ordering a limousine to take you!"

Henry called a livery service and then went off to work at the New Jersey Symphony. I waited and waited; the limousine never showed. Finally, I got into our station wagon and drove into New York in a pouring rain. I couldn't help remembering the snowstorm that accompanied the *Beatrice* rehearsal.

(It seems I'm always dealing with the elements on big occasions...)

God, I was nervous! I tried to keep cool but the overwhelming reality of stepping onstage at the Met kept coming into my head. Remember Mr. Dick in Dickens's *David Copperfield*? He's gone a little batty because of family difficulties and though capable of talking sense, a vision of King Charles's severed head keeps cropping up in his correspondence and conversation. Well, the Met debut became my King Charles's head. It popped up in everything I saw, said or did. Although doubts crept in here and there, I'd always been confident the day would come. Now, here it was and it was making me dizzy.

What a beautiful reception I got from the artists rehearsing at the same time. Birgit Nilsson, Thomas Stewart and Plácido Domingo all came over to wish me the best. Mr.

Bing was right there, too; he shook my hand and welcomed me into the Met family. Rudolf Bing knew the importance of the personal touch and though he was subject to much criticism in his time, I liked him. I'm a liberal democrat off stage but in the opera house, I believe in dictatorship. Only a benign dictator can handle singers. Rudolf Bing was a dictator and a gentleman. While I can and have worked with people I don't like, I can't work for those I don't respect. I both liked and respected Rudolf Bing—even though he didn't bring me into his house as early as he might have.

Rehearsals began, and surprisingly few points of contention arose during the staging. Joan, Ricky and I had been down the path before and Carlo Bergonzi as Pollione and Cesare Siepe as Oroveso were the very best singers and colleagues. Naturally, there had to be trouble concerning my costume. I realize I'm not the easiest person in the world to garb, but I was no longer a compliant Valkyrie chorus girl; I wasn't going to let anyone put me into the wrong outfit. They tried. My costume was brought in and lo and behold, there was the long blond wig which had been denied Gerhilde back in Naples and which had little to do with the Adalgisa I played. As for clothing, someone determined I would shine in a gold dress. I got into it, took a peek in the mirror and blew up.

"What the hell is this all about? I look like Sophie Tucker. I'm not the last of the red-hot mammas, goddamit, I'm a vestal virgin in a temple!"

Off went the wig, off went the dress and off went the mezzo. The next day, the same garb reappeared, and the next, and the next, until one day they came back with another dress in brown. It wasn't a warm attractive shade of brown either. I'd gone from gold to mud. At this juncture, the day before dress rehearsal, I called my manager, Ronald Wilford.

"Listen Ronald, you're on! This is going to be your shining moment. If my costumes don't come in here perfect tomorrow, I'm walking!"

I meant it.

The next day, two suitable garments appeared in my dressing room, along with an appropriately virginal wig of lustrous brown tresses. Believe me, I wasn't merely having a temper tantrum. As with Tancredi's cloak, I had to put my foot down. My entire energies needed to be spent on the creation of Adalgisa, and the mechanics and accouterments had to be perfect. All I needed my first night out was a silly wig or a ludicrous dress. Thanks to Ronald, that crisis was easily resolved.

The next one involved a lot more attention and angst. It was a gamble that could make or break my debut—and this time I alone was responsible.

Adalgisa's Act I entrance follows Norma's "*Casta diva,*" the glorious hymn to the moon goddess. The stage is empty until, accompanied by a stately, poignant melody, Adalgisa enters and sings her recitative and aria, "*Sgombra e la sacra selva*" (The sacred grove is cleared). Adalgisa begs the gods to pity her for falling in love with Pollione and to purify her heart. My problem was how to present this girl to her audience for the first time. I had an idea. A long time ago, Bentz Horne told me,

"Peanut, if you want to get people's attention and hold it, sing softly."

Like a piece in a jigsaw puzzle, Dad's advice fit this situation perfectly. I decided to take a calculated risk.

Most Adalgisas enter on a crest of song and sing forcefully. To me, her entrance calls for quiet reflective singing in keeping with Adalgisa's character. The first time I took on the role, I decided to begin pianissimo, and walk slowly down to the front and center of the stage. It was risky on two counts—would it be effective and would I be heard? Even though the orchestra is silent, pianissimo from the rear of the stage might not carry over the footlights. My plan called for incredible breath support—like a control pitcher threading the ball past the batter rather than mowing him down with a fastball. In a sense, I was tossing a vocal change-up. My press agent, Herbert Breslin, cautioned that, since this was my Met debut I'd be on pins and needles anyway and my breath might be a little shaky at the beginning. Why put my technique to such a rigorous test on the first notes? Herbert's comments made me uneasy. I valued his opinion and he'd planted a seed of doubt. I vacillated for a brief time then made up my mind. This was the way I'd done it; this was the way I'd do it.

Dress rehearsal came and, as usual, could have been called dress bedlam. After my final exit, knowing that this would be my opportunity to hear Joan in full regalia, I slipped out into the audience to watch the last act. As I stood on the side of the orchestra in the darkened hall, someone came and stood behind me but I was too involved with listening to acknowledge anyone. At the end of Norma's plea to her father, I was so moved I said aloud, "My God, sometimes I forget how fantastic she is!"

"You are not so bad yourself, Miss Horne," said the person behind me. I turned and found myself face to face with Rudolf Bing.

Everything was set for the big night. My mother was coming east along with Auntie Maybelle and Cousin Jeanne Hokanson Hadley and her husband Jack. However, one very important person would not be at my Met debut—my husband.

The truth is, Henry and I had been experiencing difficulties for the past four years. Angela's birth brought us together in the special way a child unites parents, but our careers were getting in the way, or should I say mine was. As my star rose, our troubles deepened.

I would have had a career without Henry Lewis but he really led the way. Others, like Ricky Bonynge, "pointed" the way but Henry labored and sweated and did everything he could to teach me, often under extreme pressure. He wrote cadenzas, arpeggios and two-octave drops which were true to the period and showcased my voice. In 1962 I was asked to sing Donizetti's *La Fille du régiment* for a student perfor- mance in San Francisco. Marie, the heroine, is usually sung by a coloratura soprano such as Pons or Sills. I learned the part quickly with Henry writing cadenzas up to the last minute. A cadenza is an elaborate flourish ornamenting a final cadence at any point in an aria. In da capo arias, there are three opportunities for cadenzas—the last is reserved for the "best shot" to show off vocal virtuosity. Because of many production snags, *La Fille* was not polished for the opening—actually, it was a mess. Kurt Adler knew it; he came to me after the performance and apologized. "Even we don't do things this badly," he moaned. Because of the confusion, I had to keep changing my cadenzas, which meant that the conductor, Oliviero de Fabritiis, had to figure out how to accompany me. Cadenzas are freewheeling, still they're also supposed to adhere to the main body of the work—which definitely was not the case in this instance. At the opening performance I reached the final cadenza, crossed my fingers and launched into my vocal pyrotech- nics hoping and praying the conductor would come along for the ride. De Fabritiis did yeoman service in the pit and kept the orchestra going in the face of many surprises from Marie/me. At the curtain call, he came onstage and, as we stood hand in hand, smiling and bowing, he leaned over, kissed my hand and said,

"Signora, you don't need a conductor, you need a

prophet."

Well, Henry Lewis was my prophet and my teacher and my right hand. I depended upon him for advice and support. Sadly, because my fame eclipsed his, he was known in some circles as "Mr. Horne."

Richard Bonynge never tried to make a career away from Joan; primarily he was his wife's conductor. Henry Lewis was, first and foremost, a conductor with his own orchestra. At the beginning, his career had been tied to mine and for many years the New Jersey Symphony sold a great many tickets because of a certain featured soloist. Eventually, the situation became too much for him and though I understood how he felt, I didn't think that much could be done about it. Sometimes when people made dumb remarks about "Mr. Horne," I'd get furious and start to fight and Henry would get mad at me. One time we had a slam-bang argument after I lit into a big mouth acquaintance.

"Don't defend me," Henry said sternly. "Don't you dare defend me because there's nothing to defend. Listen, I was the main breadwinner of this family all those years. I knew if you became successful you'd make more money than I could because you're a diva. But I've got my own career, so don't defend me! If you want to make me feel good then try to reconcile your role as Mrs. Henry Lewis with being Marilyn Horne!"

He was right. I was pouring so much energy into my career, there wasn't a lot left over for my home life. I put him in the position of being "Mr. Horne" because I wanted him to conduct for me and coach me and guide me. Looking back, I'm only amazed that we lasted as long as we did; how we managed for so many years is a tribute to our love. Truly, before we got into wholesale fighting, we did have great moments together. But, apparently my Met debut was not to be one of these moments.

Henry was in London doing recording sessions with the Royal Philharmonic Orchestra—a perfect example of career conflicts. As teacher, friend and coach, as well as husband, Henry should have been with me. He'd contributed so much to my success, he should have been there to enjoy it. I knew his commitment was genuine, but somewhere in my heart of hearts I felt that the most important career moment of my life should have taken precedence over what, for him, was a relatively non-essential engagement. I remember Henry said that he didn't want to "interfere" and I began to think that taking the London assignment had been his way of removing himself from my night. Unable to face the possible hidden meanings in Henry's action, I buried the hurt and went about my business.

The Italians have an expression, *"in bocca al lupo"* (in the mouth of the wolf) which they use to wish someone good luck. I was put in the mouths of many wolves the night of March 3, 1970. I accepted gratefully though I wasn't superstitious. Unlike some performers I didn't drag along any lucky talismans or go through any pre-performance rituals, other than vocalizing. For a while I did cart around a bunch of stuffed animals that had been given me over the years. I'd throw them in a plastic bag, lug them to the performance and set them up on my dressing table. One day, I took a good look at my fuzzy zoo and realized that those little creatures weren't doing anything. I swept them off the table into the wastebasket and that was that.

On the big day, I arrived at the Metropolitan with my regular bundles containing makeup, score and a thermos of hot tea. I went to my dressing room and began to prepare. There's usually a piano in the room—if there isn't, the management is respectfully requested to get one. I vocalize anywhere from twenty to thirty minutes before a concert or an opera, and those exercises are hard. Some singers don't vocalize at all but if you don't, it sometimes can take two acts to warm up. I don't think that's fair to the audience.

After I did my vocalizing, colleagues dropped by to chat and give good wishes. Again, Mr. Bing appeared, kissed my hand and wished me well. Joan, dressed and ready to go, stopped by, hugged and kissed me, and went off to the stage. The house lights were dimmed, the overture began; my Met debut was on its way.

In a short while, I found myself standing in the wings waiting to make my entrance. I wasn't nervous anymore— eager and excited, yes, but not afraid. Immediately I put myself into the character and mood, which is easy in opera. I found that I didn't have to psych myself up that much because the composer already has done a good deal of the preparation; the music paints a clear picture. At the opening strains of Adalgisa's music, I became that young girl. I moved forward and stood behind a huge rock upstage. At the musical cue I raced around the rock and into the audience's view. The speedy entrance was my idea: I felt that Adalgisa had "forgotten" the Druid meeting because she was agonizing over Pollione. She's like someone coming in late for church services. When she rushes into the sacred grove, she expects to find everyone but they're gone; she's missed the sermon.

The house was absolutely hushed; not a cough punctuated the brief moment of silence between the opening passage and my first words. I pushed against my diaphragm, like Mrs. Luce taught me, and opened my mouth to let out a taut thread of pianissimo. As I moved into the *messa di voce*, where volume and intensity are steadily increased, then diminished, I felt the audience's presence; I was home!

Norma is a four-scene, two-act opera but the Met version was divided into four acts and after the Act III finale,

Adalgisa is finished. The finale ends with the sublime *"Mira, o Norma,"* one of the most glorious weavings of melody in all music. I sang with every ounce of available skill and by the time Joan and I ended with the brilliant cabaletta, *"Si, fino all'ore,"* everyone in the house was sky-high. The curtain fell and my debut was over.

Joan and I stood in the center of the stage, hugging each other until it was time to step before the gold curtain to take our bows. I followed her through the opening and was met by a solid wall of applause; it took my breath away. Joan stood stage right, bowing and smiling and gesturing toward me. I gazed back at her, smiling and calling, "thank you, thank you." The next thing I knew, she was gone. I was alone on the stage. I'll never forget that beautiful and generous gesture from one artist to another, one friend to another. Joan Sutherland not only was willing to share the spotlight, she turned it on me full force. I continued to bow and looked into the wings where I saw her standing and applauding. Next to her was Rudolf Bing, and next to him, his hands flashing back and forth with enthusiastic claps, stood my husband.

I turned back to look at the audience. The house reverberated with cheers and I stepped forward to the edge of the stage. In the first row sat the legendary Maria Jeritza. Suddenly she was on her feet. Following her lead, the entire audience rose *en masse*. Somewhere in the midst of that cheering, Mother and Auntie Maybelle stood applauding till their hands were sore. I looked all around that golden house from the topmost tier to the very pit and drank in every sight and every sound. This was the fulfillment of my dreams, the goal I'd pursued for so many, many years. And I knew, somehow, someway, my father was with me.

My eyes brimming with tears of joy, I stepped off the stage and walked into my husband's outstretched arms.

THE MET AND I

As we walked to my dressing room, Henry told me that the minute he realized that the recording sessions would finish earlier than he expected, he got a plane ticket and arranged for car services in London and New York to speed him directly to the performance. The best-laid plans often go awry. Henry's plane was rerouted. He lost a few precious hours; arrived in New York a little before ten and raced to the Metropolitan in time to witness the curtain call. But he was there.

My dressing room was filled with eighty, ninety, maybe a hundred floral tributes that overflowed into the hall. I plowed my way through tulips, anemones, orchids, asters, and the like, and flopped down in a chair to collect my thoughts. Onstage *Norma* was going into its final phase, but for me, the night was over; I had reached the heights. The critics and public were unanimous, *Norma* was an absolute triumph...

But the ways of the Metropolitan Opera House were continuing strange.

"Can you believe it?" I asked one newspaper reporter. "The Met has the most winning combination since Flagstad and Melchior and they haven't planned another opera for Joan and me."

Thereafter, as far as the Met was concerned, Joan Sutherland and I were separate entities. Although we appeared with each other on other stages, we never again sang as a team at the Met. The pity is, after a Chicago *Semiramide* in 1971, we did not appear together in anything for nearly a decade. Then, in September of 1982, we were reunited for the San Francisco Opera's production of *Norma*.

I went to the West Coast feeling a bit sad as well as excited—Joan was fifty-six years old, perhaps the oldest woman ever to sing Norma, and I was forty-eight. I couldn't help thinking this might be the last of our *Norma*s. Ha! The performances were dazzling; we may even have sung better than ever, including our original Metropolitan triumph. My premonition, however, proved correct. We never again sang *Norma* together.

The day after my Met debut, Rudolf Bing called Ronald Wilford and told him that my fee—seventeen hundred and fifty dollars per performance—was ridiculous. He tore up my contract and advised Ronald that in the future, like any superstar, I'd be paid the top fee, four thousand dollars. This procedure usually is reversed; personal managers call opera directors to get higher fees. By initiating the upgrade, I think Rudolf Bing was trying to make amends for the unnecessary delay in my debut. He also was a shrewd businessman and this was smart public relations. My overwhelming triumph would have allowed my manager to negotiate my salary into the stratosphere—Bing wisely took the opportunity to be magnanimous. Put it this way, he waited a long time to open the door, but once I was on the threshold, he swept me up and carried me into his house.

Rudolf Bing always remained the gentleman but was not above trying to pull off the occasional cozy deal. Later that year, I was to sing at the Royal Opera House in Covent Garden. At that time Covent Garden was still London's central produce market, made famous in the musical, *My Fair Lady*. Before I left for England, Mr. Bing telephoned me at home.

"Hello, Miss Horne, I've called to offer you a wonderful opportunity."

His voice was warm and cordial but surrounded by a strange, hollow sound.

"Mr. Bing? You sound as though you're down a well."

The minute the words were out of my mouth, I realized the General Manager was on a speakerphone. Others, assistants and members of the board, I guessed, were listening in—I could hear them tittering in the background. Nonetheless, Mr. Bing proceeded with the conversation as though it were strictly *entre nous*.

"Well, Miss Horne, I called to tell you we're putting together a June festival and I'm prepared to offer you Rosina in the *Barber*."

Immediately, I was on to him. Obviously, Bing had thrown my name before the lions in his office. He called me and not my manager because he had to go directly to the source to impress the gentlemen gathered around the amplifier. I was sure he'd checked my schedule and knew damn well I was busy. Maybe he thought a direct plea from him would get me.

"When was that?" I asked innocently.

"This June," he reiterated.

"I'm so sorry, Mr. Bing, I'm not available. I'll be at Covent Garden."

"My dear Miss Horne," answered the General Manager, readying his putdown of any other opera house, "what do you do at Covent Garden?"

"Why, I sell fruits and vegetables, Mr. Bing."

My phone audience went from titters to roars of laughter—and Bing joined in.

For the next few years, I had long stretches of work at

the Metropolitan. This enabled me to turn down European engagements and stay home, which in turn allowed me to take part in Angela's growing-up years.

Angela was around seven when I began to travel again, but I still tried to be available for her, especially at critical times. Given the perimeters of our "artistic nest," she got all there was to give. I had to rely on household help and that was often a headache. One time, Marty Katz and I were at the airport in Tampa, Florida, when I called home.

"How's everything," I asked Henry.

"Uhh, okay except that couple we hired before you left just quit."

I burst into tears, a scene that was repeated many, many times as I tried to balance child-rearing with career needs.

The Lewis household had become a staple of Sunday magazines. We were good copy and journalist after journalist extolled our life together making much of our "salt and pepper" marriage and its product, Angela.

On the surface we were a neat, tidy package of artistic personalities getting along as marrieds and professionals. I was Mrs. Bubbly Loudmouth, Henry was Mr. Reserved Intelligence and Angela was Baby Snooks. At age seven, Angela had this to say in magazine series on children of famous parents:

> She sings and Daddy conducts. Mom uses her voice. I think that's harder than conducting because you're using up your voice when you sing. My Mom sure sings loud. I can sing higher than she can and I like rock "n' roll because I like to jazz around.

We weren't trying to pull the wool over anyone's eyes; in many respects we were a happy family. Henry and I were still good friends and colleagues and willing to share our thoughts. When I contemplate those early seventies reports of our domestic life, I see under the tip of compatibility, the iceberg of frozen discontent. Henry's resentments were building up. He offered clues to his feelings with such quotes as:

> When she's been on tour, or like now, when she's in the middle of a heavy rehearsal schedule at the Met, she comes home and all she wants to do is sit down and put her feet up. Yet I feel okay now that my wife's home and I can relax. I mean I can understand that she's tired and all that, but I've been working hard here at home on all the millions of things I have to do with my orchestra.

"... she's tired and all that..." Right!

Henry had a picture of wife and mother in his head that I wasn't fitting properly. Anyway, even if I could have read all the danger signals clearly, there was nothing I could do. Henry and I were drifting apart.

I liked dealing with Rudolf Bing, but by the time I finally made it to the Met, he was near retirement. In December of 1970 the Board of Directors of the Metropolitan Opera had named his successor: Goeran Gentele, Director of the Royal Opera House in Stockholm, Sweden. An outgoing, energetic man, trained in the theatre, Gentele was vastly different from the reserved, autocratic Bing and his arrival was eagerly awaited.

In setting up his team, Gentele asked Schuyler Chapin, formerly a vice president at Columbia Records and recently associated with Leonard Bernstein, to be his second-in-command. In those days, most opera houses planned operas at least two or three seasons ahead, to insure the availability of performers, directors and designers. Some companies were capable of calling one or two months in advance to try to secure my services but most were reasonable. *Norma*'s phenomenal success put me on the Met's scheduling list and I tried to accommodate them first. I filled out the 1969-1970 season with *Norma* and anticipated with delight my next Met role—Rosina. In June 1970, Joan and I took *Norma* to Covent Garden. Angela and my mother came with me. Mom was in remission and had recovered enough to get around. I wanted to show her Europe and after the *Norma*, she and Angela went with Henry and me to Torino. Henry and I were recording *Le Prophète* for the RAI. Mom fell under the same Mediterranean spell as her daughter and we all had a wonderful time.

Much as I loved doing Adalgisa, I couldn't wait to get back to Rosina! As you may have gathered, the composer, Gioacchino Rossini, is especially dear to me. The son of a trumpet player and a soprano, Rossini was born in 1792 and literally grew up in the theatre. He was incredibly attractive and musically gifted, so much so that his father and uncle thought of turning him into a castrato. Mama wouldn't hear of it and saved him from the knife for which her son was eternally grateful. Rossini called himself a "lazybones," but by fifteen was an accomplished singer, could play the violin, horn and harpsichord and had become an accompanist and conductor. Between 1808 and 1828, this "lazybones" wrote forty operas. In his comic operas, (*opéra buffe*), he used animated ensembles, finales with unusual rhythms. In so doing, he put the singer at the service of music and restored the orchestra to its rightful place of prominence. His opera, *La Pietra del paragone*, written in 1812, was the first work in which he used the crescendo effect, a hallmark of his style in which the orchestra increases in sound and speed. (Don Basilio's aria, "*La Calunnia*," in the *Barber*, a prime example of crescendo, musically illustrates the rapid spread of slander.) Whether Rossini actually created the form is a matter of contention, but certainly no one used it to better effect. During his productive period, Rossini fell in love with and married the soprano Isabella Colbran. They moved to Paris where he was nicknamed "Monsieur Crescendo." He wrote many operas for his wife then tired of her and shipped her off to stay with his widowed father. After Colbran died in 1845, he married Olympe Pelissier, a professional courtesan and his long term paramour. Isabella pushed him; Olympe coddled him, which suited Rossini fine. After a brief trip to Italy in 1855, he returned to Paris where he lived until his death in 1868. At the age of thirty-seven he stopped composing operas. It's mind-boggling to think that he lived for another forty years after he quit. Rossini's reputation as an epicure and a wit flourished and he wrote occasional salon pieces but musicologists and psychologists still are trying to figure out why he stopped writing operas. One theory is that he suffered great depression and wasn't cured until five years before his death. (I can't help wondering what a little Prozac might have wrought.) My generation knew very little of Rossini except for *Il Barbiere*—and, of course, the call which signaled the arrival of "The Lone Ranger" on the radio, the rousing overture to Rossini's last opera, *William Tell*.

Rossini was twenty-three years old when he wrote *Il Barbiere*. Based on a satirical play by Beaumarchais, the opera took Rossini thirteen days to complete. In the opera, Dr. Bartolo keeps his ward, Rosina, a virtual prisoner in his home. Count Almaviva catches a glimpse of her, disguises himself as a poor student, enlists the aid of the local factotum, the barber Figaro, and seeks to win the lovely girl. After much intrigue and comedy during two sparkling, melodious acts, boy does get girl proving that love conquers all—and a bribe here and there helps clinch the deal.

Although Rosina was written for a mezzo-coloratura,

over the years sopranos have poached the role. (Sopranos are never satisfied; they have ninety percent of the operatic leads and still try to usurp the few big mezzo ones.) Delicious to sing and to act, the bounce so evident in Rosina also enlivens another of my Rossini favorites, Isabella in *L'Italiana in Algeri*. My appearance as Rosina in 1971 marked my first starring role at the Met. I was joined by a fine cast: Sherrill Milnes as Figaro, Fernando Corena as Dr. Bartolo and Giorgio Tozzi as the music master, Don Basilio. What a romp!

Short of making a Metropolitan debut, the biggest coup is appearing on opening night. Before he departed at the end of the 1971-72 season Rudolf Bing arranged for me and Jimmy McCracken to begin the 1972 season in Wagner's *Tannhäuser*. I still was flirting with soprano roles. Despite the fact that Elisabeth would be my first major venture into the Wagnerian repertoire, and therefore very challenging, I had mixed feelings about the production. *Tannhäuser* was a tired old warhorse of shabby sets and frayed costumes— definitely not a glittering vehicle.

Enter Goeran Gentele.

The Swedish director came for preliminary meetings during the winter of 1971 and we got along splendidly. He was enthusiastic about my work and I sensed that my Met career would be on the express lane. Here was a general manager ready to mount not only bel canto works but baroque and nineteenth-century French operas as well. The future looked so promising, it was almost scary. Then, Gentele announced a switch in the opening-night selection and I was walking on air.

He had accepted the *Tannhäuser* and the rest of the repertoire bequeathed by Bing because he had to, but when he discovered that the Wagner was one of the seediest in the repertoire (its selection for opening night was dubbed "Bing's

Revenge") he immediately set about remedying the situation. Of course any substitution had to suit his stars—Jimmy, the baritone Tom Krause, and yours truly.

If a mezzo said her prayers before she went to bed, they might end "…. and please, God, give me *Carmen* for opening night at the Met." Guess what? Mr. Gentele bagged *Tannhäuser* and put in—*Carmen*! Jimmy, Tom, and I quickly agreed to do the Bizet. Of course there still were snags; the current production was a disaster and Gentele had to go to the Board to get money for a new one. He got it, and then assigned himself as director. That man was gutsy! He threw himself into the project, threw out the accepted *Carmen*, and returned to the original concept. (*Carmen* premiered at the Opéra-Comique in Paris on March 3, 1875 and included spoken dialogue. Later, musical recitatives, composed by Bizet's friend Ernest Guiraud, were substituted and that version of *Carmen* remained in vogue around the world.)

First, Gentele excised the Giraud additions. Next, he engaged Leonard Bernstein as conductor and Josef Svoboda as lighting and set designer. By now we all felt certain this *Carmen* would be something special. Only one ominous note marred the general good feeling. Tom Krause's wife read cards and while casting the deck saw something awful, a catastrophe for *Carmen*. She told Tom but he kept quiet. Thank goodness, none of us knew of the prediction. Although I'm pretty down-too-earth, I have a healthy respect for the supernatural.

In the winter, spring and early summer of 1972, Gentele commuted from Sweden to New York, spending much time putting *Carmen* together. During the preliminary sessions, the work was discussed and re-discussed, analyzed and re-analyzed. A former actor himself, Gentele knew that artists and directors flourish in a give and take situation; he never said, "You have to do this" or "You have to do that." When some points were unresolved, he shrugged and said, "We'll work things out in rehearsal." Rarely had I been involved in such a splendid pre-production period; it thrilled me to be part of Goeran Gentele's operatic "dream."

That dream became a memorial.

On July 18, 1972, while vacationing in Sardinia, Goeran Gentele was killed in an automobile accident.

The sudden death of this vital man turned our Metropolitan world into a nightmare. What was to have been a monumental opening to a new, glorious era became the abandoned husk of an idea—conceived, assigned and designed but not yet executed. The driving force, the man who promised to "work things out in rehearsal," was gone. We, however, had to go on. We pooled our knowledge of the Gentele concept yet great, unknown patches remained unresolved.

Schuyler Chapin was appointed acting general manager and rumors came thick and fast as to who was going to take over the *Carmen*. Jerome Robbins was mentioned and then it was thought Bernstein in collaboration with Josef Svoboda would do the staging. For a time, one guess was as good as another. Then, I got a phone call from Schuyler.

"Jackie, we've got a director. His name is Bodo Igesz."

"Bodo who?"

That was my introduction to the thirty-seven-year-old Dutch-born stage director who had taken over for other directors in the past but had yet to do his own production. Indeed, he'd been working with Gentele on the *Carmen* and in many instances knew what the late director had in mind. So Bodo stepped in, and by August 30th we were well into rehearsal.

A number of things in the *Carmen* troubled me. To begin with, I didn't think the spoken dialogue would work. I felt that English-speaking audiences, comfortable with the

Guiraud recitatives, would be thrown by the French dialogue. I protested then yielded to Lenny. (As it turned out I was categorically wrong.) Next came my misery over the *mise-en-scène*. With all due respect to Svoboda, the stark, modern sets didn't thrill me; I would have preferred realistic ones. My biggest concern was the wall-to-wall, ceiling-to-ceiling carpeting Svoboda slapped on the set. You don't have to work for an audio engineering firm to know that such material absorbs sound. I called in Henry and Ronald Wilford, among others, to listen and was satisfied only when they assured me all was right. I let the carpet stay, with *one* alteration. In the name of interior decoration, the prompter's box had been eliminated; I wanted it put back.

The prompter's box is a small compartment usually placed in the middle of the footlights and covered on three sides. A prompter sits in the box throughout the performance. Visible only to the participants onstage, his/her job is to cue the singers by giving them the first words. In Europe, the prompter's box used to be *de rigueur*; La Scala had two of them, one for soloists and one for the chorus. In my day, many artists were so tied to the prompter they never took their eyes off him. Being from the American school, I usually didn't need one. Even so, I don't think you can do opera in a repertory company without one. The prompter holds the production together; I didn't intend to let them sweep him/her under Svoboda's carpet.

Chalk the box up as a victory for me—it went back.

I won another victory as well, and it's a good thing I did, or I might not be here telling you about it. Jimmy McCracken was a pussycat, but when he got into a part— look out! We started rehearsing the final scene in which Don José stabs Carmen as she tries to go past him into the bullfight arena. I started walking toward Jimmy when I heard a click. I looked down, and saw an honest-to-God switchblade in his hand. I instantly stopped the proceedings and called out to the director.

"There's no way you're going to get me on that stage if Jimmy McCracken has a real knife!"

Jimmy was disarmed and I lived to die again.

Jimmy really was something else. He was a performer of phenomenal intensity and that intensity backfired during *Carmen*'s jam-packed dress rehearsal. At one point, Don José starts getting passionate with Carmen and wants to make love to her. Jimmy was getting into position and at the same time trying to take off his sword so he could embrace me. The scabbard wouldn't loosen and he kept yanking, tugging and pulling as he declaimed, "*Ah, que je t'aime, Carmen, que je t'aime!*" It was irresistible.

"Sure you'll make love to me," I said loudly, "if you ever get that sword off."

Another time, at a performance, the chorus didn't hold him back and he threw me down as I'd never been thrown before. Fortunately, I'd lost the battle of the carpet so my fall was cushioned.

Jimmy McCracken was great to work with; he gave so much and cared so much that you had to love him. I admired him too. The Met treated him like a second-class citizen by denying him television roles and giving them to other tenors. Jimmy wouldn't take it lying down, and when management refused to listen, he walked away. Believe me it was their loss.

Carmen opened not on the traditional Monday night, but on Tuesday, September 19, 1972. (Monday was Yom Kippur.) Many friends including Donald Gramm, Beverly Sills, Marit Gentele (Goeran's widow) and Bob Merrill sent notes. Bob wrote, "I would have loved to kill a kosher bull for you tonight!" Another short message read, "Jackie you are a wonder. Be as wonderful tonight. Love, Lenny."

In *Carmen*, Don José, a soldier, falls in love with the gypsy Carmen. He gives up his girlfriend, Micaela; deserts the army to become a smuggler; and, when Carmen turns her attentions to the bullfighter, Escamillo, he kills her. In the Met's *Carmen*, Don José became a force to be reckoned with rather than a simple country boy falling under the spell of a hot-blooded temptress. When the curtain rose to the strains of the Fate motif and a single shaft of light fell on Jose, the audience knew something special was coming. Oh, and was it ever special!

I had learned a great deal from the 1968 production of *Carmen* that I did with Sarah Caldwell in Boston. My Carmen was neither a cardboard Theda Bara vamp, nor a spit-curled moist-lipped Rita Hayworth—she was an earthy, humorous, passionate gypsy. Thanks to Bernstein, I added something else to my portrayal. Traditionally, Carmen pretends to be using the castanets while a percussionist in the orchestra does the actual clicks and clacks. Early on, Lenny took me aside.

"Look Jackie, why don't you learn to play the castanets yourself? It'll make a big difference."

I learned and played my own castanets when I danced. Alvin Ailey choreographed *Carmen* and thanks to him the critics commended my dancing. In truth, the entire production dazzled from start to finish. David Walker's costumes— he called them "clothes"—were a Goyaesque blend of browns and blacks; and, in the last act I wore a magnificent white lace gown. I was indeed the "Bride of Death," accepting my fate, as Lenny put it, "dressed to the nines."

The public was ecstatic, the critics were ecstatic and all of us associated with the opera were ecstatic. Still, the tragic and terrible circumstances leading up to that moment were not forgotten. We all wanted this *Carmen* to be special for Goeran Gentele's sake—and it was.

After the performance, my friends, Jim Nabors and Farol and Bud Seretean gave a party in the Terrace Room of the Plaza Hotel. Although I don't like parties, this one was special. Because the curtain came down at 11:50, and because I was caught up with well-wishers, plus getting out of makeup and showering and dressing and getting back into makeup, it was 1:30 before I arrived at my own party. Not a morsel of food remained. At six a.m., I had scrambled eggs at home.

I slept most of the next day and when I awoke it was to phone call after phone call. In the days that followed, letter after letter appeared, one of which I'll share:

Dearest Marilyn,

You were magnificent. Of course I was not surprised. I hope you enjoyed the "grunt" that oozed out of the audience at the end of your first aria—it was a for-real reaction and I was proud to be a part of that happy group.

> With all great admiration,
> Lena Horne

Thus, *Carmen* thrust me squarely in front of the public, allowing me, as one critic wrote, "to dispel the benign shadow of Joan Sutherland" and emerge as a star in my own right. I was linked with Joan in the eyes of New York audiences and, much as I enjoyed playing opposite her, one cannot make a grand career as a second banana. *Carmen* changed everything. Now I was such a big deal, I could make my own decisions, and of course, I knew everything.

ENDINGS

Had Goeran Gentele lived, things might have turned out differently for me, and for the Met. His theatre experience was vast and his ingratiating personality made people want to work for him. The sweetest personality in the world, however, could have soured under the kind of financial problems brewing. Gentele came from a state-supported arts program, of the kind I had experienced in Gelsenkirchen; whether he could have handled the difficulties intrinsic to the privately endowed institution remains a matter of speculation. When Schuyler Chapin was appointed permanent general manager, I knew I had another strong ally in the main office. Sadly, Schuyler was never in a secure enough position with the Board of Trustees to get their wholehearted approval, and in three years he was ousted.

The 1972-73 season marked the Fiftieth Anniversary of the New Jersey Symphony. And, during this time, Henry Lewis was scheduled to make his Metropolitan debut conducting *La Bohème*. Michael Tilson Thomas, scheduled to take over for Leonard Bernstein, bowed out of *Carmen* and Schuyler Chapin asked Henry to take over. Thus we were together on both sides of the footlights.

Professionally, we were doing very well. According to the *Ladies Home Journal* of September 1972, the Lewises were among America's twenty-five most influential couples, along with folks like Martha and John Mitchell, Jean and Walter Kerr, and Masters and Johnson. On October 10,

1972, the clue for 30 down in the *New York Times Crossword Puzzle* was, "Miss Horne's milieu." The answer was "opera." I had arrived.

During the seventies, I sang eight roles at the Metropolitan: Adalgisa, Rosina, and Carmen, followed by Orfeo in Gluck's, *Orfeo ed Euridice*, Isabella in Rossini's *L'Italiana in Algeri*, Fides in Meyerbeer's *Le Prophète*, Amneris in Verdi's *Aida*, and the Princess Eboli in his *Don Carlo*. Not a bad lot, really, but I had to travel all over the world to do *La Donna del Lago, Semiramide, Tancredi, Orlando* and *Rinaldo*—works which would have brought credit to the New York house. Maybe Goeran Gentele would have been able to produce them—who knows?

The Met's current production of *Orfeo* entered the repertoire at the end of the Bing years and was a complete and utter failure. Putting it on the roster for the new administration surely was a cruel jest on Sir Rudolf's part. The house was committed to present *Orfeo*, but yours truly, knowing it was such a miserable realization of a great work, never should have agreed to appear in it. I was a star, though; I could do anything. Through the power of my glorious voice I would single-handedly lift this production out of the muck. See what happens when you start to believe your own press?

On October 31, 1972, along with the rest of *Orfeo ed Euridice*, Mme. Marilyn Horne came a cropper. Harold Schonberg wrote in *The New York Times* that when I went out to get Euridice, I "looked for all the world like a Brooklyn matron off to a P.T.A. meeting." Compared to some of the others, Schonberg was kind. Charles Mackerras, musical director of Sadler's Wells in London, made his conducting debut in that *Orfeo*, and though his musical contributions were well received, it was faint praise for poor Charlie. He was stuck with an ill-conceived mishmash in which the chorus sang from the orchestra pit while the corps de ballet

180

danced the action on stage. Good taste prevents me from going into more details of this disaster; all I can say is Euridice was better off in Hell than I was on that stage. Appearing in that fiasco was one of my great moments of conceit.

Rossini's *L'Italiana in Algeri* (*The Italian Girl in Algiers*— a Gentele choice for me) was quite another story. I'd started singing the role in 1964 and I adored it! Isabella, the heroine, is shipwrecked and washed up on the Algerian shore. Immediately, she sings *"Cruda sorte,"* a bravura aria that has shipwrecked many a singer. She's looking for her missing boyfriend, Lindoro, now the slave of Mustafa, the Bey of Algiers. Mustafa has tired of his wife Elvira and wants to turn her over to Lindoro while he finds an Italian girl for himself. I'm not going into all the ins and outs of this one, suffice it to say, in the end Mustafa goes back to his wife and Lindoro and Isabella sail off for Italy. Isabella, warm and loving, is a mélange of Joan of Arc, Florence Nightingale, and Susan B. Anthony. She knows exactly what she wants and makes sure she gets it—and that's how I played the role.

At the opening on November 10, 1973, Luigi Alva sang Lindoro; Fernando Corena, Mustafa; and Theodore Uppman, Taddeo. Jean-Pierre Ponnelle made his debut as designer and director. I must say Mr. Ponnelle devised quite an entrance for me.

"You'll come in and walk downstage backwards," he told me. "Then when you reach stage front, you'll turn and face the audience."

The minute I heard the word "backwards," I thought he was crazy. I did it anyway and it became one of my favorite entrances ever. (I don't know where he got the idea although someone later told me that Maurice Schwartz of the old Yiddish Theatre in New York always entered backwards. Whether he was appearing in *A Ganze Meshuggah* or *The Merchant of Venice*, a crowd would gather around him at the rear of the stage. As the crowd parted, he would back toward the footlights, gesticulating wildly, till he reached the edge of the apron, where he'd turn swiftly to acknowledge thunderous applause.)

For my money *L'Italiana* was as wonderful as *Orfeo* had been awful. Still, the reviews weren't totally laudatory: for my singing, yes; for my acting, no. The *Times* said the production was "vulgar." The public came, however, and vulgar or no, liked it. If nothing else, it provided the first opportunity in over fifty years to hear a comic masterpiece. The public won this battle and *L'Italiana* took its rightful place in the repertoire.

I continued to lead my double life, New Jersey suburban housewife on the one hand, and opera diva on the other. Fame didn't provide any diplomatic immunity in my everyday life, though. I did my own shopping and cooking and mothering and was as involved in those station-wagon pickups as any average American woman. One afternoon I might be singing for United Nations Day at the UN, the next I could be car-pooling. Like other women of that era, I seemed to spend ninety percent of my time behind the wheel. A little incident in the car gave me yet another nickname, one used only by intimates.

I had driven to South Orange Village and was circling around looking for a parking space. It was one of those "You're never going to get a spot" days, and I kept circling. I owned a Mercedes sports coupe and I loved that car. Suddenly, I spotted an opening and whooshed in. I'd just shifted into Park and was about to turn off the ignition when I looked in the rearview mirror and saw a huge Cadillac behind me, obviously waiting for the space I'd usurped. Not seeing the car before was no excuse; I couldn't stay there. I was shifting into reverse when the driver of the Cadillac got out and stormed over. He was huge and he was mad. I rolled down the window to explain but he wasn't waiting for explanations. He leaned over and growled slowly, loudly and nastily,

"You little...fat...Fuck!"

"Fat!" I bellowed, "Fat!"

That did it. I turned the ignition off, got out of the car and walked away. The big bruiser waved his fists at me.

"Go ahead, hit me, go ahead, hit me!" I taunted.

He didn't, but the air was out of my tires when I returned. There was no way I would have given that creep the space, even though he had been there first, not after he called me...fat. (The nickname, by the way is LFF but don't use it.)

About this time, Henry took an apartment in New York City—"our" pied-à-terre it said in the papers. In reality, by May of 1974, he was spending the week in the city and coming home weekends to be with Angela. We hadn't been so distanced and angry since the time we went to a marriage counselor in California. Then we were screaming at each other; now we were withdrawn, sullen, and silent. Our beautiful home in New Jersey became a fortress occupied by two armed camps, his and mine. Naturally, we tried to protect Angela, and confined our battles to the hours when she was either asleep or away. Again, a big house helped; Angela found it hard to believe when I told her how long her dad I had been estranged. Besides my anguish at home, other troubles arose... Specifically, my mother's health continued to deteriorate.

After the London *Norma* trip, she'd had more surgery and more chemotherapy treatments in California. Early in April 1973, she came east again and joined me for the Met opening at Wolf Trap outside Washington, D.C. Before that, she made a "grand tour" of her "youth," visiting relatives and friends in and around Bradford. She knew she was dying and wanted to say her farewells. The Washington visit was agony for her, yet she never stopped. In constant pain, she willed herself to keep going. She had to see everything and her courage would not yield. I watched her climb stair after stair, wincing with each step but Berneice Horne kept her stride!

That spring, I was plagued by a chest infection, aggravated, no doubt, by my mental state. My marriage was going and so was my mother. When the Met tour reached Dallas that May, I flew to Long Beach and stayed for a few days. We all knew that time was running out—Mother had maybe a month, maybe two. I planned to leave Long Beach on a Monday, sing Tuesday in Minneapolis, return to New Jersey, sing a benefit for cancer research in Toronto on Sunday, then cancel everything and return to stay with Mother until the end.

On Friday, Gloria called. Mother was in a coma. I agonized over the situation because, though Dick, Gloria and Jay and his wife were all nearby, no one other than a nurse was at the hospital. I made three phone calls to the Coast asking my brothers and sister to stay with Mother in shifts. I would cancel the Toronto benefit and arrive in Long Beach on Saturday. My siblings felt that because Mother was in a coma, there was no need for an around the clock vigil. I felt differently.

"But what if she wakes up?" I cried. "Someone who loves her should be there."

On Saturday morning, while I was preparing to leave, Gloria called. Mother had died—alone.

Now that she was gone, the immediacy of getting to Long Beach was over. I would do the Toronto benefit and then leave for the funeral. How would I do the concert? I had to.

The next evening, I walked onto the stage of the O'Keefe Auditorium.

"Ladies and gentleman, this recital is dedicated to my mother, Berneice Horne, who died yesterday of cancer."

The program included Dvorak's "Songs My Mother Taught Me."

Berneice Horne did teach me, not only songs but also how to live with dignity and courage and love. I could think of no greater tribute than to sing for her that evening.

Henry and I made one last desperate attempt to reconcile by going on a cruise with our friends the Sereteans. I wasn't keen on the idea, neither was Henry. Almost every vacation we'd taken together had been a horror. Henry didn't want to go without Angela—she was at camp—while I optimistically hoped that away from New Jersey, New York and work, we might come to an understanding. In a way we did. After a Stygian voyage, Henry returned immediately; I came home later. I told Henry there would be no more parties, no more socializing; I didn't want to put our friends through the strain of being with us anymore. The marriage was finished.

Our professional lives, however, remained entwined.

Henry was conducting *L'Italiana* at the Metropolitan, and the next months were sheer agony. I was onstage going through the motions, prancing before the public, trying to get a voice up and out over choked-back tears and emotions that were tearing me apart—and there was Henry, in the pit, looking up at me. Isabella probably saved me from a breakdown. I simply had to keep going.

At first Henry and I said nothing to anyone about our separation and kept our ends up—so well, in fact, that we fooled most people. One evening during a performance, exhausted from singing and the strain of looking at Henry, I was in my dressing room between acts. I had twenty minutes to compose myself and was trying to relax when I heard a knock on the door. Judy Blegen came rushing into the room, threw her arms around me and began sobbing.

"Jackie, you've got to help me. My marriage is falling apart. You're the only one I can talk to!"

I spent the rest of the intermission comforting Judy. I even took her home with me for the night. Neither of our marriages made it.

In October 1974, Henry Lewis and I legally separated; the divorce would come in 1979. After fourteen years, we were finished—fourteen years, and of those I'd say the first five were really happy—the rest had been a slow dance on the killing ground. Before, during, and after the official announcement, my main concern was Angela. How could I tell her we were no longer a family? I was in psychotherapy at the time and went over this subject again and again, putting off the terrible duty of breaking up my child's world. For the first time in my professional life, I was refusing and canceling engagements right and left in order to be with her. I was supposed to do Rossini's *Stabat Mater* with Riccardo Muti—for the Pope! I didn't have it. When I spoke to Ronald Wilford and told him I couldn't leave my daughter, he came through as he always did. "Jackie, your personal life comes first."

The time came when we could no longer avoid telling Angela the truth. She wasn't an imbecile, and although she'd accepted her father's absence without question, sooner or later she was going to find out. I didn't want it to be from someone else or the newspapers or television. Still, I didn't know how to it. One weekend, I was scheduled to sing a concert in New Orleans and decided to take Angela with me. My plan was to talk with her on the trip and then be with her for the weekend. I didn't want to tell her, then leave her. Off we went to New Orleans, where my resolution wavered; I fell apart. I could barely look at Angela without tears welling up. I knew I couldn't speak to her calmly so I called my shrink and cried over the phone.

"What am I going to do? What am I going to do?

The analyst was wonderfully firm.

"You must be strong," she said, "for your daughter's sake. She's at the age where you are her female role model. What you do, she will emulate. You must present a woman of great dignity and strength to Angela, someone she can look up to."

That did it. For Angela, I could be brave. For Angela, I had to be strong.

I took her with me to the concert, as I had so many times before and she remained in the dressing room doing her homework while I performed. The door was ajar and she could hear what was going on even as she worked. I finished, took my bows and went into the dressing room. I closed the door behind me and Angela looked up.

"Gee, Mom, that sounded good."

You have to understand, my daughter was very reluctant to praise. She was my most demanding critic and when she complimented me, I knew that either I'd been fabulous or she wanted something. She didn't want anything that evening, though—I think she sensed a special moment. This however, was not the moment. She had to be told about the separation, but not only by me. We returned to New Jersey. First Henry spoke with her and then I did. She refused to believe us. Finally, she accepted the fact that the Lewises were no longer a family. Never in my wildest dreams could I have imagined going through what my daughter was going through. Bentz and Berneice Horne were a permanent entity, exactly what I had wanted to be with Henry. I wanted him to stay at all costs; he felt he had to leave, and I accepted his decision. The promise of a full rich life together could not be fulfilled.

Later, when I spoke to the analyst and told her how composed I'd been, she said, "You must have had a role model yourself, a woman in your past who was strong and dignified at all cost."

I thought about it. Of course, I had a model, the woman whose quiet strength anchored my life: my mother.

I couldn't pull Angela out of school or leave her in the care of others, so I withdrew from out-of-town engagements to remain at home. An *Orfeo* was scheduled in Chicago. I called the late Carol Fox of the Chicago Lyric Opera and told her why I couldn't make it. She was so kind and understanding, I could have hugged her.

My next major assignment was a revival of Ambroise Thomas's *Mignon* in Dallas, Texas. I had reservations about the event anyway because Sarah Caldwell was hired to direct and conduct. I'm afraid Sarah wasn't high on my list—even with its many admirable touches and effects, her Boston *Carmen* had been utter chaos. Miss Caldwell's flair did not include preparation: we'd been so under-rehearsed, we didn't even make it through the final scene until the actual performance. We were musically secure only because Henry was in the pit. All I needed in my present state was to be in Sarah Caldwell's hands. Another sad event tainted the *Mignon*. Larry Kelly, the founding and guiding light of the Dallas Opera, was mortally ill with cancer. But even my sympathy for Larry couldn't move me. I was traumatized and terrified that I couldn't handle the *Mignon*. My inability to perform, I later realized, was a combination of my desire to be with Angela and my own depression. I called Ronald on a Friday and told him to cancel. I spent the weekend at home and on Monday, went to the Met for rehearsal.

Matthew Epstein, then working for Columbia Artists Management, came over to me.

"Jackie," he said, "I hear you canceled *Mignon*. It's a mistake. You should do it."

"Pushy kid," I thought to myself, but I listened as he continued.

"It's only three weeks away, don't abandon it. It's good for you as well as Dallas. My God, it's been mounted for you! Come on, reconsider."

Matthew is not easy to dissuade once he sets his mind on something, and obviously he'd set his mind on my doing *Mignon*. He sincerely believed I should go to Dallas and he convinced me, too. I phoned my manager from the Met.

"Ronald, call Nicola Rescigno and tell him I've reconsidered. I'll do the *Mignon*."

By the time I arrived in Dallas, Larry Kelly was dead. The production was a testament to life, however, my life— and a new one began in Dallas.

189

NOTES ON NEW BEGINNINGS

Mignon, based on Goethe's *Wilhelm Meister*, premiered in Paris at the Opéra-Comique on November 17, 1866, with Célestine Galli-Marie in the title role. Mignon, a child of noble birth, was stolen by gypsies and in the course of the opera is reunited with her father, Lothario. He's been wandering around the country in a daze looking for her. At the end, his senses return and he gives his blessing to the union of his daughter and a young student, Wilhelm Meister.

All my fears about Sarah Caldwell materialized on the first day in Dallas. She brought out her score, put it on a desk, and opened it—to a resounding "crack." The spine had borne its first pressure—the inside of that book obviously had not seen the light of day. Sarah was a number, all right. Sometimes I wonder if she'd have been better off if she got a bunch of kids together and an old barn and said, "Okay, let's put on an opera." She did some wonderful things, I know, but I was from another school and I couldn't deal with her laissez-faire attitude. On this occasion, however, Miss Caldwell's modus operandi took a back seat where my attentions were concerned. Something else materialized in Dallas—a certain bass I'd met once before.

When I heard that Nicola Zaccaria would be singing Lothario, I said to myself, "Well, he probably doesn't have any voice left, but he'll bring great authority to the role." I was convinced that Zaccaria, a La Scala fixture for years, had to be at least sixty. At our first meeting, I'd thought he was good-looking but I was attached to Henry then, both emotionally and musically. Put it this way, in those days I saw when men were attractive, but that was all.

As fate would have it, only two members of the *Mignon* cast were staying at the Sheraton Hotel—myself and Nicola Zaccaria. Every evening after rehearsals, he'd come over and respectfully ask me to join him for dinner, and I would respectfully answer that I was getting some newspapers and going to bed. I was, too. I'd buy papers and magazines and go up to my room where I'd read, study, and cry until I fell asleep. One night, we were both at the hotel newsstand at the same time, and he repeated his offer. I smiled and shook my head.

"No, no," I said. *"Tante grazie, ma no, Lei e troppo simpatico."* ("No, thank you very much, but no; you're too kind.") Zaccaria spoke Italian, Greek, French, some German, but not much English. My onstage Italian was pretty good; I wasn't as secure offstage. I wanted Zaccaria to know that I liked him but that he was too threatening. He understood. Bowing politely, he turned and walked away to the elevators. I watched him as he moved through the lobby with long, vigorous strides. He wasn't sixty, not by a long shot. Actually, he was fifty, ten years older than I, and like it or not, I was attracted to the handsome basso.

Mignon orchestra rehearsals were held in an auditorium at Southern Methodist University. One afternoon I arrived early and was waiting for the rest of the cast when Zaccaria came into the hall. Always impeccably dressed, he looked especially handsome that day. He was carrying a large white carton like the ones used by bakeries. Smiling broadly, he motioned for me to come over.

"Vieni, signora, e guarda, questa pasticceria greca, magnifica, per piacere."

He had brought Greek pastries and was offering some to me. I put down my score and went over to his side. He opened the box and put it on a table. As I leaned over to take a look, Nicola Zaccaria took me in his arms, pulled me toward him and kissed me passionately...

That afternoon I did something wild in Dallas—I fell head over heels in love, madly in love, like a teen-ager. Nico swore I only went for him because of the pastries, but I'm not so sure. For one week a forty-year-old, world-famous singer couldn't sleep or eat—I even lost ten pounds. If anyone had told me I'd be wooed and won over *baklava* in Dallas, I'd have laughed in his face. I guess that's what made it so wonderful, it was so unexpected. With Henry, my feelings grew out of a long, long friendship; with Nico it was BAM! In the twinkling of an eye, the scorned wife became the lovesick mezzo. Don't forget, my self-esteem as a woman was at an all-time low when Nico came along; he made me feel like a woman again, more like one that I'd ever felt before. Perhaps I was ready to be a woman.

And to think I almost had canceled!

After *Mignon*, I returned to New Jersey. I was on such a high I could have flown without a plane. Nico and I played father and daughter in the opera, but when the curtain fell, we were more like Romeo and Juliet. He made that stay in Dallas glorious. I literally was a new woman when I returned. The new woman was greeted by the same old child, however. I had to cool my ardor, at least for a while. How could I tell my daughter I'd fallen for another man, especially a daughter who adored her father and, like so many children of divorce, still hoped her parents would reconcile.

My marital connection severed, I set about putting myself on an independent path. I contacted my lawyer and my accountant and with their help made myself a totally separate financial entity from Henry Lewis. As each detail of my life started to iron out, I came to realize how totally dependent I had been upon my husband. No wonder he wanted out! Living proof of the Cinderella complex, I wanted my man to take care of me; what's more, I truly believed he was more capable than I of doing so. Now it seems asinine. What's so terrible about making your own decisions? The worst that can happen is—you can be wrong.

When I married Henry, I didn't trust my feelings, my gut reactions and judgments. I'm sure this had something to do with my wanting to present myself to the world as a less intelligent person than I actually was. More than once my parents cautioned me: "It's okay to go out and become famous, Jackie, but don't change. Don't get too big for your britches." What they'd really been saying was: "Don't get too far away from us." As a result, I'd trusted Henry's opinions more than my own. To keep from getting too big for my britches, I'd held back, hiding behind a curtain woven of feminine doubts and fears. I woke up when Henry walked out.

As years go, 1975 was pretty good. I won a Grammy nomination for a recording of French and Spanish songs with Marty Katz and I was singing regularly at the Metropolitan. In May, Joan Sutherland, Luciano Pavarotti, Franco Corelli, Jimmy McCracken and I joined the company for a three-week tour of Japan. Joan sang Violetta in *La Traviata*; I sang *Carmen*, which Henry conducted. Angela came with us. Funny, Henry and I were getting on much better since the separation; the trip was strictly professional, still, Angela was thrilled that we all were together again.

During the first intermission of one *Carmen*, the principals—Jimmy, Adriana Maliponte, Guillermo Sarabia, Henry and I were invited for an audience with the Emperor of Japan and the Crown Prince. Japanese royalty didn't go backstage, so it was arranged for the teen-age heir apparent, and present ruler, to greet us in a private room. They never told us the room was on top of Mount Fuji! We were so winded from running around onstage and running up the mountain that by the time we reached the Prince, all we could do was stand there and pant.

In the fall, I arrived in Houston to appear in Handel's *Rinaldo*. David Gockley's Houston Opera has a history of innovative productions and I liked working there. Also, it was the precursor of my bringing *Rinaldo* to the Met. Around this time, I had the opportunity to give a boost to one of the most amazing singers who ever appeared on the operatic stage.

After my Texas engagement, I stopped in to see Charlie Riecker, a great friend in the Met management, to talk about things in general—including the scheduled revival of Meyerbeer's Le *Prophète*. Naturally, we talked shop (a.k.a. gossip). Charlie bemoaned the fact that Birgit Nilsson had dropped out of *Tosca* to prepare for Sieglinde. He desperately needed a star to put in the role of Puccini's glamorous heroine. (*Tosca*'s a part I'd always wanted to do but it was out of my league.) I had a suggestion. I'd recently seen a fabulous *Tosca* in Dallas with Magda Olivero in the title role. The Italian superstar had sung in places like New Jersey and Texas, and every time she appeared, her performances sold out. She practically gave acting and singing lessons while onstage; honestly, you could learn more from watching an Olivero performance than from reading most books on those very subjects. She had a huge cult following in the United States, yet she'd never appeared at the Met. Charlie was a little skeptical about bringing her there, mostly because of her age. I pushed and he called Schuyler Chapin. Schuyler dropped by and I continued extolling Olivera. Finally, I convinced them that she was a trump card. The upshot was, at the age of sixty-five, Magda Olivero made her long-overdue Metropolitan debut as *Tosca*. She sang five completely sold-out legendary performances before wildly enthusiastic audiences. What a thrill for them and for me!

In 1976, along with Leontyne Price, I went to Salzburg for a lavish, stylized production of *Aida*. But first, a word about my appearances in the Verdi repertoire. With hindsight, I realize that, save for Dame Quickly, I never had great success vocally, and I think I know why. I never "put both feet in," so-to-speak. I always kept one foot in the bel canto and Baroque partly because I didn't want to force my voice to be heard over the orchestra. Pouring forth big sound all night would have been vocal suicide. I was in good company. Enrico Caruso, no power slouch, once sang in a *Lucia* in Rio de Janiero with the baritone Titta Ruffo. Ruffo put out like thunder and in trying to keep up with the baritone, Caruso lost his voice for the evening. The tenor swore he'd never again sing *Lucia* with Ruffo.

Amneris is a great part, one of the meatiest in the mezzo canon so when I was asked to do it again at the Salzburg Festival under Herbert von Karajan's direction in 1979, I agreed. I was convinced that this would be a great *Aida*; first, because of von Karajan who, I assumed, would add a lyrical touch, and second, because Mirella Freni and José Carreras, artists of delicacy and fine tuning, would be singing Aida and Radamès.

When I got to Salzburg and took one look at the size of the augmented chorus, I knew I was in for the big-band sound. Von Karajan had quadrupled the volume—disaster for the mezzo's middle voice. Sure enough, when we started with the orchestra, the sound boomed from the pit. Von Karajan might as well have taken a cannon and shot me in the throat. And that's the way it went, except for one extraordinary performance after the opening. That evening, everything seemed so much easier; my voice felt like it was soaring out and over the pit. Then, it dawned on me. For some reason the orchestra was playing a thousand times softer that it had been. This, in fact, was how I expected it to be when I agreed to do the *Aida*. I was in heaven. It was a quick trip. That was the one and only time von Karajan gave me a chance. The rest of the performances returned to fortissimo. I couldn't help ruminating about how much I'd been looking forward to working with von Karajan whose reputation as a "singer's conductor" had been touted by everyone, including Nico. He'd appeared often with Karajan and told me that I was in for a marvelous experience. It was far from "marvelous." After the curtain call at the final performance, von Karajan came over. He thanked me politely (I have to tell you von Karajan never looked you in the eye—at least he never looked me in the eye. Shifty, I'd call him.) and then completely floored me when he added, "I would like you to do Quickly next year, Frau Horne."

I mumbled something like "we'll see," but in my heart I knew I never wanted to sing for him again. I was sad that my experience with the singers' conductor had been so disappointing—more than that, disillusioning.

Not surprisingly, the reviews for my Amneris were so-so. I certainly was not the darling of the Austrian music world. Everything seemed grim and, overcome by the Teutonic rather than the bucolic atmosphere in Salzburg, I got progressively more irritated and experienced a variety of contretemps that fueled my ire. It was only question of time before I exploded.

The evening after the *Aida* opening, Nico and I, along with my friends Mimi and Merritt Cohen, returned to the parking garage located inside a mountain. The place was pitch-black; not one miserable little bulb illuminated the vast area. [Digression: Europe and Illumination. Whenever I checked into European hotels, the first thing I did was go out to buy light bulbs and replace the ones in the room. The Continental idea of bright seemed to be something like 15 watts.] With great difficulty, we finally located the car. We got in and drove around looking for the exit. We circled and circled until completely by accident we found the *ausgang*. Alas, none of us had any change to put in the automatic toll machine.

"The hell with it," I said to Merritt. "It's getting late. Just lift up the barrier and let's get out of here."

He got out of the car and tried to push up the long wooden arm blocking the way. Before you could say *Götterdämmerung*, an attendant roared up on a motorcycle and began shouting in German. I got out of the car, stormed over to the parking-lot attendant and let him have it.

"I am *Frau Kammersängerin Horne*," I trumpeted in German (and in a voice that easily could have carried over a Karajan orchestra). We cannot get out of this place. Open that gate!"

Immediately the attendant leaped from his cycle, rushed over to the barrier and raised it. Typical—this guy knew how to take orders, period. Merritt got back into the car, and as we drove past the attendant who, I must add, was standing at attention, Nico leaned out the window and yelled, "Nazi!"

This incident further stoked my fury and by the time my scheduled recital with Marty Katz arrived, I'd about had it with Salzburg and its citizens. That evening, Marty and I stood offstage waiting to go on, and all my pent-up fury over the *Aida* turned to resolution and determination. As we stepped out, I said over my shoulder,

"Okay, Marty, let's get 'em!" I never talked like that before a concert—usually I said "good luck," "*merde*" or

197

"oy vay."

We walked on to a polite smattering of applause. Marty sat down at the keyboard and I took my place in the welcoming crook of the piano. I opened with Orlando's aria, *"Nel profondo cieco mondo"*—all black notes! I soared into the rest of the program and as each number finished, polite applause gave way to pandemonium. At the end I had to sing eight encores. Jimmy Levine was out there and I threw him a kiss during the fifth encore. Matthew Epstein sat in the second row and kept nodding his head in approval as I returned to sing more numbers. After the eighth encore, he shook his head. I knew he was right; I stopped. I swear, if he hadn't been there, I might have sung all night.

I had redeemed myself in the ears of the Salzburg public. They witnessed one of the greatest recitals I ever gave or—*auf wiedersehen*, modesty—one of the finest ever given. My success more than made up for von Karajan's *Aida* and I was thrilled that Marty, my dear friend and great accompanist, shared in that triumph. (Hey, if you want to check it out, the recital is available on CD.)

Later that year, I made my peace with Verdi in a Dallas *Aida* where I sang Amneris to critical acclaim. The conductor, Nicola Rescigno, kept the decibel level of the orchestra within the range of the human ear and the tempi he established were consistent, not idiosyncratic. Bottom line? — given the proper setting, I could do Amneris damn well!

Le Prophète should have been a resounding success for me. A grand opera in the great French tradition, it has everything going for it. The central role of Fides, mother of the hero, Jean, was associated with four great artists who sang most of the fifty-six performances given at the Met up to 1928, the year it left the repertoire, Of the four mezzos, Marianne Brandt, Ernestine Schumann-Heink, Margarete

Matzenauer and Louise Homer, I was most drawn to the incomparable Schumann-Heink.

Ernestine Schumann-Heink has been described as "a great natural phenomenon, like Niagara Falls." Beloved by colleagues—Caruso adored her and called her Nonna (grandmother)—her fame went beyond the opera house. In her day, she truly was a "household word." Every Christmas she sang *"Stille Nacht"* (Silent Night) over the radio and it was said that Christmas wasn't Christmas without Schumann-Heink. During the First World War when anti-German sentiment was so rabid that sauerkraut became "victory cabbage" ("freedom fries," anyone?), Schumann-Heink's popularity didn't slip a notch. In fact, she gained in the public's affection because of her personal quandary. She had many children via three husbands and her sons were in both the German and the American armies! Mme. Schumann-Heink also was noted for her ample proportions, another reason I felt drawn to her. Once, while rehearsing for a concert with a symphony orchestra, she made a spectacular entrance. Unable to thread her way down the narrow aisle between the string sections, she smacked, banged and barreled her way down to the front, leaving a trail of displaced chairs and musicians. When at last she reached the podium, the concerned conductor surveyed the wreckage, leaned over and said most gently,

"Perhaps, Mme. Schumann-Heink, you should come in sideways?"

"But Maestrrrrrro," replied the contralto, "I haf no zidevays."

Actually, I should have taken a cue from Ernestine and "sidestepped" my Fides; I should have canceled the first performance. I had a terrible case of bronchitis which I might have been able to overcome in a role like Rosina but it was sheer stupidity for me to try to take on a blockbuster like

199

Fides.

Fides is a dramatic tour de force laced with bel canto flourishes, indeed, when we saw the old orchestral scores for the first time, we were shocked to discover that all the excruciatingly difficult vocal flourishes had been cut. We immediately restored them! Fides should not be approached in anything less than perfect health. If I had had any sense I would have followed the advice Dr. Kriso gave me in Vienna all those years ago. I felt the responsibility of a new production created for my benefit, however. For years, I had waited and prayed for this role and the maturity to do it. I couldn't let it go. I had to do it and do it as originally written. Rumors that I was in vocal difficulty began to circulate after the opening. I got another cold and barely got through the run. I should have stopped, but I couldn't—I wouldn't. I actually was booed at the Met, booed! Finally, I had no choice; I canceled everything for five weeks. By the end of those five weeks, I felt better; then and only then did I really begin to sing. Francis Robinson said that my Fides "did not suffer by comparison with Schumann-Heink and Matzenauer." Speaking of Francis, what a special person he was, one who truly knew, loved and promoted opera. Before he died he sent me a lovely autographed picture of Schumann-Heink on the arm of one of her three husbands.

Did I learn my lesson from the Fides? Did I turn from Verdi and Meyerbeer to embrace bel canto and only bel canto? My next role at the Metropolitan was as Princess Eboli in Verdi's *Don Carlo*. Look, I never said I was above reproach. On opening night, February 5, 1979, the verdict was: Verdi, si: Horne, no. My "Veil Song" was well received but I took it on the chin principally because I had committed the unpardonable operatic sin—I had transposed Eboli's big third act aria, "*O don fatale*," down a minor third. Why? Because I no longer was comfortable singing in what had become the "accepted" key. Furthermore, I remembered that my dear old coach Fritz Zweig had told me that the composer himself sanctioned a transposition. Verdi transposed down a full tone and a half. Moreover, until the 1950s "*O don fatale*" was sung in the lower key at the Metropolitan. Honestly, I wish some of my critics had taken the trouble to do the kind of research I did in preparing my roles. Oh well, as an American poet once wrote, "Between me and my critics, I leave you to decide."

In August 1978, Marty and I, along with Nico, went Down Under for a recital tour. Joan sent a welcoming note to the Sydney airport but our meeting had to wait because we left immediately for Perth. The recital odyssey was both arduous and rewarding. Australia was a funny combination of modern and old—some of the buildings were modern and most of the plumbing was old. In Melbourne we stayed on the thirteenth floor of a new Hilton Hotel, which didn't bother me. My superstitious Greek friend, however, was convinced we were in for a run of bad luck. We unpacked and settled in. Late that evening, I turned on the television, got onto the bed, flopped back on the pillows and flipped around the stations hoping to catch a good movie. All of a sudden something gray whizzed by the front of the set and that something had four scurrying little legs and a long tail. I leaped to my feet on top of the bed, grabbed the phone and called the front desk.

"This is V.I.P. Horne," I shrieked into the receiver. "You send someone up here fast. There's a rat in this room."

Nico came in to see what the screaming was about and after my breathless explanation he paddled around the room in his bare feet looking for the creature. I called Marty and he started laughing. Soon, a pair of bellboys appeared and joined in the search. Sure enough, the rat (mouse) came scooting out across the floor and dashed under the sofa. The bellboys gave chase and cornered the thing, but it slipped away under a radiator.

"Sorry, Madame," said one bellboy. "He's eluded us. We'll try again tomorrow."

"Fine," I answered, "you try again tomorrow for the person who's staying in this room, because it won't be me!"

At three a.m., Nico and I marched through the corridors in our pajamas, followed by an entourage of bellboys laden with luggage.

Of mice, and then mobs.

The next day, returning to the hotel from a rehearsal, we ran into a street demonstration. The Australian Prime Minister was staying at our hotel and protesters had tied up the streets. Nico, Marty, and I were in a limousine provided by the Australian Broadcasting Company, a stretch vehicle about as long as a city block, very fancy. The driver inched his way through the crowd until it became impossible to move. I had a performance that evening and, while I'm sympathetic to most good causes, I need my rest—ergo, I needed to get to my room. Spotting a policeman, I opened the window to ask for assistance. As I did, some demonstrators shouted, "Look at the rich folks in their fancy car!" and other phrases of a similar nature, put far less politely. I leaned out of the window and beckoned to one of the hecklers. He looked at his friends, shrugged his shoulders and swaggered over.

"Do you speak English?" I asked him sweetly.

"Yeah," he answered.

"Good," I said, raising my voice. "Up yours!'

The crowd roared, parted like the Red Sea, and let us by. Sometimes, talking tough is the only way to get results. I talked tough, sang well and had a marvelous time.

We returned to Sydney and checked into our hotel. Joan

was appearing as Norma in the great gull-winged opera house while my recital was in the Concert Hall—both events were sold out. After our performance, Marty, Nico and I went to stand in the wings for the last act of *Norma*. It was typically Sutherland—stupendous. When the opera ended, we went back to her dressing room and found that Joan, along with a close friend Chester Corone, had prepared and was about to preside over a dinner in our honor. Imagine, she'd sung the most demanding role in the repertoire and now she was catering.

We left Sydney on September 1, and after an all-night flight arrived in Los Angeles. My brother Dick picked me up at the airport. Dick was such a busy guy he had little time to spare, so we usually had to be content with phone calls or catch-as-catch-can dinners whenever I stopped in L.A. This was Labor Day Weekend, however, and Dick was free. We drove to his house where I spent a delightful two days. The weather was beautiful, and Dick, Joanne and I sat out by the pool from morning to dusk, laughing, talking, and reminiscing. Really, it was the first opportunity I'd had in years to enjoy my brother's company.

On September 24, 1978, I was in Canada to perform *Mignon*. That evening, on impulse, I called Dick to say "hi." We had a long conversation. The next morning, I went out early and returned to the hotel suite to prepare a late breakfast. The television was on in the living room, and I heard a bulletin about a plane crash in San Diego.

"Nico," I called out, "did you hear that? Another of those damn little planes caused a major accident."

We sat down to eat. Our meal was interrupted by a phone call from someone at the opera house.

"Miss Horne, would you please call Mrs. Horne in Los Angeles?"

Not knowing which "Mrs." Horne had called, Jay's wife

or Dick's, I phoned Joanne.

"Hi, Joanne, it's Jackie," I said when she answered. "They told me to call you."

After a pause, Joanne asked if I'd heard about the plane crash.

"Yes. Isn't it awful, was anyone hurt?

There was another long pause.

"Jackie, there are no survivors. Jackie, Dick was on that plane."

I screamed and screamed.

The horror of that moment may have been dulled by time, but it will never, ever, leave me.

The next evening I sang *Mignon* in a fog. I couldn't believe it; I wouldn't believe it. I could not acknowledge Dick's death.

"I've accepted it, Jackie, but you won't and you've got to," Joanne warned me.

I remember finding some consolation in music, especially in Mahler's *Resurrection Symphony*. The words, "You will rise again, oh my dust, oh my dust," provided a link for me. I clung to that uplifting quality in Mahler and though it sustained me, I still couldn't face the reality. My denial went on for four years. Finally, most curiously, I came to grips with his passing.

In October 1982, I began using hypnosis as a method to lose weight. The hypnotist introduced me to something called "Frozen Glove Therapy."

While in a self-hypnotic state, the subject puts on a glove and in the introductory session as I drew the glove over my hand, the therapist told me to imagine it was a boxing glove.

"Feel the silken warmth of the inside of the glove," she told me.

I followed her directions and suddenly found myself weeping uncontrollably.

"What's the matter?" she asked.

"I'm remembering," I answered, "I'm remembering."

The only time in my life I ever had boxing gloves on was in Bradford when I was a kid. Dick let me wear his and pretended to spar with me. In my hypnotized state, I returned to that incident; in doing so, at last I was able to fully grieve for my brother.

I took my time putting my New Jersey house on the market partly because I clung to the comforting familiarity of my home and my friends but mostly I wanted Angela to finish elementary school. In 1977, I sold the house and moved into a duplex apartment near Lincoln Center. I'm still there!

Angela and I settled in and I continued to perform all over the country—and the world. Besides appearances in *L'Italiana* and *Il Barbiere* at the Met, I sang in Houston and Dallas, and most significantly, in Italy—my musical home.

Between operas, recitals and recordings, I spent a healthy part of the year in Italy. I may have been better known there than I was in America! And I sure was treated royally— even by the notorious Parma opera house. The Parma fans are among the toughest; stories of their inhumanity to vocalists fill books. One of the most famous concerns the tenor who sang his aria three times because the audience kept calling for encores. At the end of the third round, the tenor stepped forward and cried,

"Thank you. Thank you. Please, please, I can do it no more!"

"You'll do it till you do it right!" screamed someone from the balcony.

Another time, porters at the railroad station refused to carry the bags belonging to a baritone because they thought he sang so badly. Imagine my delight, after my recital, when the opera house paid my hotel bill, in full—an unheard of procedure if not specified in the contract. They liked me, they really liked me.

While I enjoyed singing in Italy, I must admit it was more difficult dealing with La Scala than any other place on earth. (Maybe that was part of the fun.) The Milan house had flair and style and a lot of skullduggery went on, as well. Consequently, an incredible. expenditure of energy and a hearty dose of subterfuge went into any deal with them. I really had to be on my toes! For example, in 1980, I was singing *Il Barbiere* in Macerata, a walled city on the Adriatic coast, where operas are given in a restored amphitheatre during the summer. One afternoon, I received word that representatives of La Scala wanted to speak to me. Five gentlemen were ushered up to my hotel room and questioned me as to what I wanted to sing for my Milan engagement.

"I want an opening night in a big, new production!" (Shy, I wasn't.)

"Si, si, Signora," said the La Scala quintet, nodding their heads in unison. "But, if we do this for you, would you do something for us?"

"What?"

It turned out they wanted me to do a revival of *L'Italiana*, which I already had sung at La Scala.

"Okay, okay," I agreed. "I'll do it, but only in conjunction with another new production."

"You know, Signora, 1982 is the two-thousandth anniversary of Virgil's birth and we were thinking of doing *Les Troyens* (The Trojans). Would you like to sing both Cassandra and Dido?"

Berlioz's epic opera is so long it usually was divided into Parts One and Two and given on two separate occasions. Each part contains a mezzo plum—in Part One, Cassandra, daughter of Priam and Hecuba, who is cursed with the gift of prophecy; in Part Two, Dido, Queen of Carthage, who has a tragic love affair with Aeneas. La Scala planned to combine the two sections, present it on the same evening and was offering me a double header.

"*Les Troyens* is fine," I answered, "but I really only want to do one role. I don't like to die twice in one evening. I'll take Dido, if you please."

"Certainly!" agreed the quintet, nodding their heads and smiling. "And, Signora, how would you like to sing a recital for us, too?"

"Sure. I'll do it. Not only that—I'll do it as a benefit for the Casa Verdi!"

The La Scala group nearly keeled over at my offer. The Casa Verdi, established by the composer himself, provides shelter for musical senior citizens. I was proud to donate my services.

Within the week, a contract arrived for *L'Italiana* and the recital—no *Trojans* was listed, however. I put the contract away. After a long interval I received a call telling me that the Virgil project had fallen through—*Les Troyens* had been axed.

"Okay, okay," said Little Mary Sunshine, "I'll live without *The Trojans*. I'll do the recital and *L'Italiana*. We'll figure out something in place of the Berlioz." I wasn't concerned because I still hadn't signed any contracts.

In June 1981, Marty, Nico and I went to Milan for the recital and immediately, Marty and I began rehearsing in the opera house. The heat was so unbearable everyone had cleared out for the noon break, leaving the offices empty. Nico took the opportunity to do some judicious sleuthing. Having been with La Scala for twenty-eight years, he was very suspicious of the Virgil episode. Thus, my personal Pinkerton Man found himself in an administrative office. He happened to find himself at the desk of an executive officer and his eyes happened to fall upon the 1981-82 schedule. Berlioz's *Les Troyens* topped the list. Nico told me, and quick as a wink, I called my Italian agent. He, in turn, called La Scala.

"You cannot do this to La Signora Horne! You must always tell the straight story. If there were problems in the scheduling, you should have come to her."

Obviously, the La Scala boys reneged on their promise to me in order to suit someone else. I didn't know whom they wanted to sing Dido, but the idea that they tried to put one over rankled. They called and I put Nico on the phone. By the time the conversation ended, La Scala was ready to mount a *Rinaldo*, televise *L'Italiana* and throw in a gala. (They might have added the island of Ischia, too, had Nico kept at them.) If this seems dreadfully temperamental and ego-oriented, you surely understand by now that competition in the opera world is so fierce and managements are so devious that you must look out for yourself. Too many careers have collapsed because of bad management, bad advice, or simple naïveté.

On June 15, 1981, I gave the Milan recital, which was released as a recording and taped for television. I'm especially proud of that concert for many reasons—it was for a worthy cause, it included American songs, and I really was thin. I have to add I got a certain satisfaction from all the wheeling and dealing because I could handle it. Okay, Nico did the talking for me, but I was egging him on. In the early days, I relied on Henry and while I did my own thinking, I followed his lead and rarely took matters into my own hands. After we were divorced, I took an active interest in my affairs, particularly the financial ones. I recommend the same procedure to all other women, single or married. Sure, I made mistakes, especially in Europe and I got stung quite a few times particularly with currency fluctuations. I'd be

quoted a handsome fee but by the time I got around to col-
lecting it, the exchange rate might have taken a nosedive.
To avoid getting stuck, an artist could arrange to be paid on
the spot. Once, in Monaco, I sang at a concert attended by
Prince Rainier—his first public appearance since the heart-
breaking death of Princess Grace. During the intermission,
my assistant joined me in my dressing room. We were
shmoozing when the general manager dropped by and
handed me a large manila envelope containing my fee—in
francs. The exchange rate was pretty good then, so I really
got a stack of bills. The package was too thick to leave in
the room, and I couldn't carry it onstage. I handed it to my
assistant. She brought it back to her seat in the auditorium
and sat on it for the second half. Later, she told me that the
people behind her kept complaining that they couldn't see
the stage anymore.

All told, I found it challenging to work out the financial
aspects of my career, aided by my lawyer and accountant.
You see, I wasn't just an opera singer; I was in the business
of singing. And for a good long stretch, business boomed.

THE BODY POLITIC

On March 2, 1985, I sang with the Arkansas Symphony Orchestra in Little Rock. After the concert, I was in my dressing room getting ready to return to my hotel. Unlike post-opera activity, there's way less to do; usually it's a simple matter of changing out of a gown into a comfortable outfit. Often, I'd get held up by backstage visitors but I really didn't know anyone in Little Rock and expected to leave promptly. I was sitting in front of the mirror when I heard a knock at the door.

"Come in," I cried, turning around in my chair.

The door opened and in strode a tall, handsome man.

"Hello," he said, "I'm Bill Clinton."

"I know who you are!" I replied leaping up. "I'm a yellow dog Democrat and I've had my eye on you for quite a while, Governor."

Clinton threw back his head and laughed.

He was there to present me with, among other things, the key to the state and a charter naming me an "Arkansas Traveler."

I was honored to be recognized. The Governor was wonderfully informal and after the official presentations, we chatted for a while. Among other things, the Governor and I discovered that both of us were "night owls."

"Well," he said, "If you're ever up late and want someone to talk to, here's my number. Don't be afraid to use it."

He scribbled the number on a card and gave it to me. I

thanked him and showed him out. I was so excited I immediately got on the phone and called a friend in New York.

"Listen," I cried, "I've just met a future President of the United States."

I got back to my hotel room at around midnight emptied my purse and found Clinton's note. I looked at it for a moment and then, purely on a whim, I dialed the number. Someone answered and after a brief wait the Governor got on. For over an hour we talked about everything from politics to music. The breadth of his knowledge was dazzling. We hung up with the promise of future conversations. It never happened. It was the craziest thing; he'd either call wanting to chat or to let me know he was coming to New York and would I like to go to dinner? Would I? Sure, I would have, except I was out of town every time he phoned. My secretaries got all the calls. It happened over and over. We didn't have direct communication, but he'd occasionally clip out articles that he thought I might like to read, and send them to me. So, although our association continued, we really didn't connect again until he was elected President. Needless to say, I was a big supporter of his candidacy.

Before the actual ballots were cast, I read an article in *The New York Times* asking Clinton what he would do if elected. Reporters assessed his answers, rating them "politically correct" or not. The list was pretty extensive; one question, however, particularly intrigued me.

"If you were elected, who would you ask to sing for the Inauguration?"

"Marilyn Horne," was the reply.

"Not P.C.," was the reporter's judgment. P.C., the article explained, would have been Leontyne Price.

"Politically Correct" or not, I really was thrown by the thought that I'd be asked to do it. I couldn't imagine it. Not that I hadn't sung in Washington before; I'd performed in our nation's capital on many occasions. Actually, my first visit to the White House wasn't to sing. Richard Nixon was President and along with Angela and my niece Jana, I was on a tour arranged by the Metropolitan Opera House.

The first time I sang at the White House was at a State Dinner President Reagan gave for the Prime Minister of Sweden. State Dinners are fun because all the people you see on the news are sitting around you. This occasion was especially meaningful for me because my grandfather came from Sweden. I already knew the Reagans from California. The President was a very personable guy, warm and gracious and I found Nancy equally pleasant. At that State Dinner, I met Barbara and George Bush and liked them enormously. Then, when George Bush was elected President, I was invited to come and do a concert in the White House. By the way, I'm absolutely bipartisan when it comes to this kind of thing. I may be a dyed-in-the-wool Democrat, but if a Republican is in office, he's my President.

During our visit, we were introduced to Senator David Boren from Oklahoma and he took us on a personal tour of the Capitol. He showed us the hallowed halls, took us down to the railroad underneath the Senate and then brought us up to his office. Senator Boren's father, Lyle, had served in the Congress, and some of the furnishings in the office, including a table at which we were seated, had belonged to Lyle Boren. We learned an interesting bit of lore from David Boren: Back in the early forties, his father and Harry Truman were seated at that very table when President Roosevelt called. He needed a running mate for his last term and was asking for suggestions.

"How about Sam Rayburn?" proposed Congressman Boren.

"No," Roosevelt answered, "I already went through a

Texan with Garner."

At which point, Lyle Boren turned to Truman and said, "Hey Harry, how about you?"

And that, purportedly, was the beginning of Harry Truman's rise to the presidency.

It's a wonderful story and Senator Boren is a grand raconteur. As a result of that episode, and a few other Washington visits, I became friendly with him and his wife, Molly. When David Boren decided not to run for congress again, he was named President of Oklahoma University. Later, he invited me to sing at the opening of the University's new recital hall and to teach a master class. I've gone back each year to do the master classes and to give private lessons. The Borens have become a special part of my life.

I brought my sister and my kid brother, Jay, to the White House and after the concert, President and Mrs. Bush invited us up to their private apartments. It is one thing to be in the public part of the White House, and quite another to be in the President's private quarters. The Bushes were such gracious hosts and Gloria, Jay and I were agog. The President was particularly cordial to my kid brother. Both he and Jay were runners and I got a kick out listening to the two of them discuss equipment—which running shoe was the best, and things like that. I, in the meantime, was quite taken with Mrs. Bush's needlepoint. She told me that when they lived in China, she spent hours and hours doing it.

"Come here, Jay," said the President at one point, "I want to show you the greatest view in Washington."

He ushered my brother into his office and the rest of us followed. He was absolutely right—what a spectacular vista of the mall.

In 1992, I received the Congressional Medal of the Arts along with an illustrious roster of honorees which included Robert Shaw, Robert Wise, James Earl Jones, and Earl

Scruggs. At this gala event, I renewed my acquaintance with the Bushes and again, was struck by their gentility. (You see, I like a lot of Republicans.) Still, in 1993, I was super thrilled to be asked to sing by a Democratic President and at the very moment that the Democrats came into power. Later, I learned that within a day of his election and within the first ten minutes of the meeting to plan the inauguration, President Clinton said, "I want Marilyn Horne to sing." I was beside myself when the committee notified me that I had been chosen. All I could think of was my parents. ME, Peanut, singing at the inauguration of the (Democratic) President of the United States! I was told that I could bring one guest—a no-brainer, Angela would accompany me. For about two weeks before the ceremony, I kept going over "The Star Spangled Banner" in my head. Everywhere I went, whatever I was doing, I'd start thinking "Oh say can you see...." I was terrified I'd forget the words.

Angela and I arrived in Washington and, along with most of the performers, stayed at the Watergate. All sorts of activities were going on; I performed at a big fund raising party the night before the ceremony. The Inauguration itself took place on a really cold January day. I was prepared. I had a wool suit and a cape made for the occasion. I was protected from the weather, but not from my knees. They really were in bad shape but I wasn't going to let them stand in the way. I stood on my damaged "pins" and sang my heart out. I opened with "Make a Rainbow," a lovely song written for me by Portia Nelson. Next, I sang President Clinton's personal request, "Simple Gifts," and I concluded my portion of the Inauguration with our national anthem. I didn't forget the words. I walked away from the microphone and was embraced by President Clinton. Then, I shook hands with Vice President Gore, whom I'd never met. The outgoing President stood next to Gore. I really liked President

Bush and could only imagine how he must have felt. I gave him a big hug.

"Thank you, Mr. President," I said, "thank you for everything you've given this country."

He smiled, returned my embrace and said, "I tried my very best, Marilyn."

Following the ceremony, we attended a luncheon in the capital rotunda. I was seated at a table with Madeline Albright, Warren Christopher and Joan Mondale. I told Mrs. Mondale that I was dying for my daughter to meet the President but didn't know how to approach him. I was a little shy about speaking with him now that he was the leader of my country. (To this day, I've never called him anything other than "Mr. President.")

"You know," said Mrs. Mondale, "he eats very fast and when he's finished, he stands up behind his chair. That's a signal that people can walk up and speak to him. Keep your eye out and when that happens, take your daughter over."

I never looked at my food after that; my eyes were on the President. The minute he got up, I ran over to Angela's table, grabbed her and dragged her to him. He was as sweet and charming as always. In fact, he told Angela about my first phone call to him back in Little Rock. A state trooper came into his office saying, "There's a lady named Marilyn Horne on the phone."

"Oh my gosh," I cried. Truthfully, I had totally forgotten the episode and was amazed that he remembered.

During his terms in office, President Clinton was far too busy to keep up with me. We did have a friendship, though, and when I received the Kennedy Medal in 1995 I was pleased to have him present the award. I admit, I was a little taken aback when he introduced me by saying that as a child I had sung for Roosevelt—adding, playfully, "that's *Franklin* Roosevelt."

I'm still a number one fan of Bill Clinton's. Furthermore, I think that in the future, when the wheat and the chaff are separated, he'll be recognized as one of our finest Presidents.

REGARDING HENRY

I always said that I when I reached my fifties, I would assume the role of Dame Quickly in Verdi's *Falstaff* and in the late 1980's, as if on cue, I received two offers. Jimmy Levine asked me to sing it at the Met and Terry McEwen asked me to do it in San Francisco. Terry's offer came slightly ahead of Jimmy's and San Francisco was mounting a new production with Jean-Pierre Ponnelle directing. Jimmy, a good friend, agreed that a new production plus the opportunity to work with Ponnelle was too delicious to pass up. So I did Quickly first in San Francisco, then in Chicago and again in a production of the revival in 1996 at the Metropolitan. I loved doing it. The opera sparkles and provides many opportunities for virtuoso acting as well as singing. In Verdi's musical rendering of Shakespeare's *Merry Wives of Windsor*, Quickly plays messenger between the other wives and the amorous Sir John. In their marvelous shared scene, Quickly has a grand time pulling the wool over the knight's eyes while feigning utmost servility. She continually addresses him as "Reverenza" (your Worship) even as she ensnares him in the ladies' plot to bring him down. Truly, portraying Dame Quickly was a capstone of my career.

Along with assuming a really adored role, the mid-eighties to the early nineties marked another major phase of my life, not however, a pleasant one; indeed the exact opposite. This was "the era of the knees." Where to begin? Oh, forget it—this is an autobiography not a medical history. Let's say I'd been experiencing difficulty with my legs, specifically the knees, for a long time.

In 1994, when I created the role of Samira at the world premiere of John Corigliano's *Ghosts of Versailles* at the Metropolitan Opera, I had a show-stopping twelve-minute aria, at the end of which I had to do a kind of hootchy-kootchy dance. In order for me to perform, they wheeled me onto the stage reclining on a huge divan. I sang the first section of the aria, then I arose, went down a flight of stairs and did my dance. The divan was a godsend because it gave me a chance to rest before standing. I never could have done the entire scene on my feet. Samira, regrettably, was only one of two roles that I created. (I always say I was too busy "resurrecting.") The other was in Vittorio Giannini's *The Harvest* presented at the Chicago Lyric Theatre in November 1961. *The Harvest* opening coincided with Thanksgiving and that was all the critics needed. Reviewers couldn't resist commenting that "the turkey arrived early this year." Although *The Harvest* was a failure, I had a wonderful time during the run because Geraint Evans played the role of my husband in this "Desire Under the Elmish" mishmash. Geraint was the best of colleagues, an incredibly gifted singer and really fun to work with. Both of us were insomniacs. We'd go out to the movies late at night—this was before channels like Turner Classic Movies existed—and sit in seedy theaters surrounded by drunks and perverts. Singers traveling today are much luckier. We had to go out for entertainment; they can stay in their hotel rooms and watch television, or go on the Internet.

Later on, I reached the point where I didn't want to go out. It was all I could do to get back to my hotel room. Even though I did isometric exercises, my knees got worse and worse. My work didn't help the situation, either. Not only did I have to carry myself around, I most often appeared in operas that called for extensive costuming. I don't think people realize how utterly heavy a costume can be, especially when you're playing a man's role. Granted, the armor sometimes is painted on, still the material itself can be suffocating and carrying that burden goes right to the legs, i.e. knees. Between the elaborate headdresses and the cumbersome costumes, being onstage often became agony especially on a raked stage. Offstage, it got to the point where I was being shlepped around in wheelchairs at airports. (As I write, one of my shoulders is going. I have osteoarthritis in every joint—hopefully not in the brain.)

During the first run of *Falstaff*s at the Met, the situation came to a head. I had stayed away from medication because it made me loopy and you really have to have your wits about you when you're doing *Falstaff*. At this time, however, I was gulping Percocet like aspirin because I couldn't go on without it. I was a little out of it a lot of the time, even during performances. On opening night, without realizing it, I left out a key word in the big duet with Falstaff. In between my appearances on the stage, I'd sit in my dressing room and apply Quick-ice to my throbbing legs. I got through the run only because the pleasure of performing the part plus the Percocet made it possible.

In 1995 I was off to sing a recital in Santa Fe and planned a stay at the Pritikin Institute in Santa Monica afterward. I boarded the plane and was getting into the seat when I pulled something in my right knee. I'd had arthroscopic surgery on that knee twice, and once on the left knee, but this pain was different. I knew I'd gone beyond arthroscopy. By the time the plane landed, I could barely walk.

I did the recital and flew off to Santa Monica. I really was hobbling and in pain. I arrived at Pritikin and was shown to my room. I remember opening the window and sitting by it for an hour or so, breathing in the glorious ocean air.

219

After all that dryness in Santa Fe, the breezes came as a blessing. I needed more than a breezy blessing.

The next day I went to see a doctor.

"Your knees have had it," he told me. "You can't go anywhere. You've got to have replacement surgery."

I didn't argue. I'd put off the inevitable and was paying the consequences—big time! One thing stuck in my brain, though. The doctor told me that I should do one knee at a time. Not for me, I answered, I wanted the daily double.

"You'll regret it," he chided. "It's simply not done."

I flew back to New York and consulted with Dr. Chitranjan Ranawat at Lenox Hill Hospital early in August. After the examination, Dr. Ranawat spoke to me in his office. "You have to have surgery," he said. "And, I'm going to do the two knees at the same time."

I wanted to jump up and kiss him. We definitely were on the same wavelength. However, Ranawat was so busy he couldn't schedule the surgery until the end of October. And while I wished it could have been sooner, I had tons of singing to do between the exam and the operation to keep me occupied. To prepare for the surgery I continued to apply ice to my knees and, at the doctor's suggestion, I started pool exercises. Ranawat told me that I should do water aerobics at least four days a week and I faithfully practiced what he preached. In fact, whenever it was possible, I tried to get in the pool daily. Look, I'm not going to say the knee replacement stuff was easy; it was horrible—and it's lucky I did it all at once; I'm not sure if I could have gone through it twice. My sister Gloria came east and stayed with me for weeks on end. She was a godsend. Following the initial trauma, I made a relatively quick recovery for which I credit the water exercises which, I must add, I'm still doing almost every day.

Three weeks after the operation, I attended a recital and

two weeks after that I went to the Kennedy Center to receive my medal. I was in auspicious company; the other honorees included Jacques D'Amboise, Neil Simon, B. B. King, and Sidney Poitier. On both those occasions I had to use a cane. Eight weeks after the surgery, I threw the cane away and, in February 1996, the night before the first stage rehearsal for the Met's *Falstaff*, I took my last Percocet. The next day I ran around the stage like a wild woman—up and down stairs, in and out of doors—and I felt great! The exhilaration carried right through to the premiere. I had a ball. I was able to "fly" through the set with the greatest of ease. Henry called after the premiere saying it was wonderful to see me running around again. That was the last time I ever spoke to him.

After our divorce Henry Lewis remained a significant part of my life not only because of Angela but also because of all that we shared together. Professionally, he occasionally conducted for me and, more important, he continued to help me prepare. Socially, we saw each other because of mutual friends as well as our daughter. I always did Christmas for Angela and if he were in town, he'd come over, too. Henry kept an apartment in New York City but was in Europe a good deal of the time. Among many guest spots, he appeared at Covent Garden, The Paris Opera and the Hamburg Opera. He also was the permanent conductor of the Radio Hilversum Orchestra in the Netherlands and ongoing guest conductor of the Marseilles Opera. To a great extent, each of us was "on the road" since many of my engagements were in Europe and all over the United States.

For a while, Angela attended the Dalton School in Manhattan and divided her time between her parents. She lived with me, then when Henry returned and settled in the city, she'd go and stay with him during my tours. Angela had the same setup in both her parents' houses—her own room, her own TV, her own stereo and her own phone (pre-mobile). Still, she never liked shuttling between us and with hindsight I realize how hard it must have been for her. No wonder she opted for boarding school.

Angela transferred to Hotchkiss in the tenth grade and was graduated in 1983. Between her junior and senior years, she attended a summer theatre program at Northwestern and became friendly with another student, Lisa Houle. Lisa lived nearby and on the weekends took Angela to her home in West Chicago, Illinois. There, Angela met Lisa's brother, Andre. After Hotchkiss, Angela attended Sarah Lawrence, was graduated in 1988 and, following a brief flirtation with New York life—she was an associate editor at Bantam Books—my daughter announced that she was moving back to California. Angela didn't like the frenetic pace of the city, yet I think part of her decision had to do with getting away from me—and I don't blame her. Around the same time as my daughter's declaration of independence, I went through an alteration in my personal life.

In 1989, after nearly fifteen years, Nico Zaccaria and I went our separate ways. I felt that the relationship had changed—anyway, feelings had changed. In a way it was a clash of cultures, the old world vs. the new. Nobody's going to win that battle. It was over. And so we parted, without rancor. We've remained friends. I saw him a few times in Europe and he often calls me. Nico's 80 now and still vigorous—the only octogenarian I ever knew who has a flat stomach. For me, he'll always be the original Gorgeous Greek.

In 1990, my daughter returned to the west coast. For a while she lived with a friend in Studio City. (Funny, when Angela was born we lived in Studio City.) Andre Houle now lived in Los Angeles and he and Angela became reacquainted.

222

One thing led to another and in five years they were setting a marriage date. The wedding was to take place in June 1996 in California; Angela did most of the planning. We had some fights and arguments usual with nuptial preparations, but I knew she was happy—and so was I. After finishing my *Falstaff* engagements, I planned to join Angela on the coast and get ready for the big day. My knees were good, my daughter was getting married, and I was singing a role I'd always loved. Everything seemed rosy. My joy would come to a crushing halt.

Henry Lewis had health problems for many years. Although he was a energetic man who played tennis and always kept in trim, he also was a life-long smoker; he even smoked in bed. We really fought about that! I wasn't shy about voicing my absolute loathing of cigarettes. Henry heard me but sloughed off my admonitions.

In 1977 Angela and I were living in New York and Henry came over for a visit. He told me that he'd gone for a physical check-up. I was shocked to hear that the doctor warned him that he had the beginnings of coronary artery disease. "Every puff I take on a cigarette will shorten my life," Henry admitted.

You would think a pronouncement like that might have made him stop, and he did half-heartedly try. He couldn't give them up, though. He was hooked. In 1994, he had a piece of his right lung removed. I went over to Sloane-Kettering to visit him every evening. During our walks around the floor, I spotted another patient, Melina Mercouri, a heavy, heavy smoker. She died shortly after that. Henry's operation was successful and he stopped smoking.....for eight months. We begged him to stop for good but neither Angela or I could do anything about it.

Henry went to the opening night of *Falstaff* in January 1996, and soon after left a message on my answering machine. Because so much was going on, I couldn't get back to him right away.

"Oh Henry," I cried when I reached him on Wednesday, "I'm sorry not to have called sooner, but I've been so busy." I wanted to thank him for his warm praise; I didn't get a chance. He cut me off.

"You and your goddamn career!" he blasted. "You couldn't make the time to call me? Don't you know I'm dying?"

I didn't understand what he was talking about; I thought it was the usual Henry rant. Lest that sounds callous, we both were grandstanders and threw everything including the kitchen sink into our battles. I let him rave on a bit and then he calmed down. Basically, he was happy for my success and we had a lovely conversation. We hung up on good terms

A few evenings later, a Friday, I was preparing to go to the Met for the second *Falstaff* performance. I was running late and about to leave when the phone rang. My secretary answered. I expected her to get rid of the caller. She didn't.

"I think you have to take this," she said. "It's the police."

I took the phone.

"Miss Horne?" asked the voice at the other end.

"Yes. What is it?" I was curt because I was in a hurry.

"We're in Henry Lewis's apartment and I am sorry to have to tell you that he's been found dead."

When you hear these words, and this was not the first time that I heard about a loved one's death over the telephone, there's that instant of disbelief.

"What are you saying?" I cried.

The officer at the other end identified himself and repeated his words. I felt a stabbing pain in my stomach. How strange. Henry and I had been divorced for years, I was his ex-wife and yet, in our daughter's absence I was notified as next-of-kin. I told the officer I'd be right over.

Before I left for Henry's apartment, I tried to reach Angela but got her answering machine. The wedding was eight weeks away and Angela and Andre were living in Hermosa Beach. I left a message for her to call me immediately. Meanwhile, my secretary managed to locate Andre. He was literally boarding a plane for a long trip when he got the call on his cellphone. He stayed to comfort Angela and they flew to New York the next morning. My secretary also called the opera house. Stephanie Blythe took over the role of Quickly that evening and had a deserved and enormous success. I was thrilled for her.

When I arrived at Henry's apartment, the police officers explained that they responded to a call from the building's concierge. On Thursday, someone had come for a lesson but left when there was no response. The student simply figured that Henry had forgotten. The concierge thought the same. The next afternoon, the maid arrived and went up to the apartment. She had a key but the door was bolted from the inside. She came down and told the concierge. He phoned the police. They came, broke in and found Henry sprawled on his bed. He'd suffered a massive coronary. They looked through his address book and found my number. One of the officers recognized my name, knew of my relationship to Henry, and called me.

I waited in the living room while the police made the body ready. They took an empty body bag into the bedroom and re-emerged carrying Henry's remains. I remember watching them struggle with the burden—he was so big, six-foot-one. I couldn't believe what was happening. A kindly officer assured me that Henry probably "died instantly" in his sleep. I prayed that was so. I couldn't bear the thought of him suffering.

During the next few days, I pretty much took over—as if I were the next of kin—and made all the arrangements. The funeral took place in the Riverside Memorial Chapel. Angela and I, as well as other friends, gave eulogies. I sang "Never More Will the Wind," written for me by William Bolcom, based on a poem by H.D. We played a tape of Angela's that Henry particularly liked, a gospel song, "Shine On." Earlier in the service we played Henry conducting Verdi's "*Quatro pezzi sacri*" for chorus. I know he had played it a lot in the last months before he died, and I guess that he was preparing himself for "moving on."

Later, I spent some days with Angela at her home in Hermosa Beach. The irony is, at the same time that we were sending out wedding invitations, we were mailing thank you notes for the condolences we'd received for Henry.

Eight weeks after the funeral, Angela and Andre were married. The wedding went beautifully. I was so very touched when Angela told me that except for her Dad's absence, her wedding day was perfect. Oh, do I wish Henry could have been there! And, oh, does it tug at my heart when I look at his namesake, our grandson, and at our granddaughter, Daisy. How he would have loved them! They are his legacy, our legacy. That's the personal side of the story. Professionally, I want to repeat right here what I have said for years: Henry Lewis was the big influence on the mature part of my career; his working with me made the difference between a really good career and a great one.

Thank you, my dear Henry. God rest your soul.

VISSI D'ARTE

Generally speaking, superstars in the classical world earn a lot less than their counterparts in the popular field. There are exceptions. In my discipline, the occasional mega-superstar (e.g. a certain Italian gentleman waving a white handkerchief) can pull in as much as a rock performer; but that's unusual, most opera singers labor in the field to make, at best, a decent living. I was fortunate; all the training, all the years in the choruses and choirs, and the "galley years" in Gelsenkirchen, paid off. At my peak I received the uppermost fees then offered. Again, that's more an exception than a rule. You may have the most beautiful voice and/or a fabulous technique and you can work like a dog but unless you have a certain something—a special quality that, for want of a better word, I call "a big personality"—you may never become a major player. Maria Callas provided a good example. At the peak of her fame, she did not have a "beautiful" voice, per se, but what a personality! When you listen to her take on a number of operatic characters, it's difficult to accept other interpretations from voices ten times as easy on the ears. Thus, while a lovely voice definitely is an asset, it's not everything. I adored listening to the recordings of Conchita Supervia and Kathleen Ferrier, yet in my opinion they both had rotten techniques. Again, if you have the big personality, in many instances, a serviceable bad technique will do.

Also, in the last twenty years, there's been a change in

the way opera is produced; actually, the change really began in the fifties when singers began to be chosen for reasons other than vocal excellence. Look, I don't think that people ever were chosen purely for their voices. Other things entered into it, including looks—and most important, the "personality" factor. You can take two artists of equal vocal merit and one of them will outshine the other simply because of that unique quality. This is the case in all the arts. Sergei Diaghilev, founder and director of the legendary Ballet Russe de Monte Carlo, once was asked which of the company's two leading ballerinas, Anna Pavlova or Olga Spessivitsova, was the greater dancer. He thought for a while and then responded.

"Let's say that an apple tree stands in the middle of a field and on that tree hangs an apple. And though the apple is perfect all around, only one side faces the sun. That side is Spessivitsova."

When it comes to singing, Luciano Pavarotti had as good an explanation for being "special" as any I ever heard. He said that his vocal cords were "kissed by God."

In the past, great voices ruled the roost a bit more than they do today. You know you're not living in a golden age of singing when directors, scenic designers and costumers get more recognition than the performers. This is the age of the "concept," and in order to put their stamp on a production, some directors stop at nothing. A recent *Nozze di Figaro* in Salzburg had Cherubino sniffing the Countess's pantyhose. Excuse me? Do Mozart and his brilliant librettist, Da Ponte, need to be updated to such a bizarre degree? Look, I'm all for invention and innovation but they should SERVE the masterpiece not distort it. Along with this concept business, I get the feeling that great singing, intentionally or not, is being de-emphasized. Look at the reviews. Critics spend paragraphs talking about the conception, the direction, the scenery, and the costumes and mention the singers in a few brief lines at the end. I rest my case.

One thing's for sure, you don't go into opera to make big bucks, you do it because you have to—it's your calling. I was at the top of the operatic heap for nearly three decades and making a damn good living but I spent a lot, too, and many of those expenses had to do with my personal appearance. For all the year's recitals, factor in one or two dresses per recital, and bingo!—already you're into thousands and thousands of dollars. (In my heyday I was fortunate to have had the late Barbara Matera as my designer. Barbara was exceptional in every way and her husband and business partner, Arthur, with the help of his associate, Jared Aswegan, still carry on her tradition of excellence.) It wasn't simply dresses, either. I bought shoes by the ton. I could walk into a store and come out with a minimum of six pairs. I considered style, but comfort was more important. Standing on a stage for hours is no fun when your legs are aching. Stamina is the name of the game. Christina Weidinger, a lovely singer, told me that she was asked by Bidu Sayao, then in her late 70's, what role the younger soprano planned to sing in the upcoming season.

"Susanna," answered Christina. Susanna in *Figaro* had been one of Sayao's best-loved roles.

"Why you want to sing Susanna?"asked the petite Brazilian diva. "On stage all night. At end of opera, tired feet. No parties because feet hurt too much. Pick role that let's you rest a little."

Well, that's one way to make the choice.

A variety of other expenditures go hand-in-hand with wardrobe. Most women I know have their hair done once a week. Although I'm can do my own hair, and did so many times—even for concerts, at one time, you could find me in the beauty parlor four or five days of the week. Thank God

I did my own makeup, on and off stage, and wasn't pinned down to the makeup chair for endless hours. (The Met was an exception, with Jimmy Pinto and Victor Callegari.) Appearance aside, I wish I had a nickel for every dime I spent on transportation! I've accumulated so many frequent flyer miles I could take a round trip to the moon. And don't forget ground transport. Even in New York City where taxis abound, it's too chancy to hail them. I live around the corner from the Met but I'd never tempt fate by trying to hail a cab—I've relied on a limousine service for years. In other cities, arrangements had to be made to get me to and from and from and to, and this too, added up. Clothes and transportation are bona fide business expenses. Still, they take a huge chunk out of your pay. Also, you've got to have enough left over to cover agents and managers and publicists.

On the business side, though I tried to leave the nitty-gritty to my representatives, I couldn't always stay out of negotiations, and a few times I succeeded in putting my foot in my mouth. A memorable example took place in a dressing room at the RAI in Torino. Henry and I were recording *Le Prophète* when three RAI orchestra members came over to tell us that, even though there would be no audience, we could not stop the recording to redo things. Henry and I didn't want this. The conversation grew increasingly heated. Finally, I leaped from my chair, drew myself up to my full height, and crying, "Basta!" I marched over to a door, opened it, and stormed right into a closet! Too shamefaced to turn around, I slammed the door behind me and stood there in the dark listening to the muffled sounds of conversation as Henry ushered the gentleman out of the room.

"Okay, Jackie," he said, rapping on the closet door, "the coast is clear."

Grinning sheepishly, I emerged. Henry and I took one look at each other and burst out laughing.

Give or take a few squabbles over fees, I felt very strongly about honoring my contracts and I think my record speaks for itself. As I've mentioned, there were a few times when, for reasons of health, I should have cancelled and didn't. Except in severe cases, you usually can sing over colds, sore throats, etc. However, you shouldn't challenge ailments like nodes or anything of that sort. My philosophy was, if I sang, I sang. Rarely did I ask anyone to go before the curtain to announce that I was "indisposed." To me, that was a cop-out. Basically, only if Dr. Wilbur Gould, my throat specialist said that I absolutely, positively could not sing, did I withdraw. Dr. Gould was a dedicated, caring physician. Incidentally, a good doctor can be of immeasurable help to singers and not just medically. At the Music Academy of the West, where I now teach, we're very fortunate to have Andrew Mester as a consulting physician to the vocal students. He generously looks after them and gives a lecture at the beginning of the summer on the "care and feeding of the voice." I've heard students ask if they can go out the night before a performance, or if they can drink wine, or if they can they have sex...questions like that. Dr. Mester's answer is always the same—"*Noblesse oblige.*" He's right. When you're given a gift, you're obliged to take care of it, even if you have to deny yourself momentary pleasures.

Speaking of singers, in all honesty, I have to say I don't believe the general level of singing is as good as it used to be. Certainly there are exceptions—wonderful artists and fine teachers—yet students don't get the kind of intensive training that previous generations did, and it's not only in singing. Look at ice-skating. Years ago competitors had to go through compulsory school figures; they got on the ice, without music or fancy costumes, and cut those figures precisely or they lost points. Once the basics were finished, then they went on to the free style. True, those school figures were kind of boring to watch and no one would look at them today, yet they served a purpose. It's all changed; no matter what the line of work, we don't want to see preparations, we want to see results. We are performance driven. That isn't to say that viewers should have to watch school figures, or that audiences should have to listen to someone practice scales and breathing etc., but unless an artist is totally grounded in technique, he or she is not going to be performing in a top notch manner. Moreover, the career probably won't last. Again, there are exceptions. I think particularly of Franco Corelli. I remember hearing him when I was young and being absolutely thrilled by his voice. Even so, you could hear what sounded like a strain. Many other admirers thought his career, although glorious, would be cut short. Boy, were we wrong!

Acquiring a technique is like learning to drive a car. To drive a car, you have to learn how to put it in gear, how to work the accelerator pedal and the brake, how to turn left and right, how to back up and park, etc. You can't drive without knowing all those things. Similarly, in singing you have to know how to breathe, how to support, how to place the tone, how to sing high, middle and low; how to sing soft and loud; how to sing fast and slow—all of this has to be learned. Then when you get it all under your belt, you're free to perform. You don't go on cruise control; you simply attain a certain confidence, which allows you to concentrate on the end and not the means. Unfortunately, singers who really haven't mastered the basics frequently perform blockbuster roles in blockbuster houses. Moreover, today's artists have so many things to deal with. Look at the competition. Who wants to go to the opera every Friday night when you have a half-dozen other possibilities from which to choose—including television and on-line activities that can be enjoyed without stirring from your living room?

Producing opera in itself has become problematic especially in the kind of economy we're experiencing right now. Big contributors have cut back and subscribers are choosier, or not subscribing. We're watching our pennies, and when that happens, the arts are affected—especially one as expensive as opera. What's more, singing has become a year-round profession. Previously, most musicians, including singers, took summers off. Some singers often took the opportunity to learn new roles during the summer months while others took jobs outside the profession. Then along came the summer festivals and we were in it up to our ears. At first, the festivals proliferated in Europe—Bayreuth, Salzburg and Glyndebourne, etc. In this country we had Tanglewood, Ravinia, the Hollywood Bowl—not much else, and they usually lasted a few weeks, not the entire summer! These days every other town has a music festival and musicians are working all year, which is a mixed blessing.

Once upon a time, a fountain of voices gushed out of Italy. Then, the government cut back subsidies for conservatories and provincial opera houses, and the music dried up. At the same time, music in Europe's eastern zone flourished—the communist regimes supported opera houses and paid for singers' and musicians' training. Consequently, the big voices are coming out of places like Russia, Bulgaria, Czechoslovakia, Hungary, and Romania. [N. B. I'm not advocating communism, I'm just stating facts.] It's also a fact that American opera singers are acknowledged to be among the greatest in the world—they may even be the greatest. And we should not forget that they are musical descendents of native artists who may not have dominated world stages, but were indeed, world class. I'm not talking about singers from the distant past, either. I'm speaking of immediate predecessors like Eleanor Steber, Dorothy Kirsten, Risë Stevens, Robert Merrill, Leonard Warren, Jan Peerce and

Richard Tucker, artists who were forced to stay at home because of World War II.

LET'S LOOK AT THE RECORD

I never officially declared a farewell to opera. I did, however, bid a formal adieu to my beloved Rossini. I'd been anticipating this moment and was leading up to it, gradually. While I still could do some operatic roles without undue stress, I had to work harder and harder to achieve the bravura singing Rossini demands. I slaved because I didn't want to give any less to the composer closest to my singing heart. Then I didn't want to struggle anymore. At my final performance of *Il Barbiere* at the Metropolitan Opera, I interpolated my own lyrics into one recitative, saying, "Tonight I sing for you my last Rosina." It was. In 1993, I announced that my appearance as Isabella in *L'Italiana* at Covent Garden would be my Rossini swansong. It was.

I said hello to Gioacchino Rossini when I sang *Cenerentola* in Los Angeles in 1956; thirty-seven years later, I said a fond and grateful goodbye. Later, it occurred to me that Rossini stopped writing operas at the age of thirty-seven. I don't know if there's anything significant in the number, all I know is, Rossini served me well and I believe I served him as well. Once he was out of my performance life, I did odds and ends, the *Falstaff* at the Met and the role of Geneviève in *Pelléas et Mélisande*. Although the Met really didn't have anything for me after that, offers still came from Europe. For the first time, however, I found myself weighing the possibility of doing an engagement rather than eagerly accepting it. Why should I sing the roles that I was famous for without the facility that had been a hallmark of my voice?

When I was in full career, the voice was never out of my head—it was a constant in the back of my mind. What do I have to sing next? What shape am I in? What condition is my voice in? Do I have to practice? In full career, you can deal with this subliminal nagging because you are empowered by your talent not to mention your "youth." As I grew older, additional questions, ones which never entered my mind before, whirled in my brain: Did I want to transpose this aria down a half step? Did I want to change this cadenza? Did I want to do this, that or the other thing with the score? Compromise became the name of the musical game and for a while, I made the necessary concessions. I dropped Rossini, then I stopped doing parts that called for extensive high notes. Yet even as I adjusted my repertoire, I had to factor in other particulars—like travel.

I never was a traveler by choice. When I was a little girl I didn't like being away from home, I didn't even want to spend the night at my grandmother's. When I grew up, I journeyed all over the world and while I enjoyed seeing other countries, I traveled because of my career. After four decades of roving, did I want to schlep to the airport and fly off to live in a hotel for four or five weeks away from home in order to sing eight performances of something that I'd sung many, many times before—probably better? Was it worth it?

In 1996, I developed a swelling on my vocal cord. I had to stop singing for a while till the inflammation went down. It did and I started singing again. The swelling returned. It was on an area where it could easily cause a rupture. So I stopped singing again. After an extended vocal rest (plus some cortisone) the swelling went away for good. All of this occurred within weeks of Henry's death. Call it coincidence, call it psychological, whatever; all I know is, I got very reflective. And though I did a lot of concert and recital singing after I gave up opera, the question kept coming up: Was it worth it?

One day, it wasn't. And, since I didn't want to be one of those singers whose farewell appearances last for years, I simply stopped singing opera.

I honestly admit that in the midst of my career, I didn't give a thought to "teaching" or "giving back" or anything like that. Why would I? I was too busy doing. I did, however, take a few sidesteps off my beaten path. In the early 80's, at the suggestion of Herbert Breslin, I produced as well as sang in a series of three Rossini operas at Carnegie Hall. At the time, I asked Matthew Epstein to help—in his position at Columbia Artists Management, he knew the young singers who could understudy. The Rossini concerts were a resounding success. That was enough for me; I wasn't interested in producing operas. Matthew, on the other hand, grooved on it! He created and presented his own mini-series at Carnegie Hall and eventually became one of the big players in opera production. At present, among other endeavors, he's Artistic Director of the Chicago Lyric Opera and Artistic Consultant to the Santa Fe Opera.

I too have adjudicated in various vocal contests—among others, the Cardiff Singer of the World contest. I first went there in 1993 along with Joan Sutherland, Gérard Souzay and three or four others—musicologists from China and Eastern Europe. Matthew Epstein, at that time the Artistic Director of the Welsh National Opera, was heading the jury. On the last evening, we judges were having dinner at the restaurant in the concert hall. The room was filled with people. Our table was somewhat separated from the rest of the diners, many of whom kept looking our way, to get a glimpse of Joan, I'm sure. We were waiting for dessert and coffee when Matthew, with his usual brio, appeared carrying a sheaf of papers.

"I thought it would be a nice gesture," said the impresario as he passed the papers around the table, "if all of us sang the Welsh National Anthem before the prizes are given."

I took a look at the sheet I'd been handed. Matthew had the music printed out so that we could sight read. The staff was there, the notes were there, and underneath were the words—in Welsh. At a signal from Matthew, Joan, Gérard, the others and I tentatively and quietly, began to sing. We struggled through it once, mostly trying to figure out how to pronounce the words, and were about to go at it again, when a gentleman appeared at our table, and bowed.

"Excuse me," he began, "my friends and I..." and here he gestured towards a table where fifteen to twenty men and women were seated, "...would like to sing our anthem for you. Would that be all right?"

"Yes, yes, please do," all of us enthused.

The gentleman bowed again before returning to his table. He said something to the group, and then, as one, they rose, turned to face us and immediately began singing their anthem in those glorious stentorian voices which seem to be a birthright of the Welsh. The rafters rang, and chills went down my back. All I could think of was John Ford's film, *How Green Was My Valley*. When the last note faded away, we judges burst into cheers. What a moment! I love the warmth of the Welsh people, which is what Shaw was getting at when he said, "The Welsh are Italians in the rain."

Judging is one thing, teaching is quite another. In my heyday, I barreled along my career path with blinders on as far as what would happen after I stopped performing. I never consciously thought about teaching, yet I always was intrigued by the mechanics as well as the science of singing. As my sixtieth birthday approached, I started reflecting a bit more. I'd had a fabulous and fantastic life in music. Was I going to sit at home and receive faxes, telegrams and flowers? Somehow it didn't seem the right way to celebrate. I wanted to give something back, but how? I began talking to friends and colleagues, and a theme emerged.

Once upon a time in America, music was everywhere, classical as well as popular; recitals were a common occurrence even in small towns. Not only was the recital trail a training ground for aspiring artists, renowned performers also journeyed from place to place. Major cities had concert series in performance halls and if the halls didn't exist, well, dancers like Alicia Markova and musicians like Isaac Stern performed in local high schools. I did my share of those recitals, and loved doing it. Of course television just about killed this kind of entertainment. Why go out and see one or two artists when you could see an entire symphony orchestra on a box in your living room? By the time I retired from opera, I was convinced that recitals were an endangered species. (Little did I know that classical music itself was getting closer to extinction!) I got on my white horse and decided to ride off and rescue the recital! Where to begin?

A little over a year before I turned sixty, my dear friend Farol Seratean died. Farol had left me $50,000 in her will to be used for my favorite charities. The lightning bolt came. I called her estate lawyer and asked him if I could use the bequest as seed money to start a non-profit foundation.

"Absolutely," he answered.

In November of 1993, we called a press conference to announce the establishment of The Marilyn Horne Foundation. On January 16, 1994, on a bitter cold Sunday afternoon, the Foundation officially was launched during my sixtieth birthday celebration in Carnegie Hall. What an amazing occasion! Montserrat Caballé, Flicka von Stade,

Helen Donath, Ruth Ann Swenson, Sam Ramey, Jimmy Levine, Marty Katz, and Warren Jones were among the performers. The audience was full of celebrities from the classical music world. My colleagues performed brilliantly in an atmosphere that gave new meaning to the word *gemütlich*. I must share one moment. A few up-and-coming artists also were on the program that Sunday including a beautiful young soprano. Before she did her turn, she stood on stage, looked out at the audience and said,

"In case you're wondering, it is truly awesome, terrifying and humbling to sit here while your idols get up and perform, and then sing yourself. I'm dying, and I just wanted you to know that in advance."

And then Renée Fleming sang.

The Marilyn Horne Foundation's mission is to support, encourage, and preserve the art of singing through the presentation of vocal recitals and related educational activities. Truly, it is one of the positive forces of my "golden age." (Whoever thought up that expression for the senior years? I much prefer Bette Davis's quote: "Old age is not for sissies.") We've established artist residencies throughout the country with local presenters, co-sponsored grants that allow the presenters to produce recitals and educational programs with young artists whom the foundation has selected. We've had a close and wonderful association with the Juilliard School, where most of our gala recitals and master classes have been held. Besides our young singers, many established artists have performed for the Foundation—and a good number have conducted master classes. We've been fortunate to count Carnegie Hall among our allies, and recently formed a new partnership with that august institution. (I'm so looking forward to the MHF recitals in the recently completed Zankel Hall.) The Foundation is sup-

ported by donations from individuals, foundations, corpo-
rations and government entities. I'm inordinately proud to
be associated with this magnificent effort and if this is beginning to sound like a pitch, so be it—all donations are
gratefully accepted!

1994 was a big year in many ways. Besides turning 60
and launching the foundation, I was named Director of the
Vocal Program at the Music Academy of the West (where I
had studied with Lehmann in 1953; I now had her job). My
dear friend Lotfi Mansouri, recently retired General Director of the San Francisco Opera, who also studied with
Lehmann at the Music Academy, said to me, "Jackie, this is
pure kismet." I guess it probably is. I had only a few weeks
to spare from my performing schedule that year, but by 1997,
I was able to spend the entire summer in Santa Barbara.
(Not hard to do, even with all the work.) In the summer of
2003, I was busy with the Music Academy and, at the same
time, had the great pleasure (and the great effort) to help
put together a commemorative album of my recordings for
Universal Records. I had to listen to myself at all stages of
my career and select from them. You know what? I was a
damn good singer.

In over four decades, I sang at least a thousand opera
performances and gave over 1300 recitals. This does not
count all of the performances from age 2 to 20, nor does it
include endless orchestral performances, benefits, recording sessions, and lord knows what else! Now I'm out there
to make sure that the next generation of artists has the opportunity, if not to beat my record, then at least to match it.
That's why I teach.

It's funny, when I started the foundation I didn't think
of myself as a teacher. Now I realize that I like giving back,
and that's really what teaching is. When I listen to singers,
while the voice comes first, I'm looking for that personality

241

too. After that, I look for musicianship. A person may have a lovely voice but does he/she possess an innate musicality? Frankly, I'm a sucker for a great instrument yet even if the person has a great instrument, he/she must also have a solid musical foundation. I don't enjoy teaching singers who aren't grounded. They need to learn the basics and they have to know the different styles—singing Handel is way different from singing Puccini. Speaking of composers, I'm often asked who my favorites are. I know everyone expects me to say Rossini, but the truth is I could exist on Bach, Mozart and Beethoven. For what it's worth, if I were on a desert island and could have only one piece of music with me, I'd choose Bach's *St. Matthew Passion* because that's the greatest music of all time.

In working with singers who are either on the brink of a career or already in it, I tell them there are no shortcuts to greatness. Excellence is the key word and they cannot jump over the steps. Despite the odds, I still retain the hope that great singing will come through. That's why I urge them forward and while I do it as gently as possible, one can't always be too "gentle," as the following story will show.

During a master class in Montreal, I sat at a desk at the side of the stage with music in front of me and a pencil in my hand. A tall slender young woman with long blonde hair walked out from backstage. She wore a stunning short strapless gown and my first thought was, if her talent equals her looks, this kid is it. She introduced herself, announced her selection, and leaning into the crook of the piano, she began to sing.

The voice was okay, but something was missing. I waited until she finished and after praising what she did well, I stood up and walked over to offer my suggestions. She towered above me.

"Look, you simply have to have support for the voice

and you've got to get it from here!" I placed my hand on her waist and pressed firmly against her body. "Now, push!" I exhorted.

"But, Miss Horne," she said smiling nervously, "if I do what you say, my dress will fall down."

The audience roared. I wouldn't be deterred.

"Okay, I tell you what. I'll hold up your dress, you get your support going!" Thus saying, I reached over, grasped her bodice with both hands, lifted it, and nodded to the accompanist to begin playing.

"You see," I shouted over the applause as she finished a much improved rendition, "it's all about *support!*"

You know what?—that says a lot. It *is* all about support, and that's why, at seventy, I'm still singing! Sure, Berlin, Rogers, Carmichael, Arlen, Gershwin and Simon have replaced Rossini, Handel, Donizetti, Bellini, Verdi and Bizet, but I'm still here. Also, I must add that I'm thrilled to be performing along with artists like the fabulous Don Pippin, my conductor, pianist and arranger. Oh, and sixty-five years after I started out as a sister act with Gloria, I'm singing with a new female "partner"—the incomparable Barbara Cook. Part of the reason I so enjoy working with people like Don and Barbara is the fun we have together. The work is hard and we have to go at it seriously, yet there's always room for laughs. I'm still a "cut-up," I guess, but one who's able to get serious when she has to. After all, that's the way Bentz Horne brought me up.

In all these endeavors, I am so fortunate to have the support of my friends, my colleagues, and my extended family, which of course includes my beautiful, gifted daughter (she just received her Doctorate in Psychology), my handsome, brilliant son-in-law, and my two darling grandchildren. Truly, I'm blessed.

In the final analysis, I think I was put on this earth first to sing, and then, for as long as I'm able, to support those who come after me—perhaps not as literally as the young lady in Montreal, but to assist in every way to make sure that the song continues.

DISCOGRAPHY

WORK	PRODUCED BY Cast or orchestra/role taken by MH	DATE /OPERA OR CONCERT (SELECTIONS)	Conductor(Accompanist) / Composer	
Four Russian Choruses, Three Souvenirs	Columbia ML-5107	1955/1956 Concert	Stravinsky	Stravinsky
Gesualdo: Madrigals and Sacred Music	CBS Odyssey 32886 Gesualdo Madrigal Singers	1955/1956	Stravinsky/Craft	Gesualdo
Wesendonck Lieder, Kindertotenlieder	Decca/London OS26147 Royal Philharmonic	1968/1970	Lewis	Wagner, Mahler
French and Spanish Songs	Decca/London OS-26301	1972/1974 Concert M. Katz, piano		Bizet, Debussy, De Falla, Nin

Lieder	Decca/London OS26302	1972/1974 Concert	M. Katz, piano	Wolf, Schubert, Schumann, R. Strauss
El Amor brujo	CBS/Odyssey/Columbia MBK44721 New York Philharmonic	1975/1978 Concert	Bernstein	De Falla
Giovanna D'Arco and Rossini Songs	Cetra/CBS M37296	1981/1982 Concert	*L'ultimo ricordo, Se il vuol la molinara, Canzonetta spagnuola/La passeggiata, Adieux à la vie, La pastorella, Addio a Rossini* M. Katz, piano	D'Arco, Rossini
At La Scala	Cetra/CBS M-37819	1981/1983	Concert/Recital M. Katz, piano Purcell, Handel, Beethoven, Alvarez, Turina, Montsalvatge, Granados, Obradors, Rossini, Duparc, Poulenc, Copland, Donizetti, Foster	
Carmen Jones	RCA	1954	Carmen (voice-over)	Herschel Gilbert Bizet
Folk Songs of the New World	Capitol	1954		Roger Wagner

DISCOGRAPHY

Title	Label / Details	Year	Notes
Lullabies from Round the World	Tom Thumb Records T302	1956	
Elektra	Cetra / with Borkh, Madeira, Lorenz	1957 / MH: Fourth Maidservant	Mitropoulos Strauss
Laud to the Nativity	Capitol / Los Angeles Philharmonic	1960	Oratorio/Symphony Wallenstein Respighi
I Pagliacci	Live Recording/GOP / Del Monaco, Bastianini MH: Nedda	1962	Opera De Fabritiis Leoncavallo
Giulio Cesare	Decca/London OS25876 / Sutherland, Sinclair MH: Cornelia	1963	Opera Bonynge Handel
The Age of Bel Canto	Decca OSA1257 / Sutherland, Conrad/London Symphony	1963	*Meraspe* (Lampugnani), *Semele* (Handel), *Artaxerxes* (Arne), *Angela* (Boieldieu/Gail), *Semiramide* (Rossini), *Beatrice di Tenda* (Bellini), *Lucrezia Borgia* (Donizetti), *Bolero* (Arditi) Bonynge
Norma	Decca/London 425-488-2 (highlights 421 886-2) / with Sutherland, J. Alexander, Cross	1964 / MH: Adalgisa	Opera Bonynge Bellini

	Label/Number & Performers	Year	Description	Conductor/Composer
Presenting Marilyn Horne	Decca OS 25910	1964	Recital: *Semiramide* (Rossini), *Le Prophète* (Meyerbeer), *La Clemenza di Tito* (Mozart), *Les Huguenots* (Meyerbeer), *L'Italiana in Algeri* (Rossini), *La Figlia del reggimento* (Donizetti) *La Cenerentola* (Rossini)	Lewis
Beethoven: Ninth Symphony	Decca/417-755-2 Sutherland, King, Talvela Vienna Philharmonic	1965	Symphony	Schmidt-Isserstedt Beethoven
Mozart: *Requiem*	Decca/London Weekend Classics 417-681-2 Ameling, Benelli, Franc	1965	Oratorio	Kertesz Mozart
Souvenir of a Golden Era (Rossini), *Semiramide*	Decca BA-322 411829-1/OS 25967 Montecchi (Bellini), *L'Italiana in Algeri* (Rossini), ("Sappho," Gounod), *Le Prophète* (Meyerbeer), *Alceste* (Gluck), *Il Trovatore* (Verdi)	1965	*Il Barbiere di Siviglia* (Rossini), *I Capuleti ed i Montecchi* (Bellini), *Fidelio* (Beethoven), *Otello,* (Rossini), *Tancredi* (Rossini), *Orphée et Eurydice* (Gluck), *Sapho* (Gluck), *Il*	Lewis
Anna Bolena	Live Recording/Standing Room Only-LCD 149-3 Suliotis	1966	Opera	Lewis Donizetti

248

DISCOGRAPHY

Our Garden of Hymns w. Tennessee Ernie Ford	Capitol ST2845 Tennessee Ernie Ford	1966		Facinato
Semiramide	Decca/London 425-481-2 Sutherland, Serge, Malas, Rouleau MH: Arsace	1966 Opera		Bonynge Rossini
Arias from French Opera	Decca	1967	*Werther* (Massenet), *Mignon* (Thomas), *Carmen* (Bizet), *Samson et Dalila* (Saint-Saens)	Lewis
La Gioconda	Decca 430-042-2/London OSA 1388 Tebaldi, Domiquez, Bergonzi, Merrill, Ghiuselev MH: Laura	1967 Opera		Gardelli Ponchielli
Sings Bach and Handel Arias	Decca/London OS29277 / OS26067 Vienna Cantata Orchestra	1967	*Magnificat*, Christmas Oratorio, St. Matthew Passion, Messiah, *Rodelinda*, Opera Selections	Lewis Bach/Handel
Verdi: *Requiem*	Decca/London 411-944-2 Sutherland, Pavarotti, Talvela	1967 Oratorio		Solti Verdi

DISCOGRAPHY

Don Giovanni
Decca
Sutherland, Lorengar, Bacquier, Krenn, Gramm MH: Zerlina — 1968 — Opera — Bonynge — Mozart

L'Italiana in Algeri
Live Recording/Arkadia 462
Bottazzo, Petri, Mazzini, Monachesi MH: Isabella — 1968 — Opera — Franci — Rossini

Anna Bolena
Decca
Suliotis, Ghiaurov, J. Alexander MH: Giovanna Seymour — 1969 — Opera — Varviso — Donizetti

La Prise de Troie/
Les Troyens
Live Recording
Gedda, Luchetti, Massard MH: Cassandre — 1969 — Opera — Prêtre — Berlioz

L'Assedio di Corinto
Live Recording
Sills, Diaz, Bonisolli MH: Neocle — 1969 — Opera — Prêtre — Rossini

Les Troyens
Live Recording/Melodram MEL-37060 — 1969 — Opera
Rome Italian Radio Symphony — Berlioz

Le Prophète
Live recording/ MYTO Records MCD 90318 (Qualiton) 1970 — Opera
Gedda, Rinaldi, Amis El Hage MH: Fides, Turin Radio Symphony, Lewis — Meyerbeer

Royal Family of Opera Decca/London RFO-S-1 — 1970 — Compilation

Title	Recording	Year	Type	Conductor	Composer
Marilyn Horne Sings *Carmen*	Decca/London 21055 Molese MH: Carmen	1970	Opera	Lewis	Bizet
Marilyn Horne: Rossini Opera Arias and Mahler Rückert Lieder	Live/Arkadia GI808	1971	Concerts in Italy		
People	Live recording	1971			
You Could Drive A Person Crazy, Bye, Bye Baby	Live Recording Farrell, Burnett, Channing	1971			
Carmen	DG 427-440-2 McCracken, Maliponte, Krause MH: Carmen	1972	Opera	Bernstein	Bizet
Man of la Mancha	Columbia S31237 Tucker, Kahn, Nabors	1972	Crossover	Weston (?)	
Sings Rossini	Decca/London 417-1372/411-8281 1972 *L'Assedio di Corinto, la Donna del lago*			Lewis	Rossini

DISCOGRAPHY

Cendrillon	Live Recording Von Stade, Grist MH: Prince Charmant	1973	Opera		Lewis	Massenet
Il Barbiere di Siviglia	Live Recording MH: Rosina	1973	Opera	Una voce poco fa	Schippers	Rossini
Marilyn Horne's Greatest Hits	London OS 26346	1973	Arias from *Il Barbiere de Siviglia, Les Huguenots, Carmen, Norma, Orfeo ed Euridice, Mignon, Semiramide*			
Marilyn Horne Sings Rossini	Decca 6.48134	1973	Various from *Barbiere, Semiramide, L'Italiana, Tancredi, Cenerentola, Otello, La Donna*			Rossini
A la Scala	Live Recording	1975	Recital		M. Katz, piano	Rossini, Dvorak, Arne, popular
La Navarraise	RCA Domingo, Milnes, Bacquier MH: Anita	1975	Opera		Lewis	Massenet
Rinaldo	Live Recording Ramey, Mandac, Rodgers, Walker MH: Rinaldo	1975	Opera		Foster	Handel

DISCOGRAPHY

	Year	Concert/Recital	Conductor	Composer
Scheherazade, El Amor Brujo CBS 76707	1975	Concert/Recital	Bernstein	Ravel, Falla
Il Trovatore Decca/London 421-310-2 Sutherland, Pavarotti, Wixell, Ghiaurov MH: Azucena	1976	Opera	Bonynge	Verdi
Le Prophète CBS M3K-34340 McCracken, Scotto, Hines MH: Fides, Royal Philharmonic	1976	Opera	Lewis	Meyerbeer
Mahler's Second Symphony DG 427262 Neblett, Chicago Symphony	1976		Abbado	Mahler
Suor Angelica CBS Scotto, Cotrubas MH: Zia Principessa	1976	Opera	Maazel	Puccini
Il Trittico CBS M3k-35912 Scotto, Cotrubas	1977	Opera	Maazel	Puccini
Lucrezia Borgia Decca/London 421-497-2 Sutherland, Wixell, Aragall MH: Orsini	1977	Opera	Bonynge	Donizetti
Mahler's Third Symphony RCA RCD2-1757 Chicago Symphony	1977		Levine	Mahler

Mignon
CBS 4 34590
1977 Opera
Vanzo, Zaccaria, Welting, Von Stade MH: Mignon
De Almeida Thomas

Orlando Furioso
Erato ECD-88190
1977 Opera
Los Angeles, Valentini Terrani, Zaccaria, Bruscantini MH: Orlando Scimone Vivaldi

Rinaldo (Houston)
Live Recording
1977 Opera
Handel

Tancredi
Live Recording
1977 Opera
Rinaldi, Casellato MH: Tancredi, Rome Opera
Ferro Rossini

*Rückert Lieder,
Lieder eines
fahrenden Gesellen*
(Songs of a Wayfarer)
Decca/London 430135
1978
Los Angeles Philharmonic
Mehta Mahler

Tancredi
Live Recording
1978 Carnegie Hall Opera
Ricciarelli, Palacio, Zaccaria MH: Tancredi
Queler Rossini

With Montserrat Caballé at the Hollywood Bowl Live Record 1978 *Semiramide* (Rossini), *Norma* (Bellini), *La Gioconda* (Ponchielli), *Les Contes d'Hoffmann* (Offenbach), *La Donna del lago* (Rossini), *Samson et Dalila* (Saint-Saens), *Les Huguenots*
Foster

DISCOGRAPHY

CBS Masterworks Salzburg Festspiele — CBS #MW5 — 1979 — Compilation with various artists

Dal Vivo al Teatro Regio di Parma — Bongiovanni — 1980 — Recital: *Rodelinda, l'Assedio di Corinto* (Rossini), *Tancredi* (Rossini), *Il Trovatore* (Verdi), *Lucrezia Borgia* (Donizetti), *La Sonnambula* (Bellini), *Mignon* (Thomas), *Carmen* (Bizet), *Les Huguenots*
M. Katz, piano

L'Italiana in Algeri — Erato ECD 88200 — 1980 — Opera — Ramey, Palacio, Zaccaria, Trimarchi MH: Isabella — Scimone — Rossini

Recital in Warsaw — Muza — 1980 — *Rodelinda, L'Assedio di Corinto, Meraspe, Lucrezia Borgia, Tancredi, Carmen, Samson et Dalila,* lieder of R. Strauss, songs of De Falla and American popular
M. Katz, piano

Semiramide — Live Recording — 1980 — Opera — Caballé, Ramey, Araiza, Kavrakos MH: Arsace — Lopez-Cobos — Rossini

Semiramide Aix-en-Provence — Live Recording/HRE (Lyric) 1002-2 — 1980 — Opera — Rossini

255

Semiramide Aix-en-Provence   Live Recording/Standing Room Only-Legato Classics 509-2 1980 Opera Lopez-Cobos Rossini
Caballé, Ramey, Araiza, Kavrakos

A Salute to George London RCA/Victor ARL 1-4667   1981   *Semiramide*   Concert/Recital

Diva!   CBS M3X 79343   1981
Caballé, Cotrubas, Scotto, Te Kanawa, Von Stade

DIVA!   CBS 79343-36937   1981
Caballé, Cotrubas, Scotto, Te Kanawa, Von Stade

Great Artists at the Met: Marilyn Horne RCA Special Products for the Met Opera Guild MET 111-A 1981
From Previous recorded albums 1964-80, Bellini, Rossini, Gluck, Bizet, Meyerbeer, Bertoni

La Donna del lago   Live recording   1981   Opera
Von Stade, Blake, Raffanti, Zaccaria   MH: Malcolm   Scimone Rossini

Live from Lincoln Center Decca/London 417-587-2 / 289-458-207-2 1981   *Ernani* (Verdi), *Norma*, *La*
Sutherland, Pavarotti   *Gioconda, Il Trovatore, Beatrice di Tenda, La*
                                                         Donna del lago   Bonynge

Met Stars in Hollywood Met Opera Guild MET 205   1981   Concert: The Boy Next Door - Meet Me
Farrell, Milnes, Merrill   in Saint Louis

DISCOGRAPHY

Alternative Arias - Rossini Cetra/CBS CDC18 1982 *Il Barbiere di Siviglia, Tancredi, La Gazza ladra, Zelmira, Maometto II* Zedda Rossini

Giovanna D'Arco, Ariette Inedite Cetra LROD 1002 1982 M. Katz, piano

Handel Arias Erato/ECD 88034 1982 Recital: *Rinaldo, Serse, Partenope, Agrippina, Orlando* Scimone Handel

Il Barbiere di Siviglia Cetra/CBS M3K-37862 1982 Opera Nucci, Barbacini, Ramey, Dara MH: Rosina Chailly Rossini

In concert at the Met with Leontyne Price RCA Red Seal RCD 24609 1982 *Così fan tutte, Rinaldo, Aida* (Verdi), *Norma, Madama Butterfly* (Puccini), *Rodelinda, L'Assedio di Corinto, Les Huguenots* with Leontyne Price Levine

La Cenerentola Live recording 1982 Opera Araiza, Montarsolo, Bruscantini MH: Angelina Bernardi Rossini

Beethoven's Ninth Symphony RCA Silver Seal 60477 1983 M. Price, Vickers, Salminen, New York Philharmonic Mehta Beethoven

Title	Label	Year	Type/Work	Performers	Conductor	Composer
Christmas with the Mormon Tabernacle Choir	CBS	1983			Ottley	
Live at La Scala	CB-331 74105	1983	Recital:	M. Katz, piano		Rossini, Handel
Marilyn Horne: Aria Alternative	CBS Masterworks MK 44820/38731	1983	*Giovanna d'Arco* and opera arias	M. Katz, piano		
Padmavati	EMI 7478918	1983	Opera	Van Dam, Gedda, Berbié, Burles MH: Padmavati	Plasson	Roussel
Tancredi	Cetra	1983	Opera	Cuberli, Palacio, Zaccaria MH: Tancredi	Weikert	Rossini
Sings Arias from French Opera	Erato	1984	*Zerline* (Auber), *Samson et Dalila, la Grande Duchesse de Gerolstein* (Offenbach), *Sapho* ("Sappho," Gounod), *La Vivandière* (Godard), *Hérodiade* (Massenet), *La Favorite* (Donizetti), *Medée* (Cherubini)	Foster	
West Side Story	DG	1984	Somewhere		Bernstein	Bernstein
Semele	Live recording	1985	Opera	Battle, Blake, Ramey, Gall, McNair MH: Ino, Juno	Nelson	Handel

258

DISCOGRAPHY

Beautiful Dreamer (The Great American Songbook) English Chamber Orchestra	London 417-242-2	1986	Davis
Bianca e Falliero (Pesaro) Legato Classics LCD 138-3 Ricciarelli, Merritt, Surjan		1986 Opera	Renzetti
Mahler's Second Symphony Phillips 420824-2 Te Kanawa		1986 Boston Symphony	Ozawa Mahler
Ermione (Pesaro) Legato Classics LCD 159-2 Caballé, Merritt, Blake, Morino MH: Andromaca		1987 Opera	Kuhn Rossini
Music for Life DG 427-386-2		1987	Concert/Recital: Copland's Long Time Ago, Simple Gifts, At the River
Music for Life DG 429-392-2		1987	Concert/Recital: Copland's Long Time Ago
Rossini Arias London 421306-2 Royal Philharmonic/L'Orchestre de la Suisse Romande		1988	Lewis
A Salute to American Music-Richard Tucker Foundation Gala XVI RCA Red Seal 09026-61508-2		1991	Concert/Recital: God Bless America

Title	Label / Catalog	Year	Notes
Canciones-Songs-Melodies Decca 433 917-2	Berganza, Lorengar, Te Kanawa	1992	Concert/Recital
Marilyn Horne: RCA Red Seal Rossini Celebration		1992	22 Rossini *Canti*
Grandi Voci: Marilyn Horne London 440 415-2		1994	Arias by Handel, Rossini, Bizet, Saint-Saens, Gounod, Gluck, Mozart
Stelle della Lirica Vol. IV Marilyn Horne, Rossini Renaissance Live Recording/LV 979 1994 Documents Live Recordings, Italy			Abbado, Lewis, Schippers
The Men in My Life RCA Jerry Hadley, Thomas Hampson, Samuel Ramey, Spiro Malas		1994	Gemignani
Top Ten Mezzos 2 London 443 378-2		1994	Compilation
World of Opera Favorites Decca 448 053-2		1995	Compilation
Great Opera Duets Decca 448 058-2		1996	*Semiramide* Compilation

Rossini Heros and Heroines — London 289 458 219-2 — 1998

Treasures of Baroque Opera — London 289 458 217-2 — 1998 — Compilation — Baker, Berganza, Bott, Greevy, Kirkby, Pavarotti, Shirley-Quirk, Souzay, Sutherland

Rossini Gala, Spectacular Arias — Decca 289 458 247-2 — 2000 — Compilation — Berganza, Corena, Ghiaurov, Nucci, Pavarotti, Sutherland, Tebaldi

The Glories of Handel Opera — Decca 289 458 249-2 — 2000 — Compilation — Berganza, Bowman, Kirkby, Pavarotti, Sutherland, Tebaldi

Songs of Flowers, Bells and Death — Albany Records TROY415 — 2001 — Silent Boughs (1963) "To Jackie" — Lewis, William Kraft — Los Angeles Chamber Orchestra

L'Italiana in Algeri — Opera d'Oro OPD-1382 — 2003 — Opera, at La Scala, live — Abbado — Rossini — Alva, Montarsolo, Dara, Rinaldi MH: Isabella

Airs d'Operas I Solisti Veniti — Erato NUM 75047 — W. L. Foster

All Through The Night (Lullabies) — RCA 09026-61278-2 — Brohn, Katz

Ave Maria (The Ultimate Sacred Christmas Album) — London 465932 — Compilation: O Thou That Tellest Good Tidings, Vienna Cantata Orchestra — Lewis — Handel

DISCOGRAPHY

Christmas Adagios   London 468503. *Christmas Oratorio*, BMV 248, No. 19 *Schlafe mein Liebster*
Compilation, Vienna Cantata Orchestra
Lewis   Bach

Bianca e Falliero (Critical Edition)   Ricordi/Fonit Cetra RFCD 2008   Opera
Ricciarelli, Merritt, Surjan
Renzetti

Brahms Alto Rhapsody   Telarc CD-80176
Atlantic Symphony
Shaw   Brahms

Brahms Viola Sonatas/Songs Op. 91   BMG/RCA 09026-61276-2   Concert with Pinchas Zukerman
M. Katz, piano   Brahms

Carols from Christmas Past   Investors Savings and Loan Association

Classic Opera: Mozart, Haydn, Gluck   London 421-329-2
Popp, Sutherland, Berganza, Burrows, Fischer-Dieskau

Dvorak, Schumann, Mendelssohn   BMG/RCA 09026-61684-2   Concert/Recital
Von Stade   M. Katz, piano

Falstaff   RCA Red Seal 09026-60705-2   Opera
Panerai, Sweet, Titus, Lopardo   Davis   Verdi

Favorite Rossini Arias sung by Favorite Artists   Sony Classical SMK 48399   *O patria; Di tanti palpiti; Una voce poco fa*
Ricciareli, Ramey, Baltsa

Golden Opera   London 421-322-2   *Habanera; Mon coeur s'ouvre à ta voix*
Sutherland, Pavarotti, Popp, Crespin, Fassbaender, Bergonzi, Corelli, Milnes

Great Opera Duets   London 421-314-2   *Norma* Duet
Sutherland, Freni, Ludwig, Pavarotti, Del Monaco, Bergonzi, Bastianini, Fischer-Dieskau

I Capuleti e i Montecchi (Selections)   Carnegie Hall   Live Recording/GDS Opera   Lewis
New Jersey Symphony

Il Mito dell'Opera, Arias of Bach, Handel, Rossini   Bongiovanni GB 1061-2

Il Trovatore (Scenes and Arias)   London 421-310-2   Opera   Bonynge   Verdi
Sutherland, Pavarotti, Wixell, Ghiaurov

La Bohème; Giuseppe Di Stefano GDS 21027   Opera   Molinari-Pradelli   Puccini
De Los Angeles, Konya, Bastianini, Evans

L'Assedio di Corinto   Live Recording/Mel Dram 27043   Opera   Schippers   Rossini
Sills, Bonisolli, Diaz

L'Assedio di Corinto, La Scala   Live Recording/Legato Classics LCD 135-2 Opera   Rossini

DISCOGRAPHY

L'Opéra Français
London 421-876-2
Crespin, Sutherland, Resnik, Pavarotti, Corelli, Di Stefano, Krause, Ghiaurov

Marilyn Horne
Live Recording/Standing Room Only-Legato Classics SRO 822-1
(from live performances, 1966-1979) Arias of Bellini, Berlioz, Wagner, Verdi, Massenet, Strauss, Berg

Marilyn Horne in Concert (1967/1969) Live Recording/Voca 115CD Beethoven, Wagner, Berlioz

Marilyn Horne Sings Opera Arias Erato 88085

Marilyn Horne: Rossini Celebration RCA Red Seal Concert/Recital M. Katz, piano

Marilyn Horne—Rossini, Bellini, Verdi Giuseppe Di Stefano GDS 1207 Lewis, Rescigno, Alessandro

Met Stars in the New World Met Opera Guild 216CD Jeanie with the Light Brown Hair Concert/Recital

Norma
Live Recording/Frequenz 043-020 Opera Bonynge Bellini
Sutherland, Bergonzi, Siepi

Opera Arias
RCA Gold Seal 60022
Von Stade, Miguenes, Esham, Domingo, Raimondi

264

Opera Weekend	Decca/London 421-018-2	Habanera		Various
Orfeo ed Euridice (also Highlights)	Decca 417-410-2 / London OSA1285 (OS-26214 highlights) Opera Lorengar, Donath, Royal Opera House Orchestra		Solti	Gluck
Presenting Marilyn Horne	Royal Opera House Orchestra, Covent Garden London OS 25910 *La Figlia del Reggimento, La Clemenza di Tito, L'Italiana in Algeri, La Cenerentola, Les Huguenots, Le Prophète, Semiramide,* Royal Opera House Orchestra		Lewis	
Recital	Erato 4509-98501-2 DDD Concert/Recital		L. Foster	Donizetti, Gounod, Offenbach
Rinaldo (La Fenice)	Nuova Era 6813/14 Opera Gasdia, Palacio, Weidinger, De Caroles		Fisher	Handel
Rossini Bicentennial Birthday Gala	EMI Classics 0777 7 54643 2 0 Von Stade, Blake, Merritt, Hampson, Ramey, Voigt		Norrington	
Rossini Recital	RCA Red Seal 09026-60811-2 Concert/Recital Vienna Cantata Orchestra		M. Katz, piano	Rossini
Semele	DG 435 782-2 Opera Battle, Ramey, Aler, McNair		Nelson	Handel

Tancredi Fonit Cetra/CBS CDC 19 Opera Rossini
Palacio, Zaccaria, Berli, Di Nissa, Schuman

The Art of Marilyn Horne London OS 29277 Opera

The Best of the Roger Wagner Chorale Capital SP 8682 He's Gone Away

The Damnation of Faust; Les Troyens (Highlights) Live Recording/Arkadia CDMP 461-4 Opera Berlioz
Gedda, Soyer, Petkov, Luchetti, Clabassi, Verrett, Massard

The King and I Phillips 438-007-2 Mauceri Rodgers/Hammerstein
Andrews, Kingsley

The Rose Tattoo (Soundtrack) Columbia CL727 MH sings opening credits

Verdi: *Requiem* Live Recording/Myto Records MCD 90525 (Lyric) Abbado Verdi
Scotto, Pavarotti, Ghiaurov, RAI Roma Orchestra

We Wish You A Merry Christmas CBS 321 Various

INDEX

OF NAMES APPEARING IN TEXT

Index

Index

270

ACKNOWLEDGMENTS

How can I acknowledge all those who have helped me along the way? If it were a Rossini aria, I might have sung their praises *prestissimo*, but to write down all the names would fill another book!

Please, dear friends, family, colleagues, and you "wonderful people out there" at Baskerville Publishers and Zachary Shuster Harmsworth, write your names in the space below, and know that I thank you from the bottom of my heart!

—Marilyn Horne

EDITORS' ACKNOWLEDGMENTS

Singing opera is a lot harder than publishing books, which may account for the fact that there are fewer people for us to thank. Besides those recognized on the title page of this volume for their contributions, Sue Terry (a research specialist) deserves special mention for providing helpful information just when it was needed; Jane Poole and Robert Cahen were also most helpful. Susan Landis of the Marilyn Horne Foundation, already mentioned on the title page for her contribution to the discography, was tireless in providing answers to our questions as well as in securing rights and permissions.

Without these good people we could not have met our deadlines.

—The Editors